# Tomorrow's
# **Drivers**

Tomorrow's
Drivers

# Tomorrow's
# Drivers

**Duane R. Johnson**
**Donn W. Maryott**

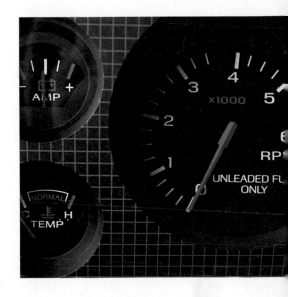

**Eighth Edition**

## GLENCOE
### Macmillan/McGraw-Hill

New York, New York   Columbus, Ohio   Mission Hills, California   Peoria, Illinois

**Duane R. Johnson** was Professor of Safety Studies at Northern Illinois University in DeKalb and has taught driver and traffic safety education at the high-school level in Michigan and Illinois. The owner of several automotive-related businesses, he continues to serve as a consultant to industry, higher education, and state departments of education. The author of over a dozen articles in professional journals, Dr. Johnson is a nationally recognized expert in traffic and safety education and a pioneer in motorcycle rider education.

**Donn W. Maryott** is Director of Prelicense Education Programs for the New York State Department of Motor Vehicles. He served as Director of Education Programs for the Office of Alcohol and Highway Safety and was with the New York State Education Department and the Pennsylvania Department of Education. A former President of the American Driver and Traffic Safety Education Association, Mr. Maryott is still active in that and other professional organizations. He has taught in California and New York at the college and high school levels.

Imprint 1992

Copyright © 1986 by the Glencoe Division of Macmillan/McGraw-Hill School Publishing Company. Copyright © 1986 by Houghton Mifflin Company. All rights reserved. Printed in the United States of America. Except as permitted under the United States Copyright Act of 1976, no part of this publication may be reproduced or distributed in any form or by any means, or stored in a database or retrieval system, without prior written permission of the publisher. Send all inquiries to: Glencoe Division, Macmillan/McGraw-Hill, 936 Eastwind Drive, Westerville, Ohio 43081.

ISBN: 0-395-36067-6 (Student Cloth)
ISBN: 0-395-36068-4 (Student Paper)

11 12 13 14 15   RAND   00 99 98 97 96 95 94 93

# Contents

# Unit 3 Driving Environments

# Unit 4 Driver Responsibilities

## Unit 5  Owner Responsibilities

# Preface

The eighth edition of *Tomorrow's Drivers* is designed to acquaint students with the driving techniques and strategies that prepare them to become safe, responsible drivers. Through clear explanations, thought-provoking activities, and colorful photographs and illustrations, this program will help students develop sound driving skills and sharpen their perceptual and judgment skills. Driver responsibility is the concept stressed throughout the book—not just the legal responsibilities of drivers, but the social responsibilities as well.

### Special Features of the Student Textbook

The student textbook has been completely revised to make it more readable, more attractive, and more comprehensive than the previous edition. Preview questions that can be used to generate class discussion and promote further investigation of specific topics have been added at the beginning of each chapter. End-of-chapter activities have been strengthened to provide for reinforcement and application of essential skills and understandings. This variety of learning activities eliminates the need for a separate student activities workbook.

Other new features of the textbook include practical tips on car maintenance, safety, and fuel savings in each chapter. In addition, interesting career vignettes have been added at the end of each unit. The career pages give students an insight into the people, planning, and effort that go into making the driving environment safe.

The inclusion of an In-Car Guide and chapter tests in the student text makes *Tomorrow's Drivers* a self-contained learning package. The In-Car Guide, located in an easy-to-access section at the back of the book, provides performance checklists of basic driving manuevers. The easy-to-use checklist format makes this section ideal for use in the in-car portion of the driver training program.

### Supporting Materials

In addition to the student textbook, the *Tomorrow's Drivers* package includes an annotated teacher's edition and two sets of printed chapter tests. The teacher's edition contains the complete student text with annotations in the margin suggesting additional topics for discussion and emphasizing and expanding important points in the textbook. The separate teacher's section lists the objectives for each chapter and provides additional teaching suggestions. A resource guide to supplemental audiovisual materials is also included, along with answers to the tests and student activities.

The two versions of the printed chapter tests provide evaluation opportunities beyond those available in the textbook. They can be used for either review or evaluation.

The supporting materials enhance the effectiveness of the student textbook, assisting the teacher and student in the investigation of the skills, laws, responsibilities, and safe practices of the driving task. The ultimate goal of the program: a safe, enjoyable learning experience that will better prepare tomorrow's drivers for the challenges of the highway.

# 1 Getting Ready to Drive

Chapter 1    # Driving in the Highway Transportation System

- **What things have you learned as a pedestrian, a bicyclist, and a passenger that might help you as a driver?**
- **How much time each week do you spend in a car, van, bus, or other vehicle? How will this change once you learn to drive? Why?**

**When you're the driver, you have new freedom, new rights, and new responsibilities.**

Our society is a mobile one. Cars, subways, buses, trains, and planes transport millions of people each day. Air travel makes it possible to fly from Houston to Toronto for a business meeting and return home the same day. Commuter trains carry workers from distant suburbs and even other states to their jobs in the city. But by far the most common means of transportation is the personal automobile.

It is likely that you have already spent a great deal of time as a passenger in a car. And you are probably looking forward to the day when you will be the one at the wheel. As one of tomorrow's drivers, you will enjoy the freedom of choosing when and where you might travel. With that freedom you will gain many new responsibilities. This book can help you become a skillful, responsible driver. It can help make each trip a safe, enjoyable experience.

# Understanding the Highway Transportation System

The **Highway Transportation System (HTS)** is made up of vehicles, roadways, and the people who use them. Through the HTS and the laws that regulate it, people and goods travel quickly and safely to their destination.

How important is the HTS? Think for a moment how important it is to you. How did you and your friends get to school today? How do members of your family get to work? How does the food you eat get to the store? How do you get to the movies or to a friend's home? No doubt you are one of the millions of people who depend on the vehicles and roadways of the HTS for your transportation.

## People

People are HTS users. They operate cars, trucks, motorcycles, mopeds, and bicycles. They walk, run, and skate across and along the roadways. They ride as passengers in cars, vans, and buses.

In a single day, you may use the HTS as a driver, a pedestrian, a passenger, and a cyclist. In each role, your purpose and concerns are slightly different. These differences can lead to conflict — especially when HTS users do not treat each other as courteously as they should. Think of the pedestrian who stands too close to the curb, making it difficult for drivers to turn. Think of the driver who honks rudely at a bicyclist to move out of the way. Are you considerate of other highway users?

**The HTS is made up of three parts: people, vehicles, and roads.**

## Vehicles

There are more motor vehicles registered in the United States than there are people licensed to drive them. Their numbers include cars, trucks, and vans. There are also bicycles, tractors, and mopeds. And there are motorcycles, recreation vehicles, and even an occasional wheelchair. Wide variations in size, weight, and purpose of vehicles lead to wide ranges in their performance.

Although there are many types of motor vehicles to choose from, cars and vans are used for 85 percent of all personal travel.

**As a driver, you should know what to expect from other vehicles on the road.**

Vehicles on the nation's roadways also vary in condition. Some are new; some are old. Some are luxury cars; others are economy models. Regardless of age or price, vehicles not kept in good condition can cause inconvenience or danger to other highway users. What kind of job will you do of maintaining and controlling your vehicle?

# Roads

There are approximately 4 million miles of roads in the United States. If you were to drive 40 miles per hour (mph) 40 hours a week and 50 weeks out of every year, it would take you 50 years to cover every mile of road!

Roads vary in condition, size, and use. Some roads wind leisurely through residential neighborhoods, while others direct high-speed traffic through commercial areas. Some have divided lanes and well-maintained surfaces. Others are narrow, rutted, or even unpaved!

Because of their design and condition, some roads contain more hazards than others. Highway users cannot change the condition of a road. However, they can and should adjust their speed and driving habits to the conditions. In this book, you will learn how to identify and handle various road hazards.

# Keeping the HTS Efficient

As you can see, the HTS is a complicated network of people, vehicles, and roads. It is amazing that the HTS operates as safely and efficiently as it does. There are failures, however. Let's look at some causes of failures in the HTS and ways to prevent them.

# Causes of HTS Failures

Any part of the HTS — a user, a vehicle, or a road — can break down, causing a failure. A driver may be traveling too fast, a car may have a flat tire, or a road may be closed for repairs. A failure may result in a traffic jam or a collision. Some collisions are minor, but too many are more serious, causing injuries and death. And frequently, the victims are young people. Traffic collisions account for 40 percent of the deaths in the age group from 16 to 22.

An HTS failure typically has multiple causes. Think how easily one thing can lead to another. For example, say you reach over to change stations on your car radio. When you look up, you see that the traffic light ahead has turned red. You step hard on the brake, causing the car to skid into the intersection. Another driver already in the intersection has to swerve to avoid your car. The result is a series of events that may lead to one or more collisions.

Drivers cause most HTS failures. Common errors include failing to stay in the proper lane, failing to yield the right of way, driving too fast for conditions, and driving on the wrong side of the road. Often these errors can be traced to the driver's use of alcohol or other intoxicants. Some driver errors result from inexperience or overconfidence. Whatever the cause, the effects of driver error are costly — in terms of loss of life, property damage, and medical costs.

**Alcohol is involved in over 50 percent of all traffic crashes.**

**Road signs and pavement markings are two elements that help keep the HTS running smoothly.**

# The Three E's = Efficiency

Collisions and other HTS failures can be prevented. The keys to an efficient HTS are engineering, education, and enforcement.

## ● Engineering

Engineers are responsible for better designed vehicles, roads, and traffic-control systems. Today's cars, for example, are more economical, more comfortable, and safer than vehicles built in the past. Automotive engineers have developed numerous features to protect a car's occupants in the event of a collision. The safety belt is the single most effective safety device in your car. Newly designed safety belts are more comfortable to wear, yet they hold occupants securely in an emergency. Other safety features include energy-absorbing front ends and padded steering wheels. These features absorb some of the force of impact in a collision, reducing the seriousness of injuries.

Engineers have worked to improve other automotive design features as well. For example, radial tires provide better

**Crash barriers reduce the impact of a collision resulting in less damage and injury.**

traction and actually increase gasoline mileage. Fuel-efficient front-end designs use the force of the air to improve traction and handling.

Highway engineers apply their engineering knowledge to the design of safer roads. Today's highways are constructed with such safety features as banked curves. Older roads are rebuilt and repaired as necessary to keep them safe.

Traffic engineers correct existing roadway conditions in several ways. They may install traffic signals at a busy intersection. They may set aside special turn lanes to improve traffic flow. Simply by erecting a no-parking or no-left-turn sign, traffic engineers can keep traffic moving smoothly.

## ● Education

Everyone who uses the roadways — whether as a pedestrian, cyclist, passenger, or driver — needs to learn to use them safely. Your traffic safety education may have begun on your ride home from the hospital in an approved infant safety seat. Your education continued when you were shown how to cross a street properly. If you've ridden a bicycle in traffic, you've had to learn to obey traffic laws

**Driver education students must put theory into practice behind the wheel.**

**Law enforcement officials make sure that drivers obey the law.**

and signals. With each experience, you've learned more about how highway users behave.

There are many things you will read in this book that can help you be a safer driver. However, more important than what you know is how you act behind the wheel. In driver education, you will have many opportunities to think through traffic situations to identify possible problems and solutions. The problem-solving skills you develop in your course will enable you to act responsibly behind the wheel.

## ● Enforcement

Traffic laws help regulate the behavior of highway users. Can you imagine how confusing it would be if you could not predict the likely behavior of other highway users? Think how difficult it would be to cross a busy intersection.

Unfortunately, not all highway users know or obey traffic laws. For this reason, there are state and local police and the courts to enforce them. Merely by their presence, police can deter many would-be violators. For example, road blocks may discourage drivers from driving after drinking.

In addition to seeing that laws are obeyed, police aid stranded or lost motorists. They also provide assistance and coordinate emergency services at the scene of a collision. By providing such assistance to motorists, law enforcement officials keep traffic and the HTS running smoothly.

# Responsibilities of Drivers

Driving a car is a social activity. That is, it brings you in contact with other highway users. As with any social activity, your driving privilege carries with it important legal and personal responsibilities.

# Legal Responsibilities of Drivers

To ensure your safety and the safety of other highway users, there are four legal responsibilities you have as a driver. You must meet certain health standards. You must have a valid driver's license. Through automobile insurance, you must satisfy your state's financial responsibility law. Finally, you must see that the car you drive is in safe operating condition.

### ● Physical Condition

You must be physically able to drive safely and be capable of handling situations that may arise. In most states, certain physical disabilities or conditions may prevent you from obtaining a license. However, your emotional state is just as important as your physical condition.

If you are worried, angry, or even happy about something, you may find it difficult to concentrate on the road. Even a minor illness can cause you to be inattentive.

Certain prescription drugs and many non-prescription drugs can affect a driver's skills. Alcohol, even in small amounts, decreases a driver's ability to drive safely and make sound driving decisions.

### ● Driver's License

Most states and provinces require you to meet certain age requirements and obtain an instruction permit before learning to drive. To obtain the instruction permit, you must fill out an application, pay a fee, and pass a vision test. You must also pass a test covering the driving laws in your area. If you are under legal age, you may need the permission of a parent or guardian to take the test.

**Three tests are often required for a driver's license: a vision test, a written test, and a driving test.**

**Have your car inspected regularly to be sure it is in safe operating condition.**

When you do your practice driving, you are required to have your instruction permit with you. You may be limited to driving during daylight hours. Whenever you drive, you must be accompanied by a qualified instructor or other adult, according to the law.

After you have practiced your driving and met the legal age requirements, you are finally ready to take your driving exam. Generally, you need to be accompanied by a qualified adult when you go for your exam. The typical driving exam tests your ability to control the car while performing basic driving skills.

### Financial Responsibility

Every state has financial responsibility laws. According to these laws, drivers are responsible for any damage to property or personal injury that they cause while driving. Most drivers satisfy the requirements of the law through their automobile insurance.

Usually, these laws require that you carry a minimum amount of insurance. However, most vehicle owners carry more insurance than required for added protection in the event of a lawsuit.

### A Safe Vehicle

As a driver, you are responsible not only for your own actions, but for the operation and condition of your car. A vehicle with a bald tire, a defective steering system, or poor brakes does not operate as it should, especially in an emergency. Driving with a broken headlight or directional signal places you and other highway users in danger. Even if you do not own the car you are driving, it is up to you to see that it is in safe condition before you take it on the road.

## Personal Responsibilities of Drivers

Most people are aware of the legal responsibilities they must fulfill in order to be licensed to drive. However, you have other responsibilities that are not so clearly defined by law. You are responsible for the safety of your passengers and for the general safety of other highway users.

## ● Ensuring Driver and Passenger Safety

Your first concern as a driver is your ability to keep your vehicle under control at all times. The best way to ensure that you are in control is to always buckle up and to never drink and drive.

Why is wearing your safety belt so important? To operate your vehicle safely, you must be able to reach the foot and hand controls. What might happen, though, if you swerve or brake suddenly to avoid a hazard? If you are not wearing your safety belt, you could easily strike your head or slide out of the driver's seat, losing your grip on the wheel. Your safety belt, on the other hand, can keep you safely behind the wheel and at the controls.

As a driver, you have the right to ask your passengers to use their safety belts. They should wear safety belts not only for their own safety, but for yours. An unbelted passenger could be thrown toward you or strike you in a sudden stop or swerve. This distraction could cause you to lose control of the car even though you are buckled up.

**In an emergency, an unbelted passenger can interfere with a driver's ability to control the vehicle.**

## ●Improving Your Driving Skills

As you get more experience behind the wheel, your driving skills will naturally improve. You will start and stop more smoothly, and you will be able to maneuver in less space. With practice, your ability to identify potential hazards will also improve. At the same time, you will develop better judgment about the best way to handle emergencies.

The more you drive, the more confidence you will have in your ability to control your car and interact with other highway users. Be careful to avoid becoming overconfident about your skills, however. Many new drivers overestimate their abilities after driving for a few months. They may begin to take chances, stop wearing their safety belts, or pay less attention to the driving task. Keep in mind that even experienced drivers can and do have collisions.

To avoid becoming overconfident, regularly examine your driving practices. Ask an experienced driver, such as a parent or older brother or sister, to rate your driving skill every month or so. In this way you can tell which skills are improving and which need work. Pay particular attention to developing these driving competencies:

1. Wears a safety belt and positions both hands on the steering wheel to permit full control at all times. *(Chapters 2, 3, 5, 7–10)*
2. Accelerates and brakes smoothly and safely. *(Chapters 2, 3, 5, 7–10)*
3. Applies the IPDE process *(Chapter 6)* in every driving environment to identify and avoid possible hazards. *(Chapters 6–12)*
4. Drives in the proper lane and avoids other drivers' blind spots. *(Chapters 7–9)*
5. Obeys traffic laws. *(Chapter 4)*
6. Signals intentions clearly and early. *(Chapters 3, 7–10, In-Car Guide)*
7. Executes maneuvers properly and smoothly so that passengers are comfortable riding with you. *(Chapters 7–10, In-Car Guide)*
8. Shows consideration toward other highway users and tries to see situations from their viewpoint. *(Chapter 9)*

**9.** Maintains the car reliably and does not push it beyond safe operating limits. *(Chapter 14)*

**10.** Accepts responsibility for maintaining control of the car at all times by wearing a safety belt and avoiding the use of any drug or other substance that might hinder driving. *(Chapter 12)*

What kind of driver will you be? You will answer that question with your actions and decisions every time you get behind the wheel.

## Maintenance Tips

- Does your car pull to one side, even on level roads? If so, check the front tire on the side the car is pulling toward. The tire pressure is probably low. If it is not, have the car's wheel alignment checked.

- Keep your car's battery clean. Water, acid, dirt, oil, and grease on the outside of the battery can cause it to short out.

- You can prevent serious engine damage and costly repairs by keeping the engine coolant at the correct level.

- Hoses rot from the inside and belts weaken on the underside. To be safe, check all belts and hoses regularly.

## Key Ideas

- People, vehicles, and roadways make up the Highway Transportation System. We depend on it for most of our travel.
- Traffic collisions usually have multiple causes, but driver error is the leading cause.
- Auto, highway, and traffic engineers are continually improving the vehicles and roads that we use.
- Police and courts enforce traffic laws to keep the HTS running safely and efficiently.
- To be licensed to drive in most states, you must pass tests to show that you know the law and can perform basic driving maneuvers safely.
- You are responsible for driving a vehicle that is safe.
- The safety of your passengers and other HTS users depends upon the quality of your decision making and vehicle handling.

# ⇨ Gauging Your Understanding

1. What other kinds of highway users besides car drivers are you likely to meet on the road?

2. What are some of the safety features in today's automobiles?

3. Name some of the ways law enforcement officials help the HTS run smoothly.

4. What are a driver's main legal responsibilities?

5. Why is wearing a safety belt so important for the driver? For the passenger?

# ⇨ In the Driver's Seat

1. You've passed your driving test, and you're taking your friends for their first drive with you. As you get in the car, you fasten your safety belt and ask them to do the same. David claims that wearing safety belts is too uncomfortable. "You want to strangle me?" he asks. Jennifer claims it will wrinkle her clothes. Marie says, "I trust you. I'm sure you'll be careful." How would you respond to each of your friends?

2. As a driver, you are responsible for the safety of your passengers. Yet, you also have the right to expect certain behavior from them. What would you like to include in your "Bill of Rights" for drivers? That is, what five or six rules would you ask every passenger in your car to obey when you're the driver?

# Special Projects

1. Contact an automobile insurance agent in your area. Find out what discounts are available for students who complete a driver education course. Why are these discounts given? What other discounts are available for drivers with safe driving records?

2. Inspect two of the busier intersections in your area. What highway design features can you identify that appear to aid the flow of traffic? What design problems can you identify? For example, does the traffic jam up in any particular lane? What improvements would you suggest?

# Chapter 2 Getting Under Way

- Why should you become familiar with the controls and instruments of a car before you drive it?
- Cars are equipped with many different types of lights. Why?
- Why have all states passed laws requiring children to ride only in approved car seats?

Finally, the car of your dreams! You slide in behind the wheel, eager to drive the car. It starts like a dream. You fasten your safety belt, shift into gear and are off. Suddenly the sky gets dark and it begins to rain. How do you turn on the wipers? Where is the switch for the headlights? Oops, not that one. Finally, you find the right one. But wait — you have high beams on. You look for the dimmer switch, but you can't find it. Now what?

# The View from Behind the Wheel

Before you drive, you need to become familiar with the instruments, gauges, and controls of the automobile. Although there are slight differences in makes and models, similar equipment is located on or near the instrument panel of every car. The **instrument panel** (which is part of the dashboard) is directly in front of the driver. On it are mounted various indicators, gauges, and hand controls. Located beneath the instrument panel are the foot controls. Knowing the location, purpose, and operation of each indicator, gauge, and control enables you to drive safely and conserve fuel.

**Notice the differences between the standard instrument panel below and the digital instrument panel on the next page.**

# Indicators

The two indicators located on the instrument panel —
the speedometer and the odometer — tell your speed and
the distance you have traveled.

Note the odometer read-
ing in the center of the
speedometer.

## ● Speedometer (1)

The **speedometer** gives your speed in miles per hour
(mph), kilometers per hour (km/h), or both. A needle (or
bar) moves from left to right as speed increases. In some
cars, speed is shown by a lighted digital display. On newer
cars there is a red line or mark at the 55 mph point, the
maximum speed allowed by law in the United States. In
Canada, maximum speeds vary from province to province,
from 80 to 100 km/h.

## ● Odometer (2)

The **odometer** measures the total distance that the vehicle has traveled. The distance is measured in either miles or
kilometers. Some cars also have a separate trip odometer
that you can set to zero at the beginning of a trip or when
you stop for fuel. The trip odometer makes it easy to
determine the distance you have driven over a particular
period.

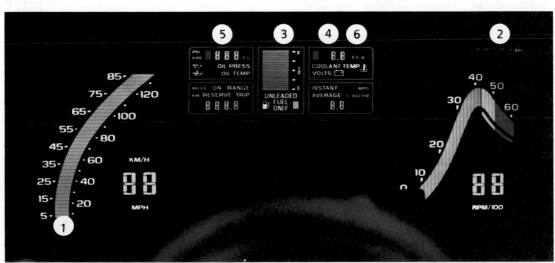

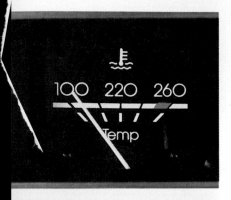

**Although they differ in appearance, both temperature gauges tell you if the engine is hot or cold.**

# Gauges

The gauges on the instrument panel show how several engine systems are operating. The information provided includes fuel level, engine temperature, oil pressure, and electrical system status. You will be a safer, more efficient driver if you learn to use the information these gauges give you.

Many new automobiles have computerized systems that monitor the operation of the car and engine for you. Even with these systems, however, you are the one who must take action when there is a problem. Consult the owner's manual of your car to determine what to do when the gauges indicate a problem.

## Fuel Gauge (3)

Most cars are powered by gasoline; some by diesel fuel; and a few by pressurized natural gas, butane, or propane. Whatever the fuel, you should always know how much is in the tank. Most **fuel gauges** have a needle that moves on a fractional scale from full (F) to empty (E). Refill the tank regularly — before the gauge nears the empty mark. If you let the tank run low, you risk running out of gas. Also, when the tank is low, water may condense inside it. In cold weather, this water may freeze and stop the flow of fuel to the engine.

## Temperature Gauge (4)

For maximum fuel efficiency, an engine should operate between 190 and 210 degrees F. The **temperature gauge** tells you whether the engine is cold or hot. In some cars a red or amber (orange-yellow) light comes on to warn you if the engine temperature goes above a safe level. If the gauge reads HOT or a temperature light comes on, stop as soon as you can safely do so. You can seriously damage an engine if you continue driving when it is overheated.

## Oil Pressure Gauge (5)

Engines need oil to reduce friction that can cause overheating and wear. The oil pressure must be high enough so that the oil reaches the moving parts of the engine. The **oil pressure gauge** warns you whenever oil is not circulating properly in the engine. If a red light comes on or the gauge registers low, shut off the engine immediately. Driving without enough oil circulating can cause severe damage to the engine.

## Alternator Gauge (6)

As the engine runs, it turns a device called an **alternator**. The alternator produces the electricity that powers the electrical system of the car. The lights and radio, for example, are powered by electricity. If electricity is not produced as fast as it is used, it is drained from the battery. When the battery is drained, the engine won't run. As you drive, check the alternator gauge periodically to see that the needle is pointing toward the positive (+) side of the scale. A positive reading indicates that the battery is charging. If the needle points toward the minus (−) side of the scale, shut off all nonessential equipment — such as the radio — that is run by electricity and see a mechanic.

In some cars a warning light is used in place of the alternator gauge. If the light glows red, follow the same steps for a minus (−) reading on the gauge.

# Controls

To drive smoothly, you need to master the vehicle controls. Cars have both hand and foot controls. Foot controls, such as the accelerator and brake, are in the same position in all vehicles. However, the location of the hand controls, such as the gear selector, may vary from car to car.

## Ignition (7)

An ignition key is required to start the engine. Insert the key in the **ignition switch** and turn it to start the engine. If the key doesn't turn easily, the car may have a locking steering wheel. Turn the key and the steering wheel at the same time to unlock the wheel.

The ignition switch also has an accessory position. Turn the key to the **accessory position** to run the electrical

**Note the various key positions on the ignition switch.**

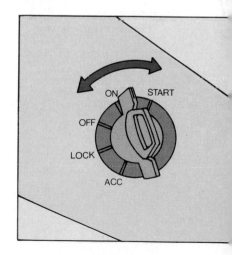

system without starting the engine. Keep in mind, though, that you can drain your battery if you operate the electrical system for any length of time when the engine is not running.

Always take the ignition key whenever you leave your car. Car theft is not impossible without a key, but it is more difficult.

### ● Steering Wheel (8)

The **steering wheel** controls the direction of the front wheels. To go right, turn the steering wheel to the right. To go left, turn the wheel to the left.

### ● Accelerator (9)

The **accelerator**, or gas pedal, controls the speed of the engine. This pedal is the foot control on the right, operated with the right foot. Pressing on the accelerator increases the amount of fuel going to the engine, causing the speed of the car to increase. Decreasing pressure on the accelerator slows the car on a level road.

### ● Service Brake (10)

**The clutch pedal is found only in vehicles with a standard transmission.**

The **service brake** is the foot control located to the left of the accelerator that slows or stops the car. When driving

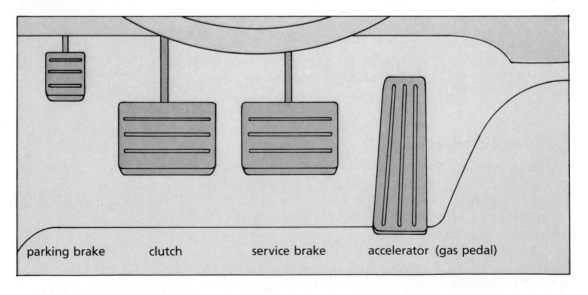

| parking brake | clutch | service brake | accelerator (gas pedal) |

any car for the first time, depress the pedal gradually and cautiously to see how much pressure is needed to bring the car to a smooth stop. If the car is equipped with power brakes, less pressure is needed to slow and stop smoothly.

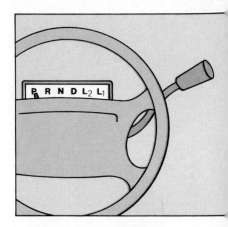

## ● Parking Brake (11)

Use the **parking brake** to keep the car from rolling when it is parked. This brake is either a pedal to the far left of the foot controls or a hand-operated lever. In some cars, the lever is to the right of the driver.

The safest way to use the parking brake is to stop the car by pressing the service brake. Then, set the parking brake by pressing the pedal with your left foot or pulling the hand-operated lever.

A warning light on the instrument panel reminds you to release the parking brake before moving the car. This light also comes on to warn you when the brake system is not working properly.

## ● Gear Selector Lever (12)

The **gear selector lever** controls the connection between the engine and the wheels. This lever is attached to the transmission. In some cars, the gear selector lever is located on the right side of the steering column. On others, it is mounted on the floor to the right of the driver.

**The gear selector of an automatic-transmission vehicle may be column mounted (top), or floor mounted (bottom).**

**Automatic Transmission.**   The gear selections on a car with an automatic transmission are: PARK (P), REVERSE (R), NEUTRAL (N), DRIVE (D), INTERMEDIATE (L2), and LOW (L1).

When a car is not being driven, it should always be in PARK. In this gear the car cannot roll. This is the only gear besides NEUTRAL in which you can start an automatic car. PARK is also the only gear that allows you to remove the ignition key. Never shift into PARK unless the car is completely stopped.

REVERSE is used to back the car. Always come to a complete stop before shifting into REVERSE.

In NEUTRAL, no power goes to the drive wheels and the car may roll. You can use NEUTRAL to restart the car without stopping if the engine fails while you are driving.

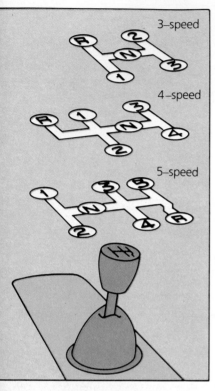

3–speed

4–speed

5–speed

**Note the different shift patterns for a 3-, 4-, or 5-speed transmission.**

DRIVE is used to move forward. To prevent the car from "jumping" forward, always keep firm pressure on the brake pedal as you shift into DRIVE. A car with a fast engine idle may "jump" even though you do not have your foot on the gas pedal.

INTERMEDIATE and LOW are forward gears that you can use when going up or down steep hills or when driving in snow or mud. Both of these gears can help to slow a vehicle if it picks up too much speed when going downhill. Of course, the brakes should still be used when necessary. Often these low gears are used when a car needs more power to pull a heavy load, such as a trailer, up a steep hill. Use LOW or INTERMEDIATE only when you are traveling at low speeds or when you need extra power. Using these gears for steady driving could result in damage to the transmission.

**Standard Transmission.**   Standard transmissions are available in three, four, or five speeds. The gear selections on a standard-shift (manual) car are: NEUTRAL, REVERSE, FIRST (1), SECOND (2), THIRD (3), FOURTH (4), and FIFTH (5).

Always start a standard transmission car in NEUTRAL. Because the transmission is not engaged to the drive wheels when the car is in NEUTRAL, there is no danger of the car "jumping" forward when the engine starts. Also remember to press in the clutch while you start the engine.

Use FIRST to move the car forward up to speeds of 10–15 mph. You can also use FIRST as a low gear for extra power when driving up hills or pulling heavy loads.

Use SECOND for speeds between 15 and 25–30 mph. You can also use SECOND as a low gear for more power or to slow the car when necessary.

In a 3-speed transmission, shift to THIRD when driving at steady speeds above 25–35 mph. In a 4-speed or 5-speed transmission, use THIRD to increase your speed to 35–40 mph.

FOURTH is for steady driving at speeds above 35–40 mph.

If available, use FIFTH for cruising at higher speeds to save engine wear and fuel.

REVERSE is used to back the car. Always come to a complete stop before shifting into REVERSE.

## ● Clutch (13)

The **clutch pedal** is located on the floor to the left of the service brake pedal. Only cars with standard transmissions have a clutch pedal. It disengages the engine from the drive wheels when changing gears and starting the engine.

# Lights and Other Signals

All vehicles are equipped with various features that help drivers communicate with other highway users. Turning on your headlights or using your turn signals, for example, can alert other drivers to your presence and your intention to change direction. Such equipment is required on vehicles because it can help prevent collisions.

## ● Headlights (14)

**Headlights** help you to see objects in your path and help other drivers to see you. At night, you must drive with your headlights on. You should also use them any time visibility is reduced, such as during a rain storm or in fog.

The headlights are controlled by a switch or knob. The switch is located on the instrument panel or on a lever connected to the steering column.

**Locate necessary controls such as the dimmer switch before you drive so you can find them easily when needed.**

Vehicles are equipped with both high-beam and low-beam headlights. When there is no oncoming traffic, you can improve vision for a greater distance by switching to **high beams**. A light (usually blue) on the instrument panel alerts you that your high beams are on. When cars are approaching from the other direction, dim your lights to low beam using the **dimmer switch** to avoid temporarily blinding other drivers. The dimmer switch is usually located on a lever connected to the steering column. In some older vehicles, it may be located on the floor to the far left of the foot controls.

## ● Taillights

All cars also have at least two **taillights** to make them more visible at night to following drivers. These lights come on when the headlights or parking lights are turned on.

**Backup lights help you see where you are backing, especially at night.**

### Parking Lights

Amber **parking lights** are located on the front of the car near the headlights. You should use parking lights only when parked. To turn on the parking lights, pull the headlight switch out halfway or twist the switch part of the way.

### Brake Lights

When you depress the service brake pedal, **brake lights** go on at the back of your car. These lights warn drivers behind you that you are slowing or stopping so that they can adjust their speed or position.

### Backup Lights

When you shift your car into REVERSE, **backup lights** in the rear of the car automatically come on. These lights help you see where you are backing at night, and also alert other drivers that you are backing.

### Turn Signals (15)

The **turn signal** (or directional lever) is located on the left side of the steering column. Turn signals are used to let other drivers know of your intention to change direction. Press the directional lever down for a left signal; raise the lever for a right signal. When the turn signal is on, blinking lights go on at both the front and rear of the car. A blinking light or arrow on the instrument panel lets you know that your turn signals are operating. When you complete a turn, always check to be sure your signal is off.

### Emergency Flashers (16)

The switch for the **emergency flashers** is usually located on the steering column. When you turn this switch on, all four turn signal lights flash. Use emergency flashers to warn other drivers that your car is not functioning properly.

### Horn (17)

The **horn** is a warning device used to alert other drivers to your presence. It is usually located on the steering wheel, but on some vehicles it may be mounted on the signal lever

on the steering column. Sound the horn only when you believe that a collision is likely because another driver or pedestrian does not see you. Don't abuse or overuse the horn. A light tap is usually all that's necessary to alert others to your presence.

**Always signal your intention to turn well in advance of the turn.**

## Controls for Safety and Comfort

Most vehicles are equipped with a number of controls that increase the safety and comfort of you and your passengers. Safety belts, for example, help protect you from injury in a sudden stop and in a collision. Heat, ventilation systems, and adjustable seats are designed to make car travel more comfortable and enjoyable. Keep in mind that the most enjoyable car trip is a safe one — so use your safety belt, even on short drives.

**Safety belts help save lives. Buckle up as soon as you get in the car.**

## ● Safety Belts

By law, car manufacturers must install lap and shoulder belts in the front seat of all new vehicles. Rear seats must have lap belts. In the United States and Canada, laws require that children ride in approved child restraint seats. Why do such laws exist? Because **safety belts** are the single best protection against injury while traveling in motor vehicles. If all drivers and passengers wore safety belts, about 25,000 lives would be saved and countless injuries would be prevented or reduced each year.

In many cars, a light, buzzer, or chime comes on when you start the car to remind you and your passengers to fasten your safety belts. Adjust the belt to fit snugly over your hips. The shoulder portion should be loose enough so that you can fit your fist between the belt and your chest.

## ● Passive Restraints

Because many people refuse or forget to wear seatbelts, engineers have developed **passive restraints** to help prevent injuries and to save lives. These passive restraints require no action by either the driver or the passengers, yet they provide protection in collisions.

**Passive safety belts** are shoulder restraints that automatically connect from the door to the seat when you close the door.

Some cars are equipped with **air bags**. In crashes violent enough to produce serious injury or death, these inflate and prevent people from colliding with the dashboard, the windshield, or other parts of the car. Air bags pop out, inflate, protect, and deflate in a fraction of a second.

## ● Head Restraints

All new cars have padded head restraints attached to the back of the front seats. **Head restraints** help prevent neck injuries to you and any front-seat passengers in a collision. In some cars the head restraints are fixed and in others they are adjustable. If you have adjustable head restraints, position them so the restraint meets the back of your head, not the back of your neck.

## ● Interior Lights

Map lights, overhead lights, and other interior lights are provided as a convenience for the driver and passengers. Because interior lights make it difficult to see the roadway clearly when driving at night, use them only when the vehicle is parked.

The instrument panel lights, which light up the instruments and gauges, come on when you turn on the headlights. Adjust them low enough (if possible) to avoid glare in your eyes. The other interior lights are generally controlled by the same switch that controls the headlights.

## ● Comfort System

Ventilation systems, heat, and window defrosters are standard equipment on today's vehicles. Many cars are also equipped with air conditioners. This equipment allows you to adjust for weather conditions that can make driving uncomfortable.

The controls for the comfort system are located on the instrument panel. Generally, you move a lever to select fresh air (vent), heat, or defrost.

**Never drive when you cannot see clearly. Wait until the defrost clears the windshield.**

Use the **defrost** to direct heat to the windshield to clear snow, ice, or moisture. Follow the specific instructions in the owner's manual of your car for the operation of the comfort equipment.

### ● Seat Adjustment

The driver's seat can be adjusted by moving a lever that is located at the front or side of the seat near the floor.

When the seat is adjusted properly, you should be able to rest your right heel on the floor at the base of the accelerator. Your left foot should rest on the floor beside the clutch or brake pedal. Your elbows should be bent when your hands are on the steering wheel.

### ● Hood Release Lever

Many new cars have a **hood release lever** under the instrument panel on the left. Pulling this lever unlatches the hood so it can be raised for engine inspection or for maintenance and repairs.

### ● Door Locks

Door locks help protect your car and the people in it. To ensure your security, always lock all doors before you drive. Locking the doors also helps prevent them from popping open in a collison.

When you leave your car, close the windows and lock the doors. Each year thousands of cars are stolen. By locking your doors, you lessen the chance of your car being one of those that are stolen.

### ● Windshield Wipers and Washers

All cars are equipped with windshield wipers and washers that are designed to keep your view ahead clear. Insects, rain, snow, and dirt can all reduce your ability to see the road ahead. Use the wipers whenever necessary to clear the windshield. If the windshield doesn't clear easily, use the windshield washer. The wipers and washers are controlled by the same lever or switch, which may be found on the steering column or on the instrument panel.

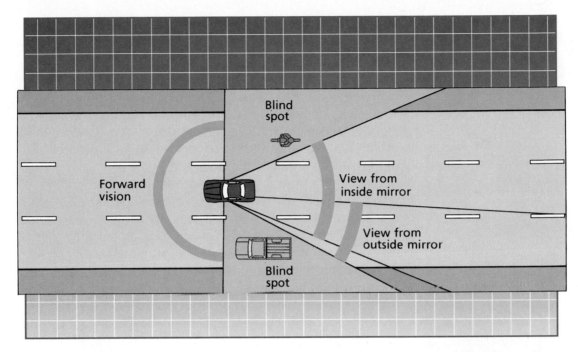

## ● Rearview Mirrors

All automobiles are equipped with an inside rearview mirror. There is also a rearview mirror fastened to the door or front fender just ahead of the driver. When you adjust these mirrors properly, you can view other highway users behind you.

Although mirrors help to minimize them, "blind spots" exist. **Blind spots** are areas behind your car that you cannot see in mirrors. After you look in the mirrors, always glance over your shoulder to check blind spots before changing lanes.

**Rearview mirrors do not eliminate the need to check over your shoulder for blind spots before changing lanes.**

# Getting Ready to Drive

Before starting the car, there are some things you should always do. Checking around your car before you enter and making the proper adjustments once you are seated behind the wheel can help you avoid problems later.

**Be sure you can hold the wheel with both hands in the correct position. Then, adjust the mirrors properly.**

# Predriving Checks

Before getting into the car, make sure that nothing is in its path. Clear the windows, if necessary. Enter your car from the curb side. If you must enter the car from the street side, approach the door from the front of the car. From this position, you can see and avoid approaching traffic. When it is safe to do so, open the door and get into the car. Close and lock the door quickly.

Once inside the car you can put the key in the ignition while you make the remaining predriving checks. Clear all objects from the front and rear window ledges. These items can block your view and also become hazards if they slide off during a sudden stop. Be sure all windows are clean.

Seat yourself comfortably with your back against the seat and your arms and legs slightly bent. Rest your left foot on the floor beside the clutch or brake pedal. Rest the heel of your right foot on the floor and the ball of your foot on the gas pedal. Grasp the steering wheel with both hands. To position your hands properly, think of the steering wheel as a clock. Place your left hand between the 9 and l0 o'clock positions. Place your right hand between the 2 and 3 o'clock positions. Move the seat forward or backward until you are comfortable and can reach all the controls. Make sure you can see over the steering wheel. If necessary, use a cushion. Adjust the head restraint so that it is directly behind the middle of the back of your head.

Once you are properly seated, fasten your safety belt and make sure that all passengers have fastened theirs. Next, check the mirrors. Adjust the inside mirror so that you can see out of the entire rear window. Adjust the outside mirror so that you can see the area to the left of your car and only a small part of the side of your car. (Refer to Manuever A in the In-Car Guide in the back of this book.)

# Starting the Engine

Before you start any car, check that the parking brake is set. Be sure the car is in PARK or NEUTRAL. If the engine is cold, set the automatic choke by pressing and releasing the gas pedal with your right foot. Then, move your foot to cover the service brake. Turn the key in the ignition to start the engine and release it as soon as the engine starts. Check the gauges on the instrument panel to be sure that everything is working properly. (Refer to Maneuver A in the In-Car Guide in the back of this book.)

Only after you have completed these safety procedures and predriving checks are you ready to begin your first drive.

## Safety Checks

- Lock your doors and fasten your safety belt before starting the engine. Remind your passengers to do the same.

- Before pulling away from the curb, press the service brake pedal down firmly to check for adequate brake pressure.

- When you play the radio or tape player in your car, keep the volume down. Remember that you must be able to hear warning sounds: car horns, train whistles, and sirens.

- In an emergency, you can slow or stop the car with the parking brake if the service brake fails.

## Key Ideas

- To operate your car safely, you need to know the location and function of all gauges and indicators on the instrument panel.
- The location of the hand and foot controls may vary from one car to another. For safety, learn where these controls are before you begin to drive any car.
- Headlights, turn signals, and other features help you communicate with other highway users. These devices can help prevent collisions.
- Safety belts and restraints help reduce injuries in a collision.
- Before you enter a car, always check to be sure there is nothing in your intended driving path.
- Adjust the rearview mirrors so that you can see any vehicles approaching from the rear.
- Always lock your car when you leave it.

## ▶ Gauging Your Understanding

1. What information do these gauges and indicators give you: speedometer, odometer, fuel gauge, and alternator gauge?

2. What are the foot controls? What is the function of each one?

3. Why are cars equipped with a horn? Describe when you should and should not use it.

4. Describe blind spots and explain how to deal with them.

5. What safety checks should you perform before getting into your car?

6. Once you are in the car, what should you do to help ensure your safety and that of your passengers?

## ▶ In the Driver's Seat

1. A light snow is falling on a cold morning. Your boss just called to ask you to report to work early. You have just 30 minutes to make it — and the ride takes 25. You grab your coat and race out the door. Your car has been parked outside all night. What should you do before you enter the car? What should you do before you start the car? What are some problems you may encounter while driving to work?

2. Your car won't start and you have to meet someone across town. You borrow your friend's car for the night with the understanding you will return the car first thing in the morning. What should you do before you drive the car? How can you determine if the car is running properly?

## Special Projects

1. Sit behind the wheel of the car you will be driving after you complete this course. Identify and locate all the controls, gauges, and lights. Compare the instrument panel with the car you drive in your driver education course. Make a list of the differences and similarities.

2. During the next week, observe the drivers you ride with to see who wears safety belts. Ask those who don't wear safety belts why they don't. Report your findings to the class.

# Chapter 3　Basic Driving Maneuvers

- What special hazards do you face when you park on a hill?
- Some people drive with only one hand on the wheel. What other bad habits have you noticed among drivers you know? Why are these bad driving habits dangerous?

Once you fasten your safety belt and start the car, the real challenge begins. The driving task becomes more complicated. Initially, it's a challenge just to move your car smoothly through traffic, staying in your lane. You must also be able to change lanes, change direction, make turns, back, and park safely. At first these basic maneuvers require total concentration. Soon, however, you'll perform them almost automatically. Then you'll be able to devote your attention to the real driving task: driving defensively, so that you and other highway users can avoid collision.

# Steering, Accelerating, and Braking

To be in control of a car, you must be able to steer, accelerate, and brake. These activities require coordination of your eye, hand, and foot movements.

## Steering

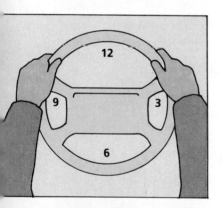

**By keeping both hands on the wheel, you can easily make steering adjustments.**

To steer a car, simply turn the steering wheel in the direction you want the car to go. You need to make slight steering adjustments to stay on course — even when your course appears to be straight. To make these adjustments easily, keep both hands on the steering wheel at all times. To position your hands properly, think of the steering wheel as a clock. Your right hand should be between 2 and 3 o'clock, and your left hand should be between 9 and 10 o'clock. With hands in this position, you have better control of your car.

As you drive, always look well ahead into the center of the lane. By doing so, you will naturally steer the car so that it follows the path of the lane. Relax your arms so you can "feel" any changes in the road and react to them. For example, you may need to make steering adjustments if you hit a bump or a pothole that throws the car off its path. Make small steering adjustments as soon as you are aware that the car is drifting out of your lane. You are likely to overreact by **oversteering** if you delay making an ad-

justment. Oversteering can cause the car to turn sharply out of your lane. Instead, make slight adjustments as needed to keep your car on course.

**Take your foot off the gas pedal to slow gradually when approaching an intersection.**

## Accelerating

The speed of the car is controlled by the amount of pressure you put on the **accelerator**, or gas pedal. In order to have a better "feel" for controlling pedal pressure, wear shoes with flexible soles and low heels. Always keep your heel on the floor.

To accelerate (increase your speed), gradually press down on the accelerator with the ball of your foot. By pressing down gradually, you keep the car moving smoothly. Also, accelerating smoothly helps save fuel. Once you reach your desired speed, you can ease up on the gas pedal slightly and still maintain your speed. Avoid sudden changes in speed by keeping even pressure on the gas pedal.

To decrease your speed gradually, reduce the pressure on the gas pedal, then use the service brake if necessary. By identifying in advance your need to stop, you can often slow enough simply by taking your foot off the accelerator.

**Check over your shoulder for approaching traffic before pulling away from the curb.**

## ● Driving an Automatic Transmission Car

When you drive a car with an automatic transmission, you do not have to manually shift gears. For this reason, automatics are easier to drive than vehicles with manual transmissions. To go forward, you simply shift to DRIVE (D) and accelerate. The car automatically shifts into higher gears as it picks up speed. As the car slows, it automatically shifts to lower gears.

**Moving the Car Forward.**   To move forward in a car with an automatic transmission, firmly press the brake pedal and shift to DRIVE. Release the parking brake. Check in the mirrors for approaching traffic and glance over your shoulder. Use a turn signal to show other drivers that you are pulling away from the curb. Just before you begin to move, look over your shoulder to check your blind spot. If no traffic is approaching, look forward into your intended path and take your foot off the brake. Gently press on the gas pedal and move into the proper lane.

**Starting on a Hill.**   When starting to move forward on a hill or other upgrade, you need to keep the car from rolling backward. Press the brake pedal with your left foot. At the same time, press the gas pedal with your right foot. Gradually apply more pressure to the accelerator as you start to release the brake pedal. Once your car begins to move forward, take your foot off the brake. You may also set the parking brake to keep from rolling backward. As you press on the gas pedal, release the parking brake. (Refer to Maneuver B in the In-Car Guide in the back of this book.)

## Driving a Standard Transmission Car

In a standard transmission car, you have to manually (by hand) shift into every gear. Each time you shift, you must first press in the clutch with your left foot and let up on the accelerator with your right foot.

**Moving the Car Forward.**   To move forward in a car with a standard transmission, press in the clutch and shift to FIRST. With your right foot on the service brake, release the parking brake. Check in the mirrors for approaching traffic and glance over your shoulder to be sure your intended path is clear. Use a turn signal to show other drivers that you are pulling away from the curb. Just before you begin to move, look over your shoulder to check your blind spot. If no traffic is approaching, look forward into your intended path. Press the gas pedal lightly as you slowly release the clutch to the **friction point**. At this point the engine and transmission engage. To move the car forward, let up the clutch beyond the friction point as you press the gas pedal gently.

When you reach a speed of 10–15 mph, shift from FIRST to SECOND. Press in the clutch and release the gas pedal at the same time. With your right hand, shift to SECOND. Release the clutch smoothly and accelerate gently.

To shift from SECOND to higher gears, follow the same procedure as for shifting into SECOND. When you are moving at higher speeds, though, remember that you should operate the clutch and gas pedal more quickly. Once you have shifted into the proper gear for your travel speed, remove your left foot from the clutch and place it on the floor to the left of the clutch pedal. Resting your foot on the clutch pedal (called "riding the clutch") causes the clutch to wear out quickly. (Refer to Maneuver G in the In-Car Guide in the back of this book.)

**On a steep upgrade, use the parking brake to keep from rolling back.**

**Starting on a Hill.**   To get a standard transmission vehicle under way on an upgrade requires skillful use of the clutch, brake, and accelerator. Keep your foot on the brake to keep the car from rolling backward. Press in the clutch and shift to FIRST. Let the clutch up until it reaches the friction point and hold it at this point to keep the car from rolling backward. Then, remove your right foot from the brake and press the accelerator to make the engine run faster. Let the clutch up slowly from the friction point as you accelerate to move the car forward.

If the upgrade is very steep, you may also use the parking brake to keep the car from rolling backward. Continue to let the clutch up beyond the friction point as you accelerate, then release the parking brake. (Refer to Maneuver B in the In-Car Guide in the back of this book.)

# Braking

Use the service brake to slow the car or bring it to a stop. Learning to brake smoothly takes practice. With experience, you can learn when to begin applying the brake and how much pressure to apply.

## ● Slowing the Car

When you step on the brake pedal, the brake lights at the rear of your car light up. In traffic, tap the pedal once or twice to alert other drivers that you are slowing.

Remember that you can save wear and tear on the brakes if you take your foot off the accelerator and slow gradually before applying your brakes.

You can slow gradually by shifting from a higher gear to a lower one — a procedure called **downshifting**. To downshift with a standard transmission, press in the clutch, let up on the gas pedal, and shift into the next lower gear. Then, press on the gas pedal as you ease up on the clutch to make the downshift smooth. In an automatic, you need only to shift to the next lower gear. Read your owner's manual to find the maximum downshifting speed for each gear. (Refer to Maneuver G in the In-Car Guide in the back of this book.)

## ● Coming to a Stop

To stop the car, apply steady pressure to the brake pedal. Just before actually coming to a stop, decrease this pressure slightly for a fraction of a second. Then, reapply pressure firmly to the brake pedal. This method allows you to make a smooth stop. (If your car has power brakes, rest the heel of your foot on the floor and use gentle toe pressure on the brake pedal. This foot position keeps you from braking abruptly.) To keep the car stopped, keep pressure firmly on the brake pedal. (Refer to Maneuver B in the In-Car Guide in the back of this book.)

# Changing Lanes and Turning

The steering wheel is used to keep the car moving on the intended path. But the more obvious purpose of the steering wheel is to steer or turn onto a new travel path. You change travel paths whenever you move from one lane to another on the same road or turn onto another road.

**Before changing lanes, check the rearview mirrors, then glance over your shoulder in the direction you want to go.**

# Lane Changes

Before changing lanes on a multilane road, check the mirrors for traffic approaching from the rear. Glance over your shoulder to make sure that no vehicles are in your blind spot. Once you are sure it is safe to change lanes, use your turn signals to let other drivers know that you are going to do so.

Remember that you do not have to turn the steering wheel very far to change lanes. Adjust your speed to enter the traffic flow smoothly as you move into the lane. As soon as you complete your lane change, check to see that your turn signal is off. (Refer to Maneuver D in the In-Car Guide in the back of this book.)

# Turning

Most travel routes require you to turn from one street to another to get where you are going. Well ahead of the turn, let other drivers know of your intention to turn. Tap the brake pedal a few times to show that you are slowing down. Then, as you approach the intersection, use your turn signal to indicate the direction of your turn. Before making *any* turn, make sure it is legal and safe. Check for hazards and be certain your path is clear of other highway users — pedestrians as well as vehicles.

When turning sharply, use the **hand-over-hand** steering method described in the In-Car Guide (Maneuver B). In the hand-over-hand method, you turn the wheel hard with one hand. At the same time, cross your other hand over to pull the wheel down farther.

When you complete a turn, "shuffle" the steering wheel to straighten it. If you need to slightly adjust your steering this way, grip the wheel with one hand firmly while sliding the other hand along the wheel to gain a new grip.

### ● Right Turns

Right turns require you to merge with traffic coming from the left and any traffic that is coming from the opposite direction and turning left. On a multilane road, you should be in the far right lane when making a right turn. Be sure to signal your intentions. Slow down before you reach the corner. Begin turning the wheel at the point where the curb or edge of the road bends around the corner. If you drive a standard transmission car, you may have to downshift as you slow down. By downshifting before you reach the corner, you have both hands free to use the hand-over-hand steering method. Turn into the lane nearest the curb that is open to traffic — usually the outside lane. (Refer to Maneuver D in the In-Car Guide in the back of this book.)

## Left Turns

When making a left turn, your car crosses the paths of oncoming traffic as well as traffic coming from both the left and right. Because so many paths are crossed, a left turn can be dangerous. To make left turns safely, begin by signaling well in advance your intention. Move your car into correct position for the turn. Many roads have separate left-turn lanes for this purpose. Slow down (downshifting if necessary) before you enter the intersection. Begin making the turn as you enter the intersection. Turn your car into the nearest lane used by traffic going in that direction. (Refer to Maneuver D in the In-Car Guide in the back of this book.)

**When planning a turn, be sure the turn is legal.**

# Backing and Changing Direction

Backing and turning around are maneuvers that require care and practice. Often there is very little space in which to carry out these maneuvers. As a result, mistakes are common. The most common mistake drivers make when backing is failing to look both ways behind them. This mistake often leads to collision with vehicles, pedestrians, utility poles, or other unseen objects.

# Backing

**What steps should you take when backing out of your driveway?**

You will begin many car trips by fastening your safety belt and backing out of your driveway. How can you back out safely? Before backing, be sure to look over both shoulders for pedestrians, obstacles, and other vehicles in your path. Then, as you back, look in the direction you are headed. By doing so, you can see whether the travel path is clear. Also, you can better control the direction of the car. When backing to the right, look mainly over your right shoulder. When backing to the left, look mainly over your left shoulder. While backing, you also should constantly check the sides and front of your car to make sure you clear all obstacles.

Always back slowly. Place your foot on the service brake pedal as you shift into REVERSE. Then release the brake but keep it covered as you begin backing. Usually you do not need to use the accelerator. If the car does not move after you release the brake, press the accelerator lightly. As soon as the car begins to move, control your speed with the brake.

A car in REVERSE steers just as it does when going forward. Just turn the wheel in the direction you want the back of the car to go. For example, when the wheel is turned right, the car backs to the right. Remember, though, that the front of the car swings in the opposite direction. Glance ahead occasionally to make sure the front end of the car is clearing all objects. (Refer to Maneuver C in the In-Car Guide in the back of this book.)

# Changing Direction

What would you do if you were driving down a busy two-way street and passed a street you wanted to turn onto? Would you back the car? Probably not. You would most likely turn around to change your direction. There are several ways to change direction on city streets. The safest way is to drive around the block. However, when you are on a dead-end street or when the street you want to turn onto is a one-way street, you cannot drive around the block. You must choose another method, such as making a U-turn or a Y-turn, or backing into or out of an alley.

Before you attempt to turn around using any method, first determine whether the maneuver is permitted. Generally, signs are posted to tell you if turns are prohibited. In some locations, however, certain turns (such as U-turns) are illegal, and you are expected to know the law.

Once you have determined that the maneuver is legal, make sure that you can perform it safely. Do not try to turn around on a street with heavy traffic. Also, be sure you have a clear view of traffic and the road in all directions. If your view is blocked by a curve or a hill, drive on until you find a safe area to make your move.

**Cars parked facing the same direction on both sides of the street should alert a driver that the street is one way.**

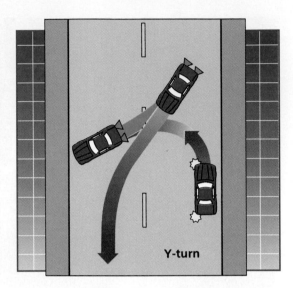

**Check carefully for traffic before making a U-turn or a Y-turn.**

## U-turn

When you are driving on a wide street with good visibility in both directions, a **U-turn** is one of the simplest ways to turn around. It is a relatively safe maneuver because it does not require you to back into or across a lane of traffic. However, a U-turn does require you to make a sharp left turn across traffic. To make a U-turn safely, make sure the turn is permitted, signal your intentions, and check for traffic in both directions. (Refer to Maneuver E in the In-Car Guide in the back of this book.)

## Y-turn

If the street you are driving on is too narrow for a U-turn, you may be able to reverse direction with a **Y-turn**. Making Y-turns can be dangerous because you must stop in and block lanes of traffic going in both directions.

Therefore, make a Y-turn only when there are no side streets, alleys, or other openings to turn into. Choose an area with light traffic and good visibility to perform your turn. Avoid roads with trees, poles, hydrants, or parked vehicles along the sides. Do not make a Y-turn if your visibility is blocked by curves and hills. Watch for approaching traffic, and be sure to signal your intentions. (Refer to Maneuver E in the In-Car Guide in the back of this book.)

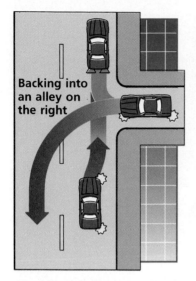

**Backing into an alley on the right**

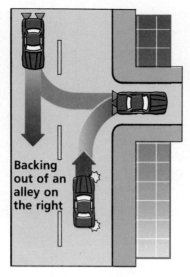

**Backing out of an alley on the right**

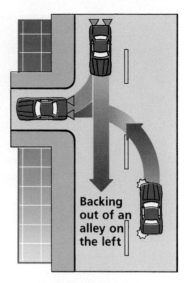

**Backing out of an alley on the left**

## ● Backing into an Alley on the Right

Another way to reverse direction is to back into an alley or opening on your right. One advantage of this method is that it enables you to enter the flow of traffic while moving forward. Remember to signal your intentions before you stop. Back into the opening slowly, checking for traffic, pedestrians, or objects in your path. (Refer to Maneuver E in the In Car Guide in the back of this book.)

## ● Backing out of an Alley on the Right

If it is too difficult or unsafe to back into an opening on the right, you may want to turn into it going forward. Turning into an opening allows you to get out of the flow of traffic quickly. You can then wait until the traffic slows to back out. This maneuver requires caution because you are backing across one lane into another. (Refer to Maneuver E in the In-Car Guide in the back of this book.)

## ● Backing out of an Alley on the Left

Sometimes you cannot find an opening on your right to turn or back into. When this is the case — and when a U-turn or Y-turn is not possible — you can turn into an opening on the left side of the street. Turning to your left takes you across a lane of traffic as you enter the opening.

**Whenever possible, avoid backing into or out of alleys to change direction.**

**When backing into traffic, use extra caution, especially if your view is blocked.**

It also requires you to back into a lane of traffic. For these reasons, use extreme caution when making this maneuver. Be sure you choose a place where you can see clearly in both directions. Also, avoid openings that have large vehicles such as trucks or vans parked at the ends. These vehicles make it difficult to see when you pull out of the opening and enter the lane of traffic. (Refer to Maneuver E in the In-Car Guide in the back of this book.)

## Parking

When you arrive safely at your destination, your next task is to find a place to park.

When selecting a place to park, avoid parking where other vehicles limit your space and visibility. Choose a space that is large enough for your car — so that you can enter and exit easily. If possible, don't park between large vehicles that may block your vision. Also avoid any spaces that have improperly parked vehicles on either side. These vehicles often make it difficult to maneuver safely.

As you search for a parking space, pay attention to changes in the traffic around you. For example, watch closely for cars getting ready to back out. Look for exhaust, brake lights, or back-up lights. Use your brake lights and turn signals to let other drivers know as soon as you can that you are going to pull into a space.

Pulling into a parking space is not difficult if you move the car slowly, know when to turn the wheels, and keep a close watch on the direction the car is moving. Although the actual procedures vary for diagonal, perpendicular, and parallel parking, the maneuvers are the same ones used in other situations. The only difference when parking is that you perform these maneuvers in a limited space.

When leaving a parking space, do so cautiously. Because there are other vehicles parked around you, your visibility is limited. Watch to be sure the front and rear of your car clear the vehicles and other objects around you.

# Diagonal Parking

**Diagonal (angle) parking** is the easiest method of parking because you simply turn into the space. When you approach a diagonal parking space, try to keep a distance of 5 to 6 feet from the parked cars. This distance allows you to see better and gives you more room to turn and pull into the space.

When entering or leaving a diagonal parking space, be sure to watch the front and rear of your car to avoid hitting cars parked on either side of you. (Refer to Maneuver F in the In-Car Guide in the back of this book.)

# Perpendicular Parking

A parking lot that is divided into **perpendicular parking spaces** can hold more cars than one with diagonal spaces. The trade-off is that parking in perpendicular spaces is more difficult because you have to turn sharply to enter them.

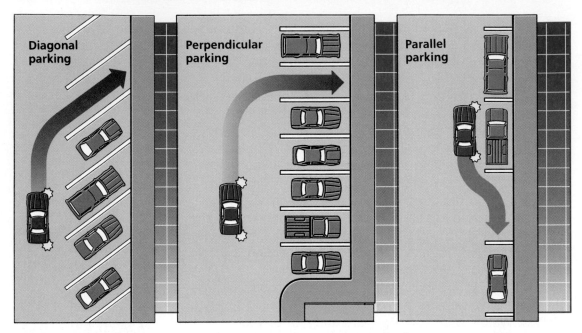

**Diagonal parking**

**Perpendicular parking**

**Parallel parking**

**Always glance to the sides to be sure your car clears other vehicles parked on either side of you.**

Before turning into a perpendicular space, move out as far as possible into the driving lane. (Wait for any approaching traffic to pass before turning.) Generally, it is better to pull into rather than back into a perpendicular space because most drivers find it easier to judge distances when moving forward. (Refer to Maneuver F in the In-Car Guide in the back of this book.)

# Parallel Parking

**Parallel parking** requires both forward and backward motion and exact steering control. Also, you must be skilled in judging distances and controlling vehicle direction. With practice and experience, parallel parking becomes easy.

When choosing a parallel parking space, make sure the space is 5 to 6 feet longer than your car. Come to a stop in front of the space. Remember that the front end of your car will swing into the lane of traffic as you back in, so be sure to check for approaching vehicles in your lane. Also keep an eye on the car parked ahead of you to be sure that the front end of your car clears it. Once you back into the space, center your car within it by pulling forward as you

steer straight ahead. Leave the same amount of space between your car and those in front of and behind you so
that you can pull out of the space easily. (Refer to Maneuver F in the In-Car Guide in the back of this book.)

## ● Parking Uphill

You must take special care when parallel parking on hills
to prevent the car from rolling downhill. When parking
uphill, be sure your car is parallel to the curb. Then, turn
the steering wheel so that the back of the front tire closest

**Use extra care when
parking on hills to pre-
vent your car from roll-
ing into traffic.**

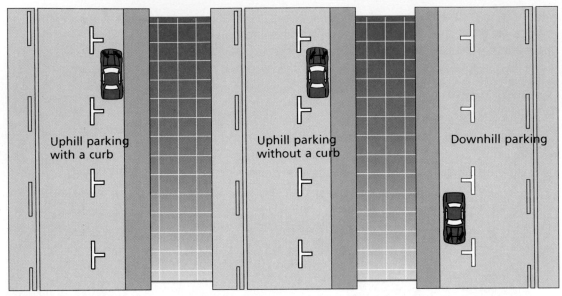

Uphill parking
with a curb

Uphill parking
without a curb

Downhill parking

**Notice how the wheels
of the cars above are
turned to prevent the
cars from rolling into
traffic.**

to the curb touches the curb. If the upgrade has no curb, turn the steering wheel so the wheels face the side of the road. If the wheels are turned this way, the car will not roll into the street if the parking brake does not hold.

### ● Parking Downhill

When parking on a downgrade with or without a curb, turn the steering wheel so that the front wheels are turned toward the side of the road. This position prevents the car from rolling into traffic if the parking brake does not hold.

## Fuel Misers

- Always accelerate gradually and smoothly to avoid wasting fuel. By slowly pressing the gas pedal instead of pushing it down hard, you can increase gas mileage.

- Travel at a steady rate of speed to save fuel.

- Let up on the accelerator as you approach an intersection. By slowing gradually, you save fuel, reduce brake wear, and make smoother stops.

- Turn off the ignition if you plan to be stopped for more than a minute. Idling uses more fuel than restarting the car does.

# Key Ideas

- Always drive with both hands on the steering wheel for maximum control.
- Slow down gradually for smoother stops, to reduce wear on the brakes, and to save fuel.
- To stop, brake early and apply steady pressure to the brake pedal.
- Check rearview mirrors and look over your shoulder to check your blind spot before making a lane change.
- Use the hand-over-hand steering method when turning.
- When changing lanes or turning, use your turn signal to alert other drivers.
- When backing, look mainly in the direction that the car is traveling. Also check the position of the front of the car as you back.
- When parking on hills, be sure to turn the wheels so your car does not roll into the street.

# Gauging Your Understanding

1. While driving straight ahead, what position should your hands be in on the steering wheel? Why?

2. What is the correct procedure for starting forward in an automatic transmission car when parked uphill?

3. While backing to the left, which shoulder should you look over? Which direction should you turn the steering wheel?

4. What is the safest way to turn around? List some of the other methods of turning around.

5. When parking your car, what should you be alert for?

6. How should your wheels be turned when parking
   a. uphill with a curb
   b. uphill without a curb
   c. downhill

# In the Driver's Seat

1. You are driving on a mountain road. While climbing a steep hill, you feel the engine start to lose some of its power. What should you do? As you start downhill, you begin to pick up a lot of speed. What should you do?

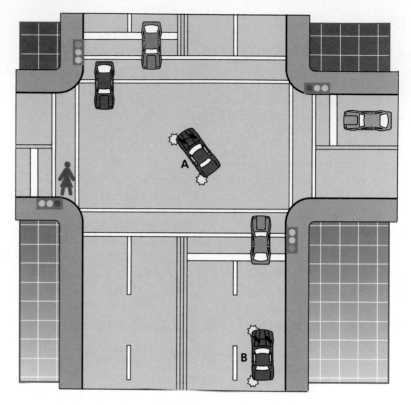

2. Study the illustration. Then answer the following questions.
   a. Is Car A in the correct position to complete a left turn?
   b. What lane should Car A turn into?
   c. What hazards should the driver of Car A watch for?
   d. If you are the driver of Car B and want to make a left turn at the intersection, what steps should you follow?
   e. What hazards should you be alert for when turning?

## Special Projects

1. Walk along a hilly street. Make note of how many parked cars have their wheels turned so the car will not roll into the street.

2. Observe anyone you ride with during the next week. Keep a record of how many drivers use the hand-over-hand steering method when making turns.

# Careers in the HTS: Traffic-Safety Education

Because the HTS is so vast, it offers a great many opportunities for employment.

Many people find careers in traffic safety education.

## Driver Education

Many high schools and professional driving schools offer courses in driver education. Instructors help students learn traffic-safety laws and how to operate a vehicle. They also teach students practical driving strategies.

To teach in a public high school, you must hold a teaching certificate. In many states, college-level driver and traffic courses are required. Some states issue special teaching licenses to instructors in professional driving schools.

In addition to schools, some companies offer driving improvement courses to their employees. A few schools and companies also offer instruction in evasive driving techniques. Safety councils often provide courses in defensive driving. In many areas, classes are provided for traffic offenders.

### Traffic-Safety Instruction

Educators are also involved in traffic-safety education at preschool, elementary, junior high, and college levels. Children are taught pedestrian, bus, and bicycle safety. At colleges, future law enforcement officials, educators, and engineers study laws, accident investigation, and other elements of traffic safety. In addition, some universities sponsor research projects to help officials define and solve problems in the HTS.

Many educators also work with various safety councils and government agencies (such as the National Safety Council). Some develop pamphlets, posters, and instructional material, while others serve as public relations officers.

### Driver Rehabilitation

Drivers with poor driving records can often be re-educated to become safe drivers.

People in law enforcement and administration help identify these drivers. Peole in medicine, social work, and psychology, help drivers cope with their problems. Educators then help them to become safe, efficient highway users.

# 2 Driving for Safety

# Chapter 4    Traffic Laws for Safety

- **What traffic problems would occur if there were no traffic lights or signals?**
- **Do you think it is possible for the same traffic laws to apply everywhere?**
- **Why are traffic signs different shapes and colors?**
- **How do speed limits control the flow of traffic?**

Think what it would be like to drive if there were no traffic laws. You could drive on either side of the road. There would be no signs to prohibit left turns or U-turns. There would be no speed limits or traffic lights. At first you might say, "Great! I can drive as fast as I want to and never have to stop for a red light." Remember, though, everyone else could do the same thing. How would you get through a busy intersection, know what highway exit to take, or know what dangers lie ahead?

# Rules of the Road

Traffic and vehicle laws are needed to keep the HTS running smoothly and safely. All states and provinces have traffic laws that must be obeyed. Before you start to drive, become familiar with these laws.

Most traffic laws are created to protect people and property. For example, maximum speed limits prohibit driving at unsafe speeds. Many of these laws are communicated to highway users through signs, signals, and pavement markings. Traffic lights and lane markings, for example, show

**Warning signs alert drivers to hazardous situations ahead.**

drivers whether certain maneuvers are allowed. Some laws are not shown on any sign, but drivers are expected to know them. These include basic driving rules, rules of right of way, and speed laws.

# Basic Driving Rules

Certain basic driving rules apply in all parts of the United States and Canada.

1. Always drive on the right side of a two-way street.
2. Unless you are on a road with more than one lane going in the same direction, pass other vehicles on the left.
3. Pass other vehicles only when it is safe to do so.
4. Always signal your intent to turn or change lanes.
5. Drive at speeds that are safe for road, weather, and traffic conditions.

# Right-of-Way Rules

When two drivers arrive at an intersection at the same time and want to turn into the same lane, which one has the right to go first? There are **right-of-way rules** that apply any time two or more highway users cross paths. Right-of-way rules apply to all highway users, including cyclists and pedestrians.

Do not assume that others will automatically obey the right-of-way rules. To avoid a collision, you may have to yield to others even though they should yield to you.

## ● Right of Way and Other Road Users

The basic right-of-way rules at intersections are:

1. Drivers approaching an intersection — with or without traffic signs or signals — must yield (give the right of way) to vehicles already in the intersection.
2. Drivers facing a stop sign or yield sign must let any traffic not facing these signs go first.
3. When two vehicles coming from different directions arrive at an intersection at the same time, the driver on the left should yield to the driver on the right.

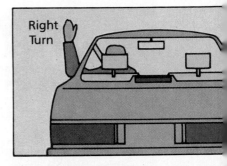

Right
Turn

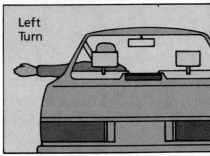

Left
Turn

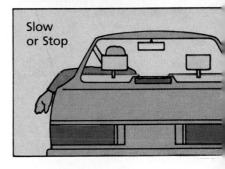

Slow
or Stop

**Hand signals help to show other drivers what you plan to do.**

**Be especially alert for blind pedestrians. Allow them extra time to cross a street.**

4. A driver making a left turn must yield the right of way to oncoming traffic that could create a hazard.
5. Drivers entering a road from a driveway or an alley must yield to traffic already on the road.
6. Drivers must yield to pedestrians in marked and unmarked crosswalks. Drivers must also yield to blind pedestrians regardless of where they cross. Blind pedestrians can be identified by white canes or lead (seeing-eye) dogs.
7. Drivers must yield to emergency vehicles (police cars, fire trucks, and ambulances) when these vehicles have their lights flashing or sirens blaring.
8. Drivers must stop when school buses are picking up or dropping off children. In most states, all traffic must stop when a school bus flashes its red stop lights.
9. Drivers facing a railroad crossing with the lights flashing and/or the gates down must stop. They must remain stopped until the lights stop flashing and the gates go up completely.

## ● Special Right-of-Way Rules

In some states there are no specific written laws for special right-of-way rules. Drivers are expected to understand that in some cases they should yield to other drivers.

For example, vehicles in a funeral procession have the right of way over other vehicles. The driver of the lead car must obey all traffic signs and signals. But the other drivers in the procession may carefully follow the lead car without stopping.

Any group of vehicles with a police escort has the right of way over other traffic. Often the police will close side streets that enter the route of such a motorcade. The route itself may also be closed to other traffic. The streets remain closed until all the vehicles have passed.

# Speed Laws

The maximum legal speed limit for any roadway in the United States is 55 mph. This limit was established to help conserve fuel. In Canada, the maximum legal speeds vary by province and range from 80 to 100 km/h. Many roadways have posted speed limits that are below the maximum legal speed. The **posted speed limit** is the maximum speed considered "safe" for the road and traffic conditions. You should not exceed the posted speed limit.

## Absolute Speed Limits

The **absolute speed limit** is the maximum (fastest) or minimum (slowest) posted speed at which you can legally drive under normal conditions. For example, expressways often post maximum and minimum speed limits. These limits establish a safe range of speeds that keep traffic moving smoothly. Because of reduced visibility, sometimes a lower speed limit is posted for night driving.

Everyone knows that you can be ticketed for exceeding the speed limit, but you can also be ticketed for driving too slowly under normal conditions. Driving too slowly can cause your car to become a hazard to other drivers. When road, weather, or traffic conditions are bad, however, the minimum speed limit is not enforced.

Just as you shouldn't drive below the minimum speed limit, you should not exceed the maximum speed limit — even when passing another vehicle. If you think you will exceed the speed limit as you pass, don't pass.

The maximum speed limit in the U.S. is 55 mph. Why do some highways post minimum speed limits?

**Always drive at speeds that are safe for existing conditions.**

**Regulatory signs help keep drivers from entering the ramp the wrong way.**

## ● Basic Speed Limit

The **basic speed limit** is not a specific, posted limit. It is the speed that is safe for existing road, weather, or traffic conditions. Although the basic speed limit can increase or decrease as driving conditions change, it is never higher than the absolute speed limit.

Under the basic-speed law, you can be ticketed for driving too fast for existing conditions, even when your speed is lower than the posted limit. For example, driving at 50 mph during a heavy snowstorm on a highway with a posted speed of 55 mph could result in a ticket. This speed would not be considered safe for the existing conditions.

# Traffic Control

Signs, signals, and pavement markings help keep traffic moving in an orderly way. By showing drivers and other highway users when and where to stop, what speeds are safe, and what dangers are ahead, they also help keep the HTS safe. In many instances, they can help you avoid being involved in collisions.

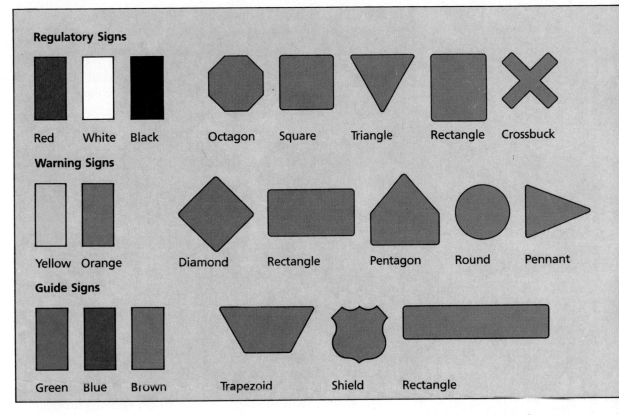

**Regulatory Signs**

Red   White   Black   Octagon   Square   Triangle   Rectangle   Crossbuck

**Warning Signs**

Yellow   Orange   Diamond   Rectangle   Pentagon   Round   Pennant

**Guide Signs**

Green   Blue   Brown   Trapezoid   Shield   Rectangle

# Traffic Signs

In 1970, new national standards for road signs were set up by the National Joint Committee on Uniform Traffic Control Devices. Based on international standards, these signs give messages in symbols. Therefore, you should be able to understand the symbols and follow road signs wherever you drive.

The color and shape of a sign enable you to recognize from far away what a sign says. For example, a diamond-shaped sign always warns of a possible danger ahead. The color orange is used to inform a driver of a detour or road construction ahead. Therefore, an orange diamond-shaped sign warns of a detour or road construction ahead. When you see this sign, you should begin slowing and be prepared to stop.

**Different colors and shapes are used to help drivers easily identify signs.**

## Regulatory Signs

**Regulatory Signs**

Speed Limit

Speed Limit

No Right Turn

Stop

**Regulatory signs** tell you what to do or what not to do. These signs have black or red markings on a white background. Signs with black markings tell you what you must do. For example, signs giving speed limits and lane use instructions have black markings on a white background.

Some signs have a black symbol (such as a horse or a truck) in a red circle and crossed by a red bar. The red bar and circle tell you what you cannot do. Signs with these markings are also known as **prohibitory signs**.

A few regulatory signs have a special shape and color. Among them are the stop, yield, do-not-enter, wrong-way, one-way, and railroad crossbuck signs.

The **stop** sign is a red octagon, or eight-sided figure, with white markings. This sign tells you to stop at the stop line or before the crosswalk if there is no stop line. If there is neither a crosswalk nor a stop line, you must stop before your car reaches the cross street. Before proceeding, yield to all traffic that does not have to stop.

The **yield** sign is a red and white triangle pointing downward. This sign warns that you should slow but need not stop unless you would interfere with other traffic. Always allow drivers with the right of way to go before you do.

The **wrong-way** sign is a red, horizontal rectangle. When you see it, do not enter the road. If you are already on the road when you see the sign, pull off the road quickly and change direction as soon as you safely can.

The **do-not-enter** sign is a white square with a red circle. Inside the red circle is a white bar and the words DO NOT ENTER. You must not enter any road where this sign appears.

Yield

Wrong Way

Do Not Enter

One Way

Railroad Crossing

A **one-way** sign is a black rectangle with a white arrow that shows the direction you can drive on the roadway.

The **railroad crossbuck** is a white **X**-shaped sign with black lettering. It warns you that a railroad crossing is ahead. Slow down and prepare to stop for a train when you see this sign.

## Warning Signs

**Warning signs** tell you about possible dangers ahead. Whenever you see one, be prepared to slow or stop. Most warning signs are yellow diamonds with black legends (words). Frequently, they contain symbols. For example, a sign warning that a roadway is especially "slippery when wet" also shows a car with wavy "skid" marks behind it.

A few warning signs have different shapes or colors. **School-crossing** and **school-zone** signs are yellow pentagons (five-sided figures) with black legends. Slow down and be prepared to stop when you see these signs.

The **railroad crossing ahead** sign is round and has a yellow background with a black legend. Be prepared to stop for trains whenever you see this sign. **No-passing** signs are yellow pennants with black legends. They are found on the left side of the road where drivers can see them more easily. In some states, however, a rectangular sign (on the right side of the road) with a white background and black lettering shows a no-passing zone.

Road construction, repair, and detour signs are always orange with black legends. They may be diamonds or rectangles. Change-of-speed signs are yellow rectangles. These signs are often found on expressway ramps, before curves, and in other areas requiring a change in speed.

**Warning Signs**

Slippery When Wet

Divided Highway

Deer Crossing

School Crossing

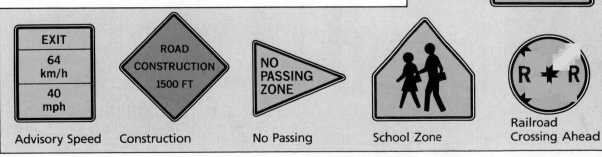

Advisory Speed    Construction    No Passing    School Zone    Railroad Crossing Ahead

## Guide Signs

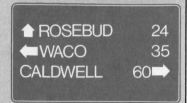

**Destination**

**Information**

**Recreation**

**Service**

### Guide Signs

Information about location, direction, types of services available, or points of interest is given on **guide signs**. These signs are usually square or rectangular and have color-coded messages.

Destination and distance signs are green with white legends. They provide you with information about route directions and the distance from one place to another.

Milepost signs are also green with white numerals. These signs are placed along the roadway at one-mile intervals. The first sign, numbered zero, is at the beginning of a route or at the west or south border of a state. Milepost signs are helpful in identifying your exact location along your route.

Rest, scenic, and service area signs are blue with white legends. These tell you where to find such services as service stations, hospitals, restaurants, and telephones. They also tell you where scenic and motorist rest areas may be found. Recreation area signs are brown with white legends.

General information signs are white with black or green legends. Green markings are often used to point the way to parking lots. Black markings are used to tell about things such as road conditions and speed-regulated areas.

A **route marker** always tells the number of the highway. The shape and color of the marker depend on the kind of highway. For example, an interstate highway is marked by a red and blue shield. A green shield shows an interstate business route. Some markers show the outline of a state.

**Route Markers**

# Traffic Signals

Traffic-control signals are also used to help keep traffic moving in an orderly way and to tell drivers who has the right of way at congested or dangerous intersections. Like signs, they are color coded. The colors used most often are red, yellow, and green. Red means stop; yellow, proceed with caution, prepare to stop; and green, go if the way is clear. Pedestrian lights are usually white or green for WALK and orange for DON'T WALK.

## ● Traffic Lights

**Traffic lights** may be located on a support at the side of the road or suspended above the middle of an intersection. They can be arranged horizontally or vertically. Red is on the top in a vertical arrangement and to the left in a horizontal one. Yellow is always in the middle. Green is at the bottom of a vertical arrangement and at the right of a horizontal one. Knowing how the lights are arranged is especially important for people who are color blind.

A green traffic light does not guarantee that your way is clear — another vehicle may still be in the intersection. Always scan the intersection carefully before you proceed on a green light. Vehicles already in the intersection must be allowed to clear the intersection before anyone else enters it. Also be alert for drivers who may not stop for a red light.

**Use extra caution when driving through busy intersections.**

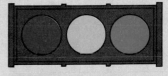

**Traffic Control Signals**

STOP    WARNING    GO

STOP. Do not turn in this direction.

WARNING. The green arrow is about to turn red. Prepare to stop.

GO in the direction indicated.

GO STRAIGHT AHEAD ONLY

GO LEFT ONLY

GO RIGHT ONLY

STOP

WARNING

GO

The yellow light helps provide a smooth, safe change in the movement of traffic. A yellow light is a warning that the light is about to change to red. Prepare to stop when you approach a yellow light. If you cannot stop safely, continue through the intersection with caution.

You must stop when the light is red. Unless there is a "No Turn On Red" sign, you may make a right turn at a red light. Before turning, though, you must come to a complete stop. Always yield the right of way to pedestrians and vehicles with the green light.

Sometimes traffic lights also have arrows. A green arrow allows you to go in the direction that the arrow is pointing. A yellow arrow indicates that traffic going in the direction of the arrow must prepare to stop and yield to other traffic. A red arrow means stop — you cannot go in this direction until the signal changes.

### Flashing Signals

**Flashing signals** are used at some intersections where traffic is not very heavy or steady. Such signals are also placed near dangerous sections of road. At a yellow flashing signal, slow down and check carefully for traffic before you proceed. Always be prepared to stop. At a red flashing signal, come to a complete stop. Then, if there is no danger from cross street traffic, you can proceed.

### Lane-Use Signals

**Lane-use signals** show which lanes are open to traffic. These are usually green arrows and yellow or red crossbars appearing directly over the lanes they control. A green arrow means that the lane is open to traffic. A lane marked by a red crossbar is closed to traffic. A yellow crossbar tells you that the lane ahead will soon be closed to traffic — leave the lane as soon as it is safe to do so.

### Pedestrian Signals

**Pedestrian lights** are usually white or green for WALK and orange for DON'T WALK. When facing a WALK signal, pedestrians have the right of way. You must yield to them as they cross the street.

**Lane use signals are designed to move cars more efficiently.**

**Pedestrian signals help control the movement of pedestrians.**

**Lane Use Lights**

| Lane open | Warning | Lane closed |

**Pedestrian Signals**

Pedestrians facing a flashing DON'T WALK signal should not begin crossing the street. Those who are already in the street, however, may continue across. You must yield to these pedestrians. When facing a steady DON'T WALK light, pedestrians must not start across the street. Drivers now have the right of way, and pedestrians are expected to yield to traffic. They may not always do so, however, so proceed with caution.

# Pavement Markings

**Pavement markings** are the yellow or white markings painted directly onto the road surface. They help to regulate traffic, define lanes, and warn drivers of possible dangers. Some pavement markings repeat information given on signs and signals. Still other markings tell drivers which

**Pavement markings are used to regulate, warn, and guide drivers.**

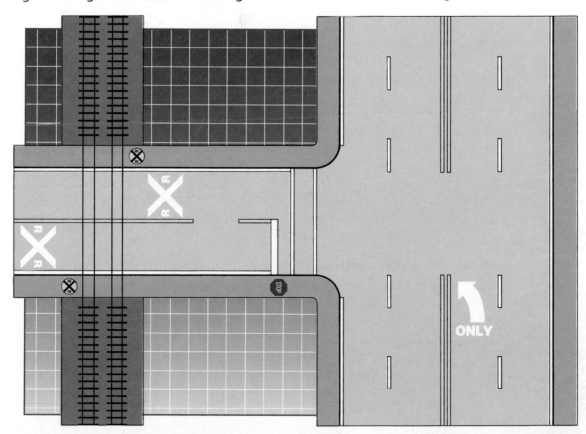

lanes they may enter and how they may use the lanes. These markings are especially helpful when visibility is poor. In some areas, raised lane separators are used to mark traffic lanes.

### Pavement Edge Lines

**Edge lines** are solid white lines along the side of a road that mark the outside edge of the road. Edge lines do not continue through intersections, so their absence helps you identify intersections. Edge lines are sometimes used to guide traffic around bridge supports or other hazards.

### Lane Markings

Lines are used to show the boundaries of driving lanes. White lines separate lanes that are open to traffic moving in the same direction. Yellow lines separate traffic moving in opposite directions. Lines can be solid or broken. Solid lines indicate that you may not cross into the other lane. When the line is broken, you can cross into the other lane after checking that your path is clear.

If there are no lane markings to separate traffic, you must judge how much of the road you may take without crowding other highway users.

Arrows are used near intersections to indicate which lanes can be used for what purpose. White lane arrows may point left or right, straight ahead, or both. Drivers in the lane must go in the direction the arrow is pointing. Sometimes solid white lines edge the lane marked with arrows. These lines serve to discourage drivers from changing lanes close to the intersection.

### No-Passing Lines

Sometimes a solid yellow line is used to separate traffic moving in opposite directions. It is illegal to cross a solid yellow line except when you are entering or leaving a roadway or making a legal turn. Often this line appears next to a broken yellow line. The solid line prohibits vehicles to the right of it from crossing the line to pass. A double solid yellow line indicates that passing is illegal for vehicles on either side of the roadway.

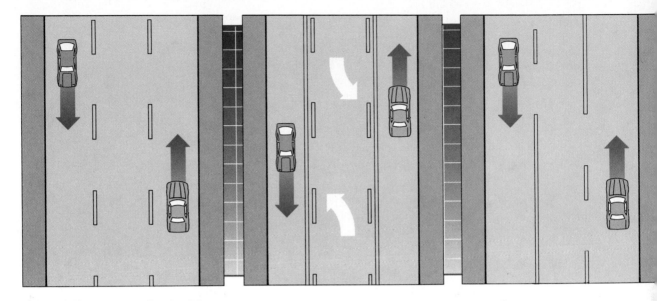

## ● Multilane Road Markings

In some areas, you may find three- or five-lane roads with traffic moving in opposite directions.

**Three-Lane Roads.** On three-lane roads, the middle lane may have broken yellow lines on both sides. In this case, drivers going in either direction may use the middle lane for passing. When the middle lane has solid yellow lines on both sides, the lane may be used only by drivers turning left. The solid yellow line may alternate from one side to another. On these roads, the middle lane serves as a passing lane for those drivers who do not have the solid line on their side.

**Five-Lane Roads.** On five-lane roads, the middle lane has solid yellow lines on both sides. There are usually broken yellow lines inside the solid lines. The middle lane can be used only to make a left turn. Enter the middle lane cautiously, since oncoming traffic can also use the lane.

## ● Stop and Crosswalk Lines

**Stop lines** are wide solid white strips. They go across only the lanes that are controlled by a signal or stop sign. Cars must stop behind these lines. **Crosswalk lines** help

**Driving on a 3-lane road can be dangerous. Pay close attention to the pavement markings.**

**When in a crosswalk and walking with the light, pedestrians have the right of way.**

guide pedestrians as they walk through an intersection. They are two solid white lines about 6 feet apart that extend across a street. Always stop before the crosswalk.

### ● Railroad Crossing Lines

In lanes approaching railroad tracks, the pavement is marked by a large **X** and **RR**. There is usually a wide stop line near the railroad crossing. When a train is coming, stop your car behind this line.

# Special Safety Laws

All drivers are expected to obey traffic control devices as well as right-of-way and speed laws. But drivers must also obey other safety laws. Over the years as unique situations occurred in the HTS, special traffic laws were enacted to help keep the system running smoothly and safely.

# DWI Laws

States and provinces recognize how alcohol and other intoxicants impair drivers' perception, driving skills, and judgment. Recent statistics show that there are over 25,000 alcohol-related highway deaths each year. In order to prevent these deaths, most states have enacted tough drunk-driving laws. **Driving while intoxicated (DWI)** is the single greatest cause of death of teenagers.

If you are arrested for driving while intoxicated, you must post a bail bond (pay a set amount) before you can be released from jail. If you are convicted, your license may be suspended for a specified period of time. In addition to losing your license, you may also have to pay a fine and/or serve time in jail. If you are convicted more than once, you may have your license revoked.

## Implied Consent

All states now have an **implied consent law**. According to this law, any person receiving a driver's license agrees to take a test if suspected of driving under the influence of alcohol. If you refuse to take the test, your driver's license can automatically be suspended — even if you were not driving while intoxicated. If you agree to take the test, the results may be used in court.

## Post-Collision Procedures

The purpose of traffic laws is to keep the HTS running smoothly. Even with these laws, though, the system does break down. Collisions are one example of a system breakdown. Because collisions do happen, special laws have been set up to help those involved.

All states require a driver who is involved in a collision to:

1. **Stop immediately.** Try to pull off the road so that you do not block traffic.
2. **Help anyone who is injured.** Send for medical help or call an ambulance if necessary. Do not give first aid unless you are qualified to do so.
3. **Notify the police** — immediately if possible. Ask someone else to do this if you are not able to.
4. **Give required information** — name, address, registration number, driver's license number, insurance company

**Breath tests are often used to determine whether a person is intoxicated.**

**Never leave the scene of a collision in which you are involved.**

name and address — to the police and to anyone involved in the collision.

While still at the scene, get the names and addresses of people who witnessed the collision. Also, record any details about the collision (time of day, road conditions, position of the vehicles, etc.) that you may need to recall later when filling out an accident report.

If you strike an unattended vehicle, try to locate the owner. If you cannot find the owner, write your name, address, telephone number, and registration number on a piece of paper and attach it to the vehicle in a place where it will be seen. Then notify your insurance company and the police.

Following a collision, you must also satisfy the state's **financial responsibility law**. Most states require drivers to prove that they are capable of paying up to $10,000 for one injured person, up to $20,000 for two or more injured persons, and up to $5,000 for property damage.

## Good Samaritan Law

If you are the first driver to arrive at the scene of a collision, you must stop and provide assistance. You should also help warn oncoming traffic of the accident ahead.

Most states have a **"Good Samaritan" law**. "Good Samaritan" laws help protect people who give first aid at the scene of a collision in any lawsuit that results from helping. This law also protects doctors, nurses, and emergency medical technicians (EMTs) who give first aid to injured people at the scene, provided that they act within their level of competence.

## Safety Checks

- Intersections are the most common sites for collisions. Always reduce your speed when approaching an intersection.

- Driving at speeds below 55 mph reduces the risk of serious injury or death in traffic collisions.

- Learn CPR (cardiopulmonary resuscitation). It can help you save a life at the scene of a collision.

- If you meet a vehicle that is going the wrong way on a one-way street, flash your headlights or tap your horn as a warning.

## Key Ideas

- At an uncontrolled intersection, you must yield to the driver on your right.
- In general, drivers must yield to emergency vehicles, school buses, and pedestrians.
- It is unlawful to exceed a posted speed limit or to drive faster than traffic and weather conditions permit.
- Traffic signs may be recognized by their distinctive shapes, colors, and symbols.
- A green traffic light (signal) means proceed, but only if the way is clear.
- You must stop at a red traffic light. Unless there is a sign prohibiting it, you may make a right turn on a red light after stopping if the way is clear.
- Pavement markings help to separate traffic, define lanes, and warn drivers of possible dangers, such as areas where passing is prohibited.

## Gauging Your Understanding

**1.** How do right-of-way rules help keep traffic moving smoothly?

**2.** List the five basic driving rules.

**3.** Under what condition can you be stopped for speeding — even though you are driving below the posted speed limit?

**4.** Describe what shapes and colors of traffic signs warn of hazards ahead.

**5.** What do the following lane markings tell you: solid lines, broken lines, yellow lines, white lines?

**6.** If you are involved in a collision, what are you required to do?

# ⇨ In the Driver's Seat

**1.** As you approach an elementary school on your right, you identify groups of children standing at the curb on both sides of the street. The posted speed limit is 25 mph. In this situation, what hazards would you look for? What steps should you take? What signs or pavement markings might help? Is the posted speed limit appropriate?

**2.** Assume that you are the driver in each situation described here. How would you respond to the various signals and pavement markings?
   a. As you approach an intersection, you notice a white arrow pointing left on the pavement ahead in your lane.
   b. You come to an intersection that has a red flashing signal, and there is no traffic coming from either direction.
   c. The lane you are driving in has a signal overhead with a yellow crossbar.
   d. You are on a three-lane road and want to turn left. The center lane has solid yellow lines on both sides.

## Special Projects

**1.** Observe a busy intersection where drivers are allowed to make a right turn on red. How many drivers come to a full stop before turning? What are some hazards these drivers should look for? Do the drivers allow enough space between oncoming cars to enter the flow of traffic safely?

**2.** As a passenger, try to identify traffic signs by shape and color before you are close enough to read them or see a specific symbol. How many different types of signs do you observe? How many shapes and colors are displayed?

# Chapter 5

# Natural Laws and Driving

- **What sensations do you feel on amusement park rides? What similar sensations occur in a moving automobile?**

- **How many factors must you consider when you round a curve? What about the load in the car? the tires? road features?**

As a passenger, you've probably noticed the way a car responds on sharp curves, going up or down steep hills, or driving on slippery or rough road surfaces. You have likely had the sensation of being pulled to the left when taking a sharp right turn, or of being pushed backward or forward when accelerating or braking suddenly. You've seen loose objects slide around or fall over when the car stops or when it turns. Chances are you have also experienced minor skids or "fishtailing" in rainy or snowy weather.

All of these events are the result of certain natural forces that influence how a vehicle accelerates, brakes, and turns. By learning about the forces acting on your vehicle, you will be better prepared to predict how your vehicle will respond in certain situations.

## Understanding Natural Laws

Several natural forces affect the handling of your vehicle. These forces include gravity, friction, energy of motion (momentum), inertia, and centrifugal force.

## Gravity

The force that pulls objects toward the center of the earth is known as **gravity**. Gravity gives objects their weight. It also causes a vehicle to increase speed when going downhill and to lose speed when going uphill. When driving, you must use your car's controls to compensate for the effects of gravity.

When you drive downhill, gravity causes your car to gain speed. You must use engine braking (by decreasing pressure on the gas pedal) or the service brakes to keep the car from building up too much speed. Downshifting (shifting to a lower gear) helps provide additional braking.

Stopping on a downgrade is also more difficult than stopping on a level surface. Leave more time and space to stop your vehicle when you are headed downhill. Also stay well behind the vehicle ahead.

Going uphill, your car is working against the pull of gravity. You must put more pressure on the accelerator to maintain speed and climb the hill. Shifting to a lower gear gives you added climbing power.

# Center of Gravity

Your car's **center of gravity** is the point around which all of its weight is balanced. Because most of today's cars have a low center of gravity, they handle well on curves and turns. Any change in a car's center of gravity affects how the car handles, especially on turns.

Adding weight to a rooftop carrier raises a car's center of gravity. This higher center of gravity makes the car less stable on curves and in sudden changes of direction. Any additional weight in a vehicle affects how it steers, accelerates, and brakes. Riding with passengers or with heavy materials in the trunk or back seat may produce noticeable changes in how the car handles.

**To keep from building up too much speed, truck drivers often must downshift on steep hills.**

**An overhead load may cause a vehicle to become unstable on curves.**

**Traction is reduced on icy surfaces. What driving adjustments should you make on an icy road?**

# Friction

The force that resists the motion of one surface against another is known as **friction**. Without friction, a car's tires would simply spin in place and no motion would be possible. It is the ability of tires to "grip" the road surface that makes it possible to control vehicle motion. This friction between the tires and the road surface is called **traction**.

Speeding up, slowing down, and cornering all put added stress on tires and affect their ability to grip the road. The design and condition of the tires also affect how a vehicle handles on the road. In addition, any material on the road — water, ice, snow, sand, oil — reduces traction.

The condition of the road also affects traction. Wet surfaces provide less traction than dry surfaces because there is less contact between the tires and the road. Bumpy roads reduce traction as well. On an uneven surface the tires must move up and down rapidly in order to stay in contact with the road. Worn or defective shock absorbers cause the tires to lose their grip on the road. Replacing worn shock absorbers helps ensure proper traction and control.

Friction plays a part in braking a vehicle as well as in moving it forward. When you apply the brakes, the friction created slows the turning of the wheels. This causes the car to slow.

# Energy of Motion

The energy that builds up in a moving vehicle is called its **energy of motion**, or momentum. Energy of motion is determined by the moving vehicle's weight and speed. The heavier a vehicle is, the more energy of motion it develops. For example, at the same speed a 3500-pound car has twice as much energy as a 1750-pound car.

An increase in speed also increases a vehicle's energy of motion. In fact, the energy of a moving vehicle is increased by the square of its increase in speed. If you double the speed of a car, you increase its energy of motion by a factor of 4 ($2 \times 2 = 4$). If speed is tripled, the energy of motion is 9 times as great ($3 \times 3 = 9$). For example, if the speed of a car increases from 15 mph to 45 mph, the car is going 3 times as fast. However, its energy of motion is 9 times as great.

A fast-moving vehicle builds up more energy, or momentum, than a slow-moving one. Therefore, it must travel a greater distance before coming to a complete stop.

For example, two vans of equal weight are on the road. One is traveling 20 mph, the other 40 mph. The one going 40 mph has built up 4 times more energy of motion. As a result, it needs 4 times the distance that the slower van needs to stop.

Not only does the car itself build up a certain energy of motion as it is driven. Whatever is inside the car also builds up momentum. Once a car has reached a certain speed, the car and its occupants will continue to travel at that speed in a straight line unless acted upon by some outside force. This tendency is known as **inertia**.

In a collision with a solid object at 30 mph, the car comes to a complete stop in about $\frac{1}{10}$ second. However, because of inertia, any unrestrained occupants continue traveling at 30 mph. An unrestrained occupant in a 30 mph

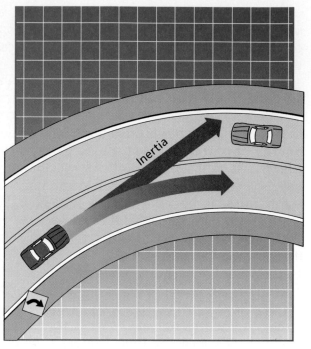

**Banked curves reduce a vehicle's tendency to slide toward the outside of a curve.**

**To compensate for centrifugal force, reduce your speed before entering sharp curves.**

crash strikes the interior of the car with a force of several thousand pounds. Serious or fatal injury is likely to result. Safety belts and other restraint systems can help reduce the seriousness of any injury. So can safety features such as energy-absorbing steering columns and padded instrument panels, which provide several inches of cushioning.

# Centrifugal Force

One of the effects of inertia is **centrifugal force**. Centrifugal force tends to push a vehicle out of a curve or turn on to a straight path. In order to maintain control on curves, you must use your vehicle's controls to overcome the effects of inertia. Gravity and friction must be strong enough to overcome centrifugal force and keep the car on the curving or turning path.

The more energy of motion a car develops — that is, the faster it is moving — the stronger its inertia. Therefore, the higher your car's speed, the more it resists being turned from a straight path. In addition to vehicle speed, there are other factors that affect the control you have over your car on a curve. One is the sharpness of the curve. The sharper the curve, the more difficult it is to overcome the car's inertia. Sharp curves require lower speeds.

The slope of the road also affects how a car handles on a curve and how difficult it is to overcome centrifugal force. On a **banked curve**, the road is built up on the outside edge and slopes down toward the inside of the curve. The downward slope reduces the car's tendency to slide toward the outside of a curve.

On a **crowned road**, the middle is built up higher than the sides. The road slopes down from the middle to each side. A car is more likely to pull toward the outside of a crowned road. The inside of a **crowned curve**, however, is almost the same as a banked curve.

A flat road has no slope at all — not even on curves. Therefore, the shape of such a road is of no help in resisting centrifugal force. You should reduce your speed significantly before entering a curve on a completely flat road. There may be an advisory speed sign posted to let you know what speed is considered safe for taking the curve.

Vehicle weight also affects your ability to control a car on a curve. As you have learned, added cargo can increase a vehicle's energy of motion or change its center of gravity. A heavily loaded car is harder to control on curves. Therefore, reduce your speed on curves more than usual when your car is heavily loaded.

An important function of the safety belt is to keep you behind the wheel and in control of the car during and after a violent maneuver or a collision. On a particularly sharp turn, the safety belt can keep you from sliding too far and losing your grip on the steering wheel.

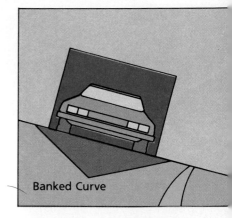

Banked Curve

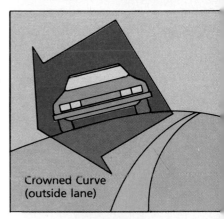

Crowned Curve (outside lane)

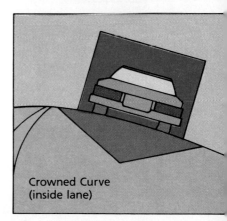

Crowned Curve (inside lane)

# Stopping Distance

**Total stopping distance** is the space it takes to stop your car once you have identified a potential hazard. This distance varies depending on such things as vehicle speed

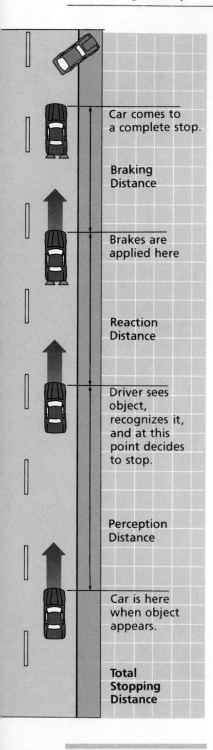

Car comes to
a complete stop.

Braking
Distance

Brakes are
applied here

Reaction
Distance

Driver sees
object,
recognizes it,
and at this
point decides
to stop.

Perception
Distance

Car is here
when object
appears.

Total
Stopping
Distance

and road conditions. The faster the car is moving, the more energy of motion it has and the longer its stopping distance becomes.

Stopping distance can be divided into three parts: perception, reaction, and braking distances.

# Perception Time and Distance

**Perception distance** is the amount of space your car travels from the time a potential problem exists to the time you perceive it and decide to take action. **Perception time**, then, can be seen as the time it takes to identify, predict, and decide. These are the first three steps of the IPDE process, which is described in Chapter 6. Perception time varies according to a driver's attentiveness, physical condition, and driving experience.

Reduced visibility can also affect perception time. Always travel at a speed that is safe for the particular weather and road conditions. When visibility is poor, decrease your speed so you can handle an emergency easily and safely.

# Reaction Time and Distance

The distance you travel between the moment of deciding and the time you start to brake is known as **reaction distance**. The time it takes to actually apply the brakes after you make your decision is called **reaction time**. Although average reaction time is about $\frac{3}{4}$ of a second, in difficult traffic situations this time can be much longer.

# Braking Distance

**Braking distance** is the distance your car travels from the time you apply the brakes until the car stops. Braking distance is directly related to speed and energy of motion. The braking distance of a car traveling 40 mph is 4 times that of a car traveling 20 mph.

The condition of your car's tires, brakes, and shock absorbers affects braking distance. Bad weather and poor road conditions increase any vehicle's braking distance.

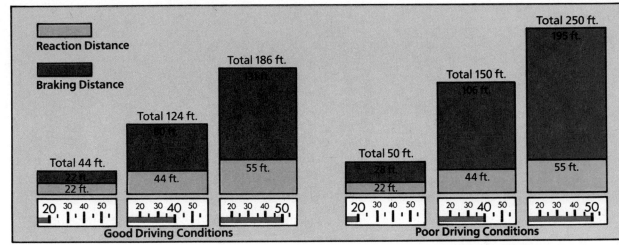

**Reaction Distance**

**Braking Distance**

Total 44 ft.
22 ft.
22 ft.

Total 124 ft.
80 ft.
44 ft.

Total 186 ft.
131 ft.
55 ft.

**Good Driving Conditions**

Total 50 ft.
28 ft.
22 ft.

Total 150 ft.
106 ft.
44 ft.

Total 250 ft.
195 ft.
55 ft.

**Poor Driving Conditions**

Gravity also has an effect on braking distance. Because of the pull of gravity, braking distances are shorter going uphill and longer going downhill. Staying a safe distance behind the vehicle ahead is the best way to ensure that you will have enough time and space to stop.

In some emergencies it may be safer to swerve, or steer around an object, rather than to stop to avoid a collision. At speeds above 30 mph, swerving time is much less than stopping time. Swerving requires less traction than braking. Also, reaction time is faster for swerving. You can turn the steering wheel more quickly than you can apply the brake.

**As speed increases, so do reaction and braking distances. Allow more space to stop under poor driving conditions.**

# Force of Impact

When a car collides with an object, it hits that object with a certain **force of impact**. The faster the car is traveling, the greater the force of impact.

## Factors Affecting Force of Impact

The weight of the car also affects the force of impact. The heavier the vehicle, the stronger the collision. When driving with a heavy load, reduce your speed to make up for the added weight.

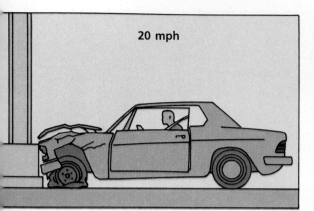

20 mph

40 mph

**The faster a car is traveling, the greater the force of impact and the more serious the damage.**

How much damage there is in a collision also depends on the object that is hit. If a car hits a solid, stationary object (such as a stone wall), all of its moving energy is converted on impact. The resulting damage is greater than if the object has some "give" to it — for example, a bush. In this case, the object absorbs most of the impact force, and damage to the car and injuries to occupants are less.

# Energy-absorbing Features in Cars

The car's design also affects how much damage results from a collision. Many new cars have energy-absorbing features. These features allow the bumper and front-end to absorb much of the force of impact in a collision. As a result, the passenger compartment of the car is less seriously damaged. Energy-absorbing features spread out the time and space in which the passenger compartment comes to a stop in a collision. Therefore the occupants are shielded from some of the impact force. Beams in the doors help prevent penetration of the passenger compartment.

# Passenger Restraint

Some safety features on the inside of the car help reduce the force of impact for the car's occupants. The most important and effective of these is the safety belt. A combined lap and shoulder belt helps keep the occupants from striking the interior of the car with a potentially fatal force.

**Passive safety belts** are found in some new cars. These safety belts fasten automatically when you close the car door. **Air bags** are now standard equipment in some cars. The bags inflate in a collision and help prevent the occupants from striking the inside of the car. These passive restraints require no action on the part of the occupants.

The most frequent cause of death in collisions is injury to the head and chest caused by hitting the steering assembly or windshield. New cars have energy-absorbing steering columns, padded instrument panels, and windshields with safety glass. These features can absorb some of the impact force. Still, use of a safety belt can mean the difference between a minor injury and a fatal one — even at speeds as low as 15 mph. Overall, safety belts can improve your chances of surviving a serious collision by 60 percent.

**Children should always ride in approved child-restraint seats.**

## Fuel Misers

● Shift to a higher gear when the recommended speed is achieved. Refer to your tachometer or your owner's manual for the recommended speed.

● Apply only enough pressure to the brake pedal to reduce excessive speed.

● Ease up on the gas pedal when driving downhill. Take advantage of the car's momentum to conserve fuel.

## ➡ Key Ideas

● Gravity increases stopping distance on downgrades.
● The higher a car's center of gravity, the more difficult it is for you to control the car.
● Increased speed and weight both result in an increase in a vehicle's energy of motion, or resistance to stopping.
● Centrifugal force resists your efforts to round a curve or turn.
● A banked curve and the inside of a crowned curve are safer to round than a flat curve or the outside of a crowned curve.
● Stopping distance is made up of perception, reaction, and braking distance. Driver alertness and experience are important factors in stopping in time.

- Today's cars contain many safety features designed to reduce force of impact. The most important is the safety belt.
- In an emergency, safety belts keep you behind the wheel.

# ➡ Gauging Your Understanding

**1.** How is a car's cornering response affected if you have 100 pounds of luggage in the roof rack?

**2.** How much greater is the centrifugal force when a car rounds a curve at 40 mph than it is at 20 mph?

**3.** Give at least four reasons why the stopping distance of your car at 30 mph may vary from one situation to another.

**4.** Explain each of the following: perception time and distance; reaction time and distance; braking distance.

**5.** To avoid a hazard, is it better to stop or swerve? Why?

**6.** What are the advantages of wearing safety belts?

# ➡ In the Driver's Seat

Refer to the illustration on page 88. Then answer the following questions:

**1.** Driver A enters the curve without reducing speed. As a result, the car swings partially into the opposite lane, just over the yellow line. How should Driver A react? What should the driver of Car B do to avoid a collision?

**2.** Assume that the road shown is crowned. For which driver is the road design an advantage? What should the driver of each car do upon approaching and entering the curve?

## Special Projects

**1.** In your area, how many curves are banked properly? Are there any crowned roads? Are there roads that would be safer if they had been constructed differently?

**2.** Observe cars at an intersection controlled by a stop sign or traffic signal. How many drivers slow down enough before stopping so the car doesn't pitch forward? How many stop beyond the stop line? How many cars stop smoothly?

# ⮕ Chapter Test 5

Name _____ Date _____

**Write "T" beside statements that are true and "F" beside those that are false.**

_____ **1.** Oil, dirt, or water on a roadway can reduce traction.

_____ **2.** The force that resists the motion of one surface against another is known as inertia.

_____ **3.** A vehicle with a high center of gravity is easier to control than one with a low center of gravity.

_____ **4.** Perception time is not affected by reduced visibility.

_____ **5.** The sharper the curve and the faster a car is traveling, the greater the effect of centrifugal force.

_____ **6.** Stopping on a downgrade is more difficult than stopping on a level surface.

_____ **7.** An increase in speed also increases a vehicle's energy of motion.

**Write the letter of the best answer in the space provided.**

_____ **1.** If a car traveling 40 mph weighs the same as one traveling 20 mph, its energy of motion is (a) 2 times greater, (b) 4 times greater, (c) 9 times greater, (d) 12 times greater.

_____ **2.** To keep a vehicle on its turning path on a curve, gravity and friction must be strong enough to overcome (a) force of impact, (b) center of gravity, (c) centrifugal force, (d) energy of motion.

_____ **3.** The space it takes to stop your car once you have identified a potential hazard is (a) braking distance, (b) reaction time, (c) total stopping distance, (d) energy of motion.

_____ **4.** The distance your car travels from the time you apply the brakes until the car stops is (a) reaction distance, (b) total stopping distance, (c) perception distance, (d) braking distance.

_____ **5.** The faster a car is traveling, the greater its (a) gravity, (b) friction, (c) centrifugal force, (d) energy of motion.

**Complete these sentences by writing the correct terms in the blanks.**

**1.** Perception  distance plus reaction distance plus braking distance equals

_____.

**2.** The middle is built up higher than the sides of a _____ road.

**3.** Applying the brakes creates _____, which slows the car down.

**4.** _____ keep you behind the wheel of your car in an emergency.

**5.** _____ varies according to a driver's attentiveness, physical condition, and driving experience.

**6.** A passive safety feature that helps reduce the force of impact for a car's occupants is the _____.

**7.** The tendency of a car and its occupants to continue to travel at a certain speed unless acted upon by some outside force is known as _____.

**Match the items in Column B to the items in Column A by placing the correct letter in the space provided.**

| Column A | Column B |
|---|---|
| _____ **1.** Inertia | **a.** Causes a vehicle to increase speed when going downhill. |
| _____ **2.** Friction | **b.** The force that resists the motion of one surface against another. |
| _____ **3.** Gravity | |
| _____ **4.** Centrifugal force | **c.** Tends to push a vehicle out of a curve or turn onto a straight path. |
| _____ **5.** Energy of motion | **d.** Tendency of a vehicle to continue at the same speed in a straight line unless acted upon by some outside force. |
| _____ **6.** Perception time | |
| | **e.** The energy that builds up in a moving vehicle. |
| | **f.** The time it takes to identify, predict, and decide. |

# Chapter 6     A Strategy for Driving

- **Some drivers concentrate only on what is going on directly in front of them. What dangers does this practice create?**
- **Driving the speed limit and obeying traffic signs are not enough to help you avoid a collision. What other things should a safe driver do?**

As you turn onto a side street, your sunglasses case slides off the seat and onto the floor. You look ahead, see the coast is clear, and then reach down to pick up the case. In less than a second, your eyes return to the road. When they do, you find that the car ahead of you has stopped to drop off a passenger. Or you look up to see a pedestrian crossing the street directly in your path. Coping with constantly changing conditions is a routine part of driving. The best way to be prepared for changing conditions is to develop a **strategy**, or plan, for driving. This strategy must include a way to identify hazards and a way to handle them safely in order to avoid collisions.

## Understanding the IPDE Process

You must constantly scan your path of travel for trouble spots. As soon as you identify a hazard, you must consider the choices open to you and then act. Usually, you have just seconds to decide and act.

**IPDE** (Identify, Predict, Decide, Execute) is a very useful strategy for driving. IPDE is a way of gathering, interpreting, and acting on traffic information. It involves identifying possible hazards and predicting how they may affect you and other highway users. Then, using this information, you must decide what action to take to avoid a collision. Finally, you execute, or carry out, your decision.

## Identifying

The first step in the IPDE process is **identifying** possible problems. As you drive, constantly search for any objects or changes in the traffic situation that are possible sources of danger, or hazards, to you. Any part of the HTS — including roads, traffic-control devices, your own car, other vehicles, and pedestrians — can become a hazard at any time. To avoid the hazard, you may have to change direction, change speed, signal others, or perform a combination of these maneuvers.

## ● Visual Lead Time

The sooner you identify a possible hazard, the more time you have to handle it. You should therefore regularly search the HTS for possible dangers. Begin by **centering** on, or looking ahead to, where your car will be in about eight seconds. This will provide you with a **visual lead time** that will help you identify a hazard before it becomes an immediate danger.

**Drivers should constantly search the roadway ahead for possible hazards.**

visual lead
required at 50 mph

visual lead
required at 25 mph

**Maintain an adequate
visual lead, especially
when you identify a po-
tential hazard such as
the cyclist ahead.**

The higher your speed, the farther you must look to see
eight seconds ahead. For example, at 25 mph, your car
travels about 37 feet per second. At this speed you must
look ahead 293 feet — almost the length of a football
field — to see where you will be in eight seconds. However,
at 50 mph, your car travels about 73 feet per second. At
this speed you must look ahead 587 feet — nearly the
length of two football fields! — to see where you will be in
eight seconds.

An 8-second visual lead is the minimum that you should
maintain on a straight road under ideal conditions. At
speeds greater than 30 mph, you probably need about four
seconds to stop your car. Since cars coming the other way
also have a stopping time of four seconds, you need a
minimum of eight seconds of lead time to prevent a collision. On the highway, you should extend this visual lead to
twelve seconds to give yourself a greater margin of safety.

Maintaining an 8-second visual lead is not always possible. On hilly or curved roads, for example, you cannot see

that far ahead at all times. Your strategy on such roads —
or whenever the view ahead is limited — should be to slow
to a safe speed.

**Checking the rearview mirror is an essential part of a driver's scanning routine.**

### Scanning

Besides centering eight seconds ahead, **scan** the immediate area around your car for possible hazards. Scan to both
sides of your lane for pedestrians or cars leaving the curb.
Check your mirrors about every five seconds to see behind
and to the left of your car. Use **ground viewing** to see
where other cars are heading by the direction of their
wheels. Glance at your instrument panel occasionally to find
what is happening in your own car.

# Predicting

**Predicting** — the second step in the IPDE process — is
the act of estimating what is likely to occur in a given
situation. Through experience, you learn how your car

reacts — how well it steers, how quickly it brakes or picks up speed. You also learn through experience what other vehicles are capable of doing. This knowledge can help you predict what may happen in a traffic situation.

For example, if you know how long it takes you to stop your car at 30 mph, you can plan the proper distance to stay behind other vehicles. If you know that a heavy truck is likely to pick up speed on a downgrade, you can keep to the right to allow the truck to pass. Predicting is an important step in your driving strategy because it enables you to think about hazards *before* they actually occur. As a result, you can reduce and sometimes even prevent the hazard.

If you had to face only one hazard at a time, you could easily predict the possible outcomes. However, often you are faced with more than one hazard and the task of predicting becomes more difficult. For example, if a car is backing out of a driveway ahead of you, you can predict that by stopping suddenly you run the risk of being hit from behind. You can also predict that swerving around the car ahead may create a conflict with traffic coming the other way. Being able to predict the possible outcome of your actions helps you to decide the safest course to follow.

# Deciding

**Deciding** — the third IPDE step — involves choosing the safest way to handle a driving hazard. Your decision is likely to result in one or more of the following actions:

1. Slowing or stopping your car.
2. Changing direction. You may have to change direction by turning, changing lanes, or swerving.
3. Signaling a warning to other drivers through the use of turn signals, stoplights, or horn.

# Executing

**Executing**, or acting on, your decision is the final step in the IPDE process. To execute a maneuver, you must use your car's controls and equipment.

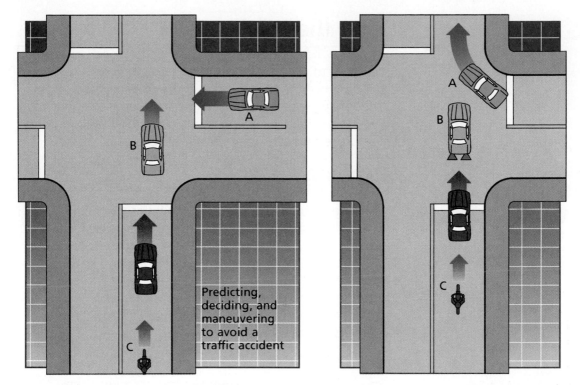

Predicting, deciding, and maneuvering to avoid a traffic accident

When faced with a critical traffic situation, you must take emergency action. And you must think and act quickly. For example, consider the steps you would take if a child suddenly ran in front of your car. Using IPDE, you would:

1. Identify the child's action as a hazard. In this case, you want to avoid striking the child.
2. Predict what could happen and consider possible ways of reducing or eliminating the danger and avoiding a collision. You could try to stop, swerve into another lane, or honk your horn to get the child's attention.
3. Decide on the best course of action for reducing the possibility of injury to the child, yourself, and other drivers. After considering your choices, you decide to brake and swerve slightly to avoid the child.
4. Execute your decision as quickly as possible by applying the brakes and turning the wheel.

Keep in mind that in most emergencies, you will have only seconds to identify a hazard and take action.

**You predict that the car on the side street will turn into your lane. By deciding to ease off the gas pedal, you allow enough space for yourself and the motorcyclist to brake moderately to avoid a collision.**

**What would you do to avoid hitting this child? What other hazards could you face?**

# Using the IPDE Process

Learning to use the IPDE process takes practice. As a new driver, you can practice the first three steps in the process — identifying, predicting, deciding — when riding with other drivers. Practice will make it easier for you to use the entire process once you are in the driver's seat.

# Handling Hazards

Working through the IPDE process helps you avoid hazards. As you maneuver your car to avoid one hazard, however, you may find you are involved in another hazardous situation. When faced with a hazard, often you must decide what course of action involves the least danger to you and to other highway users. Your decision will usually involve avoiding single hazards and either separating or compromising multiple hazards.

### ● Avoiding Hazards

You should always try to **minimize**, or reduce, the chance of becoming involved in a collision. When faced with a single hazard, you should minimize the danger of collision by changing speed or position and avoiding the hazard in the safest manner possible.

For example, Car A is parked ahead of you on the side of the road. It is blocking part of one lane on a two-lane, two-way highway. There is a driver in Car A. You, the driver of Car B, are approaching in the same lane. There is no other traffic on this straight road.

Applying the IPDE strategy, you decide to reduce the danger of colliding with Car A by pulling completely into the second lane (opposite lane). This action is safe because there is no oncoming traffic. After passing the parked car, you pull back into the proper lane. You have minimized the hazard by positioning your car in a different lane. By passing in this lane, you will not interfere with anything that the driver of Car A might do, and you avoid the possibility of collision.

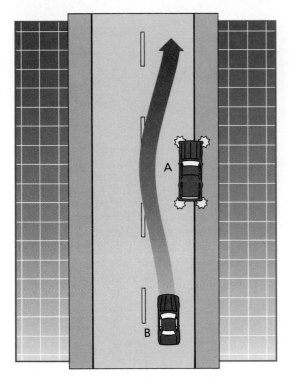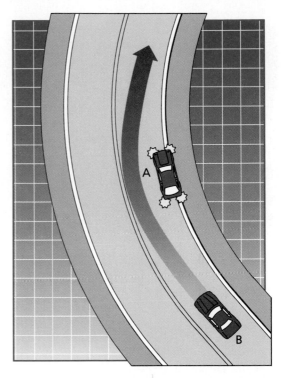

Sometimes a single hazard is complicated by other factors. A blind curve, for example, may make it difficult for you to see oncoming traffic. In this case, you would handle the hazard of the parked car differently.

Again, assume you are in Car B. Because of the blind curve, you can't tell whether it is safe to pull even partially into the other lane. In this case, you should reduce your speed and slowly pass the parked car. You might also sound the horn to signal the driver of Car A that you are passing so that he or she doesn't open the car door or pull into your path.

**Avoiding a single hazard usually involves changing speed or direction.**

## ● Separating Hazards

On the road you may face more than one hazard at the same time. When this happens, try not to cope with all of the hazards at once. Instead, deal with them one at a time. This strategy is known as **separating** hazards.

For example, suppose you are driving Car B on a two-way, two-lane straight highway. You identify Car A parked

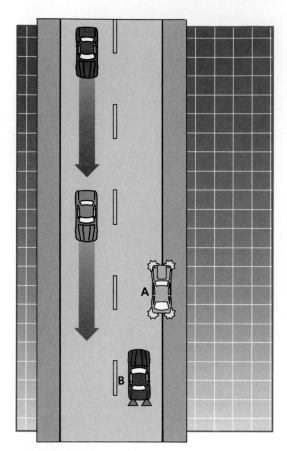

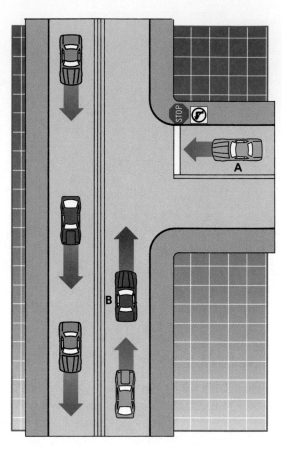

**It is usually better (and safer) to separate rather than compromise multiple hazards.**

on the side of the road in your lane. The driver of Car A is in the car. At the same time, you identify a line of oncoming traffic. You are faced with two hazards: the parked car and the line of oncoming vehicles. Because of the oncoming traffic, you cannot pull completely into the opposite lane to pass the parked car.

You decide to follow a swerving path. You slow down to let the first oncoming car pass the parked car. Doing so eliminates the first hazard.

You decide to pass the parked car before the second oncoming car becomes a hazard. You therefore move slightly into the oncoming lane, clear the parked car, and return to the original lane. This action eliminates the second hazard. By handling each hazard individually, you have successfully dealt with both.

## ● Compromising Hazards

At times you may face two or more hazards that cannot be handled separately. In such cases you must risk involvement with one hazard to avoid a more serious hazard. This strategy is known as **compromising** hazards.

For example, say that you are traveling in Car B on a two-way, two-lane roadway. A side street off this roadway is regulated by a stop sign. You identify Car A, which is approaching rapidly on the side road. The driver of Car A does not appear to be slowing for the stop sign. At the same time, you note in your mirror that you are being tailgated (followed closely from behind) by Car C. You also notice a line of oncoming traffic in the lane to the left. You predict that the driver of Car A is not going to stop.

You consider the following possible maneuvers and the risk involved with each:

1. You could continue driving at the same speed and risk getting hit broadside by Car A.
2. You could swerve into the left lane to avoid Car A and risk being hit head-on by oncoming traffic.
3. You could stop completely to allow Car A to proceed safely. By doing so, you risk being hit from behind by Car C, which has been tailgating you.
4. You could slow down, giving Car A the chance to turn and speed up before you reach the intersection. There is still a chance of a collision with Car A, however.

You decide to slow down, choosing the last option. By doing so, you avoid the risk of being hit from behind by giving the tailgater a little more time to adjust speed. The compromise is that you are not leaving as much space for Car A to maneuver.

In any hazardous situation, the course of action decided upon should be the one that involves the least amount of risk. Choosing the least amount of risk does not guarantee that no hazard will result. Sometimes compromising hazards is not successful and a collision results. For this reason, it is generally better to try to separate rather than compromise multiple hazards. Dealing with hazards one at a time reduces the chance of having a collision.

**At intersections where there is no escape route, a driver should increase following distance.**

# Managing Time, Speed, and Space

To use IPDE, you must know how to manage the space around your vehicle. You must drive at a proper speed and follow others at a safe distance. These measures will normally give you enough time to stop or swerve to avoid a hazard. There are three basic elements involved in giving yourself enough time and space to maneuver in an emergency: following distance, immediate path of travel, and total stopping distance.

## ● Following Distance

The interval or amount of space you leave between your car and the car ahead is known as **following distance**. You should follow at a distance that allows you enough room to avoid hitting the car ahead if it stops suddenly.

## ● Immediate Path of Travel

Your **immediate path of travel** is the distance your vehicle can cover in four seconds. You may need this entire distance to bring your vehicle to a stop.

## ● The Interval Rule

The distance between your car and the car ahead of you should be large enough to allow you to stop or swerve around the other car if it stops suddenly. The **interval rule** requires that you stay *at least* two seconds behind the car ahead. Two seconds is the smallest amount of time needed to stop suddenly at low or moderate speeds when road and weather conditions are good. It is also the minimum amount of time needed to swerve around an object in your path of travel.

There is a simple way to judge your following distance. First, choose a fixed object along the road — for example, a sign. When the *rear* of the vehicle ahead passes this object, begin counting. After counting two seconds (one thousand one, one thousand two), check the position of your car. If the *front* of your car is even with the fixed object, you are just two seconds behind the car ahead. If you have passed

the object, you are following too closely. Increase your following distance by slowing down.

Eventually you will no longer need to judge following distance in this way. You will know from experience whether you are following at a safe distance and you will adjust your speed as needed.

## ● Adjusting Following Distance

The interval rule can be used at any speed. However, the space required between vehicles will be greater the higher the speed. The reason is that you travel a greater distance at high speeds than at low speeds. For example, at 25 mph, your car travels about 73 feet in two seconds. At 50 mph, your car travels twice that far — about 146 feet — so the safe following distance doubles.

At times, you have to increase your following distance. When road or weather conditions are poor and visibility is limited, increase the interval to about four or five seconds. You need more time and space to stop or swerve under such conditions.

If you are being tailgated, you should also increase your following interval. Drop far enough back so that the interval between the car ahead of you and the car behind you is at least four seconds. This 4-second space provides an added margin of safety. It gives you extra distance so that you can slow gradually if the car ahead stops suddenly. By slowing gradually, you avoid being hit from behind.

**A 2-second following distance is the minimum distance necessary to stop or swerve to avoid a hazard.**

### ● Stopping Distance

**Stopping distance** is the amount of space needed to bring a car to a complete stop. The distance required to stop safely varies with speed and traction. When road conditions and traction are poor, you must slow down or stop more gradually to avoid skidding. In such cases your stopping distance is increased. Therefore, you must increase your following distance when road and weather conditions are bad. The extra distance provides you with more stopping space.

If a stationary object appears in your immediate path of travel (the space your car covers in four seconds), you may need four seconds to stop the car. If you are maintaining an 8-second visual lead, you can easily avoid hitting the object. However, consider a situation in which a car is approaching you in the same lane and at the same speed. If both you

**When being tailgated, the total interval between the car behind you and the car ahead of you should be at least four seconds.**

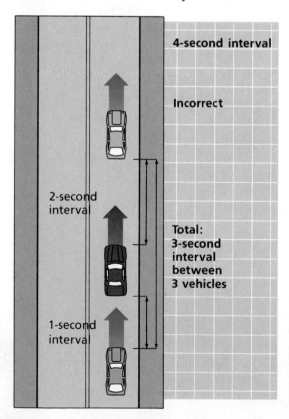

4-second interval

Incorrect

2-second interval

1-second interval

Total:
3-second interval between 3 vehicles

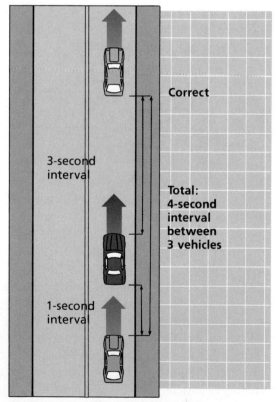

Correct

3-second interval

Total:
4-second interval between 3 vehicles

1-second interval

and the other driver are maintaining the minimum visual lead (eight seconds) you will see each other when you are only four seconds from colliding. Increasing your visual lead to twelve seconds provides a margin of safety and reduces the chance of collision.

## ● Swerving Path Time

In some situations it is safer for you to go around a hazard rather than to come to a stop. **Swerving path time** is the amount of time it takes to veer (steer) a car off the immediate travel path — usually two seconds. Returning to the original path takes another two seconds. The entire swerving maneuver therefore takes four seconds, which is equal to the immediate-path-of-travel time.

Poor traction increases the swerving path time to a total of eight or ten seconds. As with stopping distance, whenever your swerving path time increases, you must also increase your following distance. By increasing following distance, you give yourself more time to stop or swerve safely in response to objects in your path and maneuvers of the car ahead. (Refer to Maneuver I in the In-Car Guide in the back of this book.)

**A driver can often avoid a last-minute swerve by identifying farther ahead.**

## Adapting the IPDE Process

Many people work to make the HTS safe and the driving task as easy as possible. However, trouble spots remain that limit your and other drivers' ability to make the best use of the IPDE process. These limitations include reduced visibility, limited traction, areas of lateral access, limited space, and risk-taking drivers.

## Limited Visibility

Your ability to see affects the IPDE process greatly — particularly the identifying stage. You receive about 90 percent of all traffic information through your eyes. When your visibility is limited, you may not be able to identify possible hazards in time to take action. In fog or heavy rain, you may not be able to establish a sufficient visual lead. As a result, unless you reduce your speed you may not see a hazard until it is too late to avoid it.

Your ability to see may be hampered by other vehicles — especially by large vehicles such as trucks. Hills or curves may also reduce visibility. Buildings and trees might block your view. Weather and lighting conditions can also make it difficult for you to see. To adapt to limited visibility, reduce your speed or change your position so you have enough time and space to use the IPDE process.

**Increased following distance, especially behind large vehicles such as this, results in increased visibility.**

Your view of the road varies according to the type of vehicle you drive. In a low sports car, your view of the situation far ahead is limited. From a high-riding van, however, you get a better view of what's going on in front of you. Each time that you drive an unfamiliar vehicle, you may have to get used to a different range of visibility.

**What adjustments should you make for the poor road surface or limited space shown below?**

# Limited Traction

Good traction is essential to maintaining control of your car. The condition of the roadway and of your tires can affect traction. Rain, snow, and ice reduce traction. Bridges can cause special problems, since they often freeze and become slippery before other road surfaces. Traction is also poor on gravel and dirt roads, in sand, and on roads with metal grates.

Improper tire pressure affects the handling of the car. Tires with too little or too much air do not contact the road surface properly and can reduce traction. When traction is reduced, allow more time to execute your maneuvers. Once you identify the conditions that reduce traction, you can make the necessary adjustments to IPDE.

# Lateral Access

Complicated traffic scenes make it difficult to carry out the IPDE process. Areas of **lateral access** — where pedestrians or other vehicles can enter your path — can lead to many possible hazards. These areas include intersections, alleys, driveways, and merge lanes. Be extremely cautious as you approach one of these areas. Always look well ahead so that you can identify a hazard in enough time to avoid a collision.

# Limited Space

Limited space reduces the number of ways an emergency can be handled. Space is limited when an escape route to either side is cut off. Some hazardous situations can be avoided only by changing direction or coming to a sudden

stop. These actions require room to maneuver. Maneuverability can be restricted by several factors:

1. Congested roads. If another car is following too closely, for example, you cannot stop suddenly. Similarly, you cannot pull into an adjoining lane if it is crowded with cars.
2. Fixed objects, such as bridges, rock ledges, abutments, utility poles, or parked cars.

## Risk-takers

Sometimes you may unknowingly take a risk by failing to work through IPDE properly. Your failure to identify a hazard may place you and your passengers in danger. Some drivers, however, regularly take risks with little or no concern for their personal safety or that of others.

**Defensive driving will help you deal with drivers who risk their safety and the safety of other HTS users.**

Drivers who consistently exceed the posted speed limit or who ignore stop or yield signs are risking their own safety. More important, they endanger other highway users. Unfortunately, you never know when you will meet these drivers.

Since you cannot assume that all drivers will act in a safe and reasonable way, you must be alert and drive defensively. Always travel at a safe speed, maintain an adequate following distance, and identify possible escape paths.

Risk-takers complicate everyone's driving task. You must be ready at all times to adapt your own driving strategy to handle hazards caused by others.

## Safety Checks

- Before starting the car, clear the dashboard and seat of loose objects. If you accelerate or decelerate suddenly, they may fall off, distracting you, getting caught under the brake or accelerator, or injuring you or a passenger.

- To scan effectively, consciously move your eyes every two seconds.

- Practice making smooth and gradual stops. Stopping suddenly can result in being hit from behind.

 # Key Ideas

- IPDE is a driving strategy that helps you avoid collisions. It involves four steps: identifying, predicting, deciding, and executing.
- You can identify most hazards early enough to avoid them if you have a minimum visual lead of 8–12 seconds.
- Through experience and practice you can learn to predict what is likely to occur in various traffic situations.
- Once you decide on the safest way to handle a driving hazard, you must execute the maneuver safely and quickly.
- Strategies for handling hazards include minimizing, separating, or compromising hazards.
- When it is not possible to separate multiple hazards, always choose the compromise that is least hazardous to you and other highway users.
- Maintain a following distance of two to three seconds under ideal conditions; lengthen it to four to five seconds when conditions are poor.
- You must adapt IPDE to limited visibility, limited traction, limited space, areas of lateral access, and risk-taking drivers.

# ⬛ Gauging Your Understanding

1. How much visual lead time should you allow under ideal conditions? On the highway, what should you increase your visual lead to?

2. What is the minimum following distance that should be maintained under ideal conditions?

3. What should your minimum following distance be if you are being tailgated?

4. How does your vehicle's speed affect following distance?

5. What three actions can a driver take to avoid a collision?

6. Explain these terms: immediate path of travel, stopping distance, swerving path time.

7. What are some of the conditions that require you to increase your following distance?

# ⬛ In the Driver's Seat

1. It was a rainy December evening as Barbara drove to the mall to finish her Christmas shopping. Being careful of the slick roads, she kept three seconds behind the van ahead. Suddenly the van's brake lights flashed as the driver stopped to avoid a pedestrian. As Barbara's foot reached for the brake, she glanced in her rearview mirror. There were headlights right at her bumper. What should she do? How did she get in this situation? What could she have done to avoid it?

2. Look at the photograph on page 107. What possible hazards can you identify?

## Special Projects

1. Stand alongside a fairly busy street. Determine the following distances of at least 20 cars and list them on a chart. How many drivers had a safe following distance?

2. As a passenger, practice identifying, predicting, and deciding what to do in various traffic situations. Take note of whether the driver reacts the same way you would if you were driving.

# ⇨ Chapter Test 6

Name _____   Date _____

**Write the letter of the best answer in the space provided.**

_____ **1.** A driver can usually swerve around a hazard and return to the original path again in (a) 2 seconds, (b) 4 seconds, (c) 8 seconds, (d) 12 seconds.

_____ **2.** A driver must handle a single hazard by (a) compromising it, (b) separating it, (c) minimizing it, (d) strategizing it.

_____ **3.** The minimum interval at which a driver should ever follow the vehicle ahead is (a) 2 seconds, (b) 4 seconds, (c) 8 seconds, (d) 12 seconds.

_____ **4.** Before handling a source of danger, a driver must be able to (a) minimize it, (b) compromise it, (c) separate it, (d) identify it.

_____ **5.** Immediate path of travel is the distance a vehicle can cover in (a) 2 seconds, (b) 4 seconds, (c) 8 seconds, (d) 12 seconds.

_____ **6.** A driver who risks exposure to one hazard in order to avoid a more dangerous hazard is (a) compromising, (b) separating, (c) minimizing, (d) identifying.

_____ **7.** The IPDE process is completed when a driver (a) makes a decision, (b) makes assumptions about a situation, (c) uses the vehicle's controls and equipment to maneuver, (d) scans the traffic scene.

_____ **8.** A driver can note the direction of the wheels of other cars when the seeing routine includes (a) centering ahead, (b) scanning the area, (c) ground viewing, (d) checking mirrors.

_____ **9.** A driver should always try to maintain a minimum visual lead time of (a) 2 seconds, (b) 4 seconds, (c) 8 seconds, (d) 12 seconds.

_____ **10.** A driver who performs a maneuver in a traffic situation is (a) identifying, (b) predicting, (c) deciding, (d) executing.

_____ **11.** The best way to handle a situation that involves more than one hazard is to (a) compromise, (b) separate, (c) minimize, (d) identify.

_____ **12.** A driver who looks for and recognizes hazards is (a) identifying, (b) predicting, (c) deciding, (d) executing.

_____ **13.** The amount of time it takes to steer a car off the immediate path of travel is (a) stopping distance, (b) following distance, (c) swerving path time, (d) interval rule.

_____ **14.** IPDE is a (a) method of determining following distance, (b) useful driving strategy, (c) margin of safety, (d) limiting condition.

**Complete these sentences by writing the correct terms in the blanks.**

**1.** The interval rule requires that you stay at least _____ seconds behind the car ahead.

**2.** Begin searching for hazards by _____, or looking ahead to where your car will be in about 8 seconds.

**3.** Places where vehicles or pedestrians may cross a driver's travel path are known as areas of _____.

**4.** The minimum visual lead that you should maintain on a straight road is _____.

**5.** A driver who is following one car and being tailgated by another car should increase his or her _____.

**6.** _____ reduces the number of ways you can handle an emergency.

**7.** When faced with more than one hazard at a time, always try to _____ the hazards.

**8.** A driver carries out a decision by changing _____, changing _____, or _____ other drivers, or a combination of these maneuvers.

**9.** A driver may have to adapt use of IPDE because of problems caused by limited _____, limited _____, and limited _____.

**10.** When your _____ is limited, you may not be able to identify possible hazards in time to take action.

**11.** Because you cannot assume that all drivers will act in a safe and reasonable way, you must be alert and drive _____.

# Careers in the HTS: Law Enforcement and Administration

Almost everyone thinks of the police when law enforcement is mentioned. But the police are not the only people involved in regulating the HTS.

### Police

State, county, and local police officers see to it that people obey the laws of the HTS.

The police receive training in how to recognize and deal with behavior caused by the use of alcohol or other drugs. They also receive training in pursuing a driver who has broken the traffic laws.

But the police play other roles in the HTS as well. They direct traffic, investigate collisions, aid drivers in trouble, and testify in court.

To serve people in so many ways, they must be familiar with a variety of traffic laws, emergency procedures, equipment, and rules of evidence (to be used in court).

### Traffic Court

It is up to the courts to determine whether a driver is guilty of breaking a law.

Both sides — the driver and the law enforcement agency — have a chance to present their cases in court. A judge or jury then comes to a decision based on the evidence presented. If the driver is found guilty, the court imposes a sentence. For most traffic offenses, the penalty can be a fine, a suspended license, or both.

### Administration

Administrative personnel help law enforcement agencies do their jobs more efficiently.

These workers collect fees, process applications, keep records, and issue registrations and licenses.

Driver's license examiners give the visual, written, and in-car tests. They must evaluate the driver's handling skills, alertness, and regard for safety procedures and the law.

States require all motor vehicles to be registered. They also keep records of all collisions and traffic offenses. File clerks, statisticians, and computer programmers are among the people involved in this task of recordkeeping.

# 3 Driving Environments

# Chapter 7

# Driving in City Traffic

- **What predictable hazards are you likely to encounter in city traffic?**
- **How do heavy traffic patterns affect your driving?**
- **What can you do about tailgaters?**
- **Why are right-of-way laws so important?**

Can you remember your first trip to a big city? Do you remember the bright lights and city sounds, the crowded streets and sidewalks? A city can be an exciting place because of the crowds of people, the heavy traffic, and the tall buildings. A city can also be a confusing, frustrating place to drive if you are not familiar with the area. Even if you know the area well, driving in the city can be hazardous if you don't use effective strategies for driving in traffic. Often you must face several hazards at the same time. You must work through the IPDE process carefully in order to be prepared for these hazards.

# Characteristics of City Driving

Every driving environment — even a quiet city side street — has its potential hazards. Cars parked on both sides of the street create problems of limited space and reduced visibility. Pedestrians may walk between parked cars into your path. The car ahead of you may stop suddenly to park, or an oncoming car may turn left, crossing your path. Certain characteristics of city driving affect how you handle these driving hazards. These characteristics include congested streets, low speeds, and cross traffic at intersections.

## Congested Streets

City streets are congested. They are crowded with moving cars, buses, trucks, motorcycles, and bicycles. They are often lined with parked vehicles. This congestion limits the space you have to maneuver. In fact, on many city streets at almost any time of the day, it may be impossible to find an escape route.

Commercial areas of cities are usually the most congested. Traffic is heavy in such areas, and you must constantly be alert for vehicles entering or leaving parking spaces. In residential areas, traffic density is usually lower. Still, pedestrians, small children, animals, and cars emerging from driveways present special problems.

## Low Speeds

Speed limits in cities and other densely settled areas are lower than on open roads and highways. At lower speeds, you can move through congested traffic more safely. However, even the posted speed may be too fast for existing traffic conditions. When driving on city streets, reduce your speed as specific conditions require.

## Cross Traffic

**Intersections** — where two or more streets cross — are among the greatest hazards of city driving. As you drive, you have to be aware of traffic crossing the intersection from your left and right. You also have to watch for cars turning into the cross street. Cars ahead of you may slow down or stop as they prepare for left or right turns. Oncoming vehicles may turn left in front of your car, requiring you to slow down or stop.

**What are some of the potential hazards a driver faces in this congested driving environment?**

**Increased following distance enables a driver to scan farther ahead for hazards and stop if necessary.**

# Using IPDE in City Driving

Identifying hazards in city traffic is demanding. You must constantly scan the area around and far ahead of your car. Working through the IPDE process seems more difficult because you must identify, predict, decide, and execute in response to many possible dangers at once. Your strategy for driving in the city must involve leaving enough room ahead to stop if necessary and dealing with tailgaters.

# Identifying Hazards

Setting up an 8-second visual lead time is especially important in city driving. An 8-second visual lead allows you to identify hazards ahead early enough to avoid sudden speed or lane changes. If you identify a problem ahead, immediately increase your following distance. Increased following distance gives you an extra margin of safety. You may need this extra space if there is no escape route to the side, as is often the case in city driving.

## ● Oncoming Traffic

You should also be aware of possible hazards created by oncoming traffic. Oncoming vehicles might make a left turn in front of you, or pull into your lane to avoid a hazard or to pass. They might swing partially into your lane when making a right turn. To avoid conflict with an oncoming vehicle, adjust your speed and position accordingly.

## ● Following Traffic

In traffic, you should travel at about the same speed as other vehicles in your lane. By doing so, you avoid approaching too fast or crowding traffic ahead. Also, you are less likely to cause other traffic to slow down or pass you.

**Two-second Following Distance.**   Maintaining a 2-second following distance is particularly important on congested city streets. There are many areas where cars ahead of you may stop suddenly — for example, at intersections controlled by traffic lights. Therefore, you must leave room ahead to stop or swerve if necessary. Do not concentrate just on the car ahead, however. Look as far ahead as possible. Be alert for brake lights, turn signals, or any other signs of possible problems. Being aware well in advance of the need to reduce speed ahead may prevent a rear-end collision.

**Tailgaters.**   When being followed, check the position of the cars behind. If they are too close, increase your own following distance. If you have to stop suddenly, warn the driver behind by pumping the brakes so that the brake lights flash. Also, plan an escape route in the next lane or on the road shoulder. In a sudden stop, you may need to swerve to avoid being hit from behind.

# Intersections

Much activity takes place at intersections. Drivers may turn left or right or travel straight through the intersection. Often pedestrian crosswalks are located at intersections, so you have to consider foot traffic as well as other vehicles.

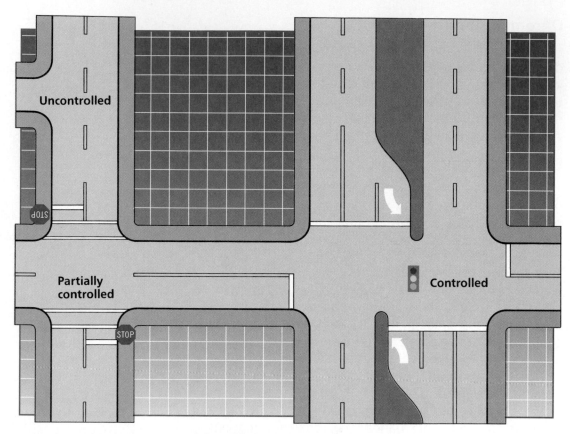

**Uncontrolled**

**Partially controlled**

**Controlled**

**Study the differences between the three intersections illustrated above.**

## ● Identifying Intersections

There are three basic types of intersections: controlled, partially controlled, and uncontrolled. Each has certain characteristics that you should be aware of in order to apply the IPDE process.

**Controlled Intersections.** You can easily identify a **controlled intersection**. These intersections are regulated by traffic lights or stop signs at all approaches. These controls are designed to regulate the flow of traffic through the intersection. Do not assume, however, that others will always obey the signs or signals they are facing. Be prepared to stop in case other drivers take the right of way when they do not legally have it. When nearing controlled intersections, take your foot off the accelerator to slow the car. Cover the brake as you look for possible hazards.

At intersections controlled by traffic lights, be alert for turn arrows and advanced or delayed green signals. At some intersections, the green signal is delayed in one direction to allow traffic going in the other direction to move ahead or turn first. Also be aware that some lights are **traffic-activated** — vehicles approaching the intersection activate, or trigger, a sensor in the pavement that causes the light to change.

Other traffic lights are set to change in a specific time — for example, a minute. Often a series of lights is preset to a rate of speed. For example, you may be able to proceed through one green light after another by driving at 25 mph. Sometimes signs are posted that tell the preset speed for a series of lights. If you travel a route often enough, you should be able to determine how lights along that route have been set.

Try to approach traffic lights so that you arrive when they are green. If you identify a red light far enough in advance, you can slow down gradually so that the light may change and traffic may begin to move ahead before you arrive. In addition to saving gas, this technique also saves wear on the brakes.

**Partially Controlled Intersections.**   At least one approach at a **partially controlled intersection** is regulated by a stop or yield sign. Drivers who face such a sign should

**Controlled intersections may be regulated by traffic lights or stop signs at all approaches.**

yield to those who do not. However, some drivers may try to pull into the intersection before uncontrolled traffic enters it. You can avoid conflicts at such intersections by slowing down and being prepared to stop, even when your approach is not regulated by a stop or yield sign.

**Uncontrolled Intersections.**   Because there are no signs or signals regulating them, **uncontrolled intersections** may be difficult to identify and should be approached cautiously. The only clues you may have that there is a road intersecting ahead are street-name signs or a long break in curbing or pavement markings. Any car already in an unregulated intersection or the car arriving at the intersection first has the right of way. If two drivers arrive at the intersection at the same time, the driver to the right has the right of way.

## ● Driving Through Intersections

Before driving straight through an intersection, check in all directions at least twice for any hazards. Do not enter the intersection unless you are certain you can cross it safely. Starting from a standstill, you can drive through a two-lane intersection in about four seconds. Completing a left or right turn safely may take up to eight seconds. Of course, such maneuvers take longer if pedestrian or vehicle traffic interferes with your progress. Also, you need more time to cross multilane intersections. Knowing how long it takes to perform these maneuvers helps you judge whether you have enough time to complete them safely.

## ● Turning at Intersections

If you remember certain pointers, making a turn can be a safe maneuver — even on a busy street. Before making any turn, be sure the turn is legal and safe. As you approach the intersection, use your turn signal to indicate the direction of your turn.

To make a right turn, position the car in the farthest right lane open to traffic and slow down. Check to the left, right, and straight ahead for any situation that may delay the turn. For example, pedestrians or bicycle riders may be

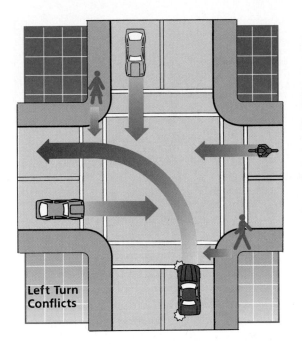

**Left Turn Conflicts**

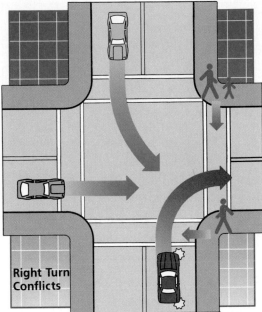

**Right Turn Conflicts**

crossing the street. You must give them the right of way. When your path is clear, turn into the closest right lane open to traffic. (Refer to Maneuver D in the In-Car Guide in the back of this book.)

Begin a left turn from the farthest left lane open to traffic in that direction. Be sure the turn is legal, and that you signal your intention. Slow down and check for pedestrians or vehicles in the turning path. Also check for vehicles that may be approaching from behind. Carefully judge how much space you need to complete the turn. Then, wait for a gap in the oncoming traffic. While waiting to turn, keep the wheels straight so that your car will not be pushed into oncoming traffic if hit from behind. Once the path is clear, turn into the nearest left lane open to traffic in the new direction. (Refer to Maneuver D in the In-Car Guide in the back of this book.)

**Always check carefully in all directions for traffic or pedestrians when making a turn.**

## Multilane Roads

Where traffic flow is heavy, highway engineers have built roads that have two or more lanes in each direction. A

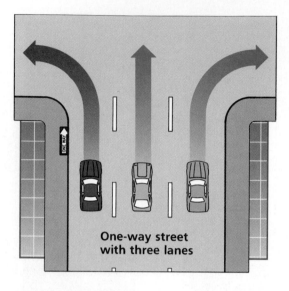

**One-way street
with three lanes**

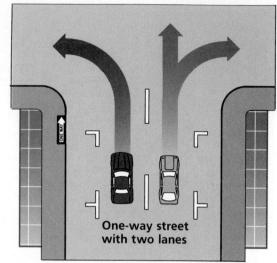

**One-way street
with two lanes**

**On a one-way street
with three lanes, use the
left lane for left turns,
the right lane for right
turns, and the center
lane for traveling
straight ahead. If the
one-way street has only
two lanes, drive in the
right lane except when
turning left.**

multilane road eliminates the hazard of crossing into on-coming traffic to pass. Not only can the road carry more traffic, it is safer as well.

Unless you plan to turn left, travel in the right lane on a multilane road. Traffic records show that this is the safer lane to drive in.

Left-turn lanes are often indicated by pavement markings on multilane streets in cities. These lanes make left turns easier and safer. Plus, there is less congestion at intersections because through traffic is not slowed by left-turning vehicles. Even if the left-turning vehicle must wait for oncoming traffic to clear, vehicles in the other lanes can continue without delay.

## One-Way Streets

**One-way streets** are common in cities because they allow a greater volume of traffic with less congestion. Since all traffic flows in one direction on one-way streets, usually there is no conflict with oncoming vehicles. If you do encounter a vehicle traveling the wrong way, however, look for an escape route to the side of the road. If there is time, warn the driver of the oncoming vehicle by sounding your horn or flashing your lights.

Most one-way streets are marked by one-way, do not enter, or no left (or right) turn signs. Even if you fail to see the sign, though, it is usually easy to tell that a street is one-way. Look for parked cars on both sides of the street facing the same direction. Signs on both sides of the street facing in the same direction are another clue.

Enter a one-way street from the travel lane closest to that street. When leaving a one-way street, use the left lane for left turns and the right lane for right turns. If the one-way street has three lanes, use the middle lane if you are going straight through an intersection. The outside lanes should be left open for cars that are turning.

Often parking is allowed on both sides of a two-lane, one-way street. On such streets, stay in the right lane except when turning left. From this position, you have a better view between parked cars and can scan intersections more easily.

## Special Hazards

Road construction often makes it necessary to route traffic around highway workers and equipment. As a driver, you will be guided by signs, cones, or a flag person at the construction area. Reduce speeds below normal levels, be prepared to stop, and look out for unexpected hazards.

When driving on narrow roads, you face the added challenge of staying on the roadway. Reduce your speed and steer carefully. Stay to the right of the yellow center line, but avoid drifting off the pavement. Road shoulders are not intended to carry moving traffic. Avoid them unless you are faced with an emergency.

On narrow city streets, you may have only inches to clear other vehicles and pedestrians entering or leaving parked vehicles. Using IPDE is very important. Try to identify hazards early and predict the conflicts that could develop. Quickly decide on your safest course of action and execute the maneuver with caution. Avoid oversteering, and keep your eyes moving.

In heavy city traffic, delays are common. Vehicles often veer suddenly into your lane or stop in your path. If your

**When driving in a city, always be prepared for special situations such as one-way streets and cars pulling out into your travel path.**

lane is blocked by a stopped vehicle, yield to oncoming traffic before pulling into another lane to drive around that vehicle. Be patient with other highway users, and learn to expect the unexpected.

# Right-of-Way Situations

City streets are congested with more than just cars and trucks. Pedestrians and bicycle, moped, and motorcycle riders also use the roadway. Drivers of automobiles, trucks, and vans must adjust their driving to enable the others to use the roadway safely.

## Pedestrians

**Pedestrians often do the unexpected. A good driver scans an intersection carefully for pedestrians who may become hazards.**

Pedestrians are sometimes careless. They may cross in the middle of a street rather than at crosswalks. In bad weather they may hurry across the street and pay little attention to traffic. They may begin to cross the street before the light changes or ignore pedestrian signals entirely.

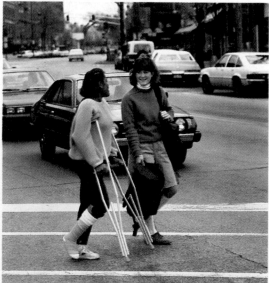

Careless pedestrians present problems for you as a driver. Be especially cautious near schools and playgrounds and in residential areas, where small children are more likely to be crossing streets. Children are also likely to run out into the street while playing. Reduce your speed in these areas and scan between and under parked cars and along sidewalks. You may see something that alerts you that a child is running into the road.

At intersections, you must yield to pedestrians who have the right of way. Carefully scan the intersection to make sure there are no pedestrians in or entering your path. Do not hug the curb near intersections, since pedestrians may step down from the curb and become hazards in the curb-side lane. When making a turn on red, remember that pedestrians have the right of way. Before you turn, permit them to clear the lane you are turning into.

Some people take much longer to cross the street than others. For example, a young adult can usually cross the street in a few seconds. However, a small child, an elderly person, or someone with a disability may need extra time.

Where there are no sidewalks, pedestrians should walk on the left side of the road facing vehicle traffic. If a cross-walk is provided at an intersection, pedestrians must use it, and they must obey pedestrian signals. If an intersection is regulated by traffic lights but has no pedestrian signals, pedestrians must cross on the green light.

You must yield to pedestrians at both marked and un-marked crosswalks. Although drivers have the right of way if a pedestrian crosses where there is no crosswalk, you should avoid conflicts and yield to pedestrians. You must always yield to blind pedestrians regardless of where thay cross. Blind pedestrians can be identified by a white-tipped cane or lead (seeing-eye) dog.

# Emergency Vehicles

When an **emergency vehicle** — a police car, fire truck, or ambulance — is approaching with its lights flashing, its siren blaring, or both, you must yield to it. If you are going in the same direction as an emergency vehicle on a two-

**Emergency vehicles have the right of way. Pull over to the side of the road when one approaches with lights flashing or siren blaring.**

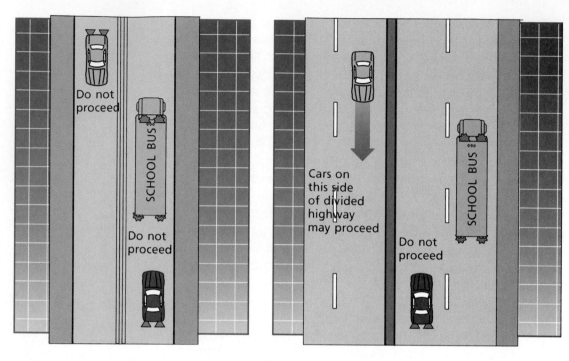

**Traffic in both directions must stop when a school bus is loading or unloading passengers, except in the opposite lane of a divided highway.**

lane road, pull over to the curb and stop. Be careful that you do not block an intersection. Remain stopped until the emergency vehicle has passed. Although it is not practical to stop on multilane highways, you must slow down and clear a lane for an emergency vehicle to pass.

# School Buses

School bus operators, like all other drivers, must obey all traffic laws, including right-of-way rules. However, most states have laws that give school buses the right of way when they are picking up or dropping off children. These laws were set up to protect those who may not yet fully understand traffic rules.

All traffic must stop when a school bus flashes its red lights. Drivers may not proceed until the lights are turned off and the bus begins moving. Usually, however, oncoming traffic on a divided highway — one with a median strip or other center barrier — need not stop for a school bus even though its lights are flashing.

**A school bus with red lights flashing has the right of way. Be alert for children who may run into the street.**

## Maintenance Tips

- If you drive regularly in heavy city traffic, have your engine oil changed more frequently than recommended in the owner's manual.

- Inspect all lights on your vehicle regularly and replace head-lights, bulbs, and fuses as needed.

- Have the brakes inspected at least once a year or when you feel or hear anything unusual when reducing speed.

## ▶ Key Ideas

- When driving in the city, you need to adapt to congested streets, lower speeds, and intersecting traffic.
- To provide an adequate safety margin, you must maintain a 2-second following distance.
- Tailgaters are a major cause of city traffic collisions.
- Several types of intersections — controlled, partially controlled, and uncontrolled — allow traffic to blend, merge, and change directions.
- When making left and right turns in city traffic, be aware of all other highway users, including pedestrians.
- Special rules apply when driving on one-way streets.

- Right-of-way rules apply to all highway users. Yield the right of way to pedestrians, emergency vehicles, and school buses with red lights flashing.

# Gauging Your Understanding

1. How does city driving differ from driving in other environments?

2. Describe the IPDE process as it applies to city driving. Give examples of the hazards you are likely to encounter.

3. What procedures should you follow as you approach a city intersection controlled by a traffic light?

4. What steps should you take as you prepare to make a left turn at an intersection?

5. Which lane should you use when driving on a one-way street?

# In the Driver's Seat

1. As you drive on a 4-lane divided road, you identify an intersection ahead with a flashing yellow light facing you. You are traveling in the left lane. A truck ahead of you in the right lane signals a right turn. The truck blocks your view of traffic coming from the right. What steps should you take to drive through the intersection safely?

2. On a congested city street, a delivery truck ahead in your lane stops suddenly. You stop so close to the truck that your view of oncoming traffic is partially blocked. How should you proceed? How could you have been better prepared for this hazard?

## Special Projects

1. Observe traffic at some of the uncontrolled intersections in your area. How many drivers observe right-of-way rules at these intersections? Which of these intersections do you think are hazardous enough to require installation of traffic controls?

2. At a controlled intersection, observe pedestrian activity. Do all pedestrians cross only at the crosswalk? What conflicts do you see created by careless or inattentive pedestrians?

# ➡ Chapter Test 7

Name _____  Date _____

**Write "T" beside statements that are true and "F" beside those that are false.**

_____  **1.** In traffic you should travel at about the same speed as other vehicles in your lane.

_____  **2.** If cars are following you closely, speed up to get farther ahead of them.

_____  **3.** Tailgaters are a major cause of city traffic collisions.

_____  **4.** City speed limits are usually higher than those on open roads.

_____  **5.** You must always yield to blind pedestrians no matter where they cross a street.

_____  **6.** A controlled intersection ensures that cross traffic will not collide.

**Complete these sentences by writing the correct terms in the blanks.**

**1.** When driving in city traffic, try to leave a following distance of at least _____ seconds.

**2.** _____ allow a greater volume of traffic with less congestion.

**3.** All traffic must stop when a _____ flashes its red lights.

**4.** Where there are no sidewalks, pedestrians should walk on the _____ side of the road, facing vehicle traffic.

**5.** If two drivers arrive at an uncontrolled intersection at the same time, the driver to the _____ has the right of way.

**Write the letter of the best answer in the space provided.**

_____  **1.** A partially controlled intersection is regulated (a) at all approaches, (b) only by traffic lights, (c) by at least one stop or yield sign, (d) only during rush hours.

_____  **2.** An intersection with traffic lights is (a) controlled, (b) traffic-activated, (c) partially controlled, (d) uncontrolled.

_____  **3.** A multilane road (a) eliminates left turns, (b) eliminates crossing into oncoming traffic to pass, (c) eliminates collisions, (d) is most dangerous.

_____  **4.** Cars already in an unregulated intersection (a) must stop if they see a car approaching, (b) should speed up to avoid a collision, (c) have the right of way, (d) are breaking the law.

_____ **5.** Intersections where two or more streets cross (a) are the safest places to drive in cities, (b) are among the greatest hazards of city driving, (c) eliminate the need to watch for cars coming from the left or right, (d) increase the flow of traffic.

_____ **6.** Always yield to emergency vehicles (a) when they approach from the opposite direction, (b) on multilane highways, (c) when they have lights flashing and sirens blaring, (d) when they are stopped on the side of the road.

_____ **7.** At intersections regulated by traffic lights but with no pedestrian lights, pedestrians must cross (a) at their own risk, (b) on the red light, (c) on the green light, (d) whenever they have a chance.

**Match the items in Column B to the items in Column A by placing the correct letter in the space provided.**

| Column A | Column B |
|---|---|
| _____ **1.** Controlled inter- sections | **a.** Roads with two or more lanes in each direction. |
| _____ **2.** Partially con- trolled intersec- tions | **b.** Are not regulated by signs or signals. |
|  | **c.** Are regulated by a stop or yield sign at one or more approaches. |
| _____ **3.** Intersections | **d.** Allow a greater volume of traffic with less congestion. |
| _____ **4.** Traffic activated | **e.** Are regulated by traffic signs or signals at all approaches. |
| _____ **5.** Uncontrolled in- tersections | **f.** Signals that are changed by an approaching vehicle. |
| _____ **6.** One-way streets | **g.** Any place where two or more streets cross. |
| _____ **7.** Multi-lane roads | |

# Chapter 8

# Driving on Highways

- You are doing 30 mph on an expressway with a speed limit of 55 mph. An officer stops you. Why?
- Why do expressways have lower collision rates than other roadways?
- As you begin to pass another car, the car speeds up. What should you do?

**Long stretches of flat road often cause drivers to become bored and less alert to potential hazards.**

City driving is most often low-speed and stop-and-go driving. But the situation is different on highways. Speeds are higher, roads are more open, and usually there is less traffic. Drivers must adapt their use of IPDE to the specific hazards they face on these roadways.  For example, at higher speeds, vehicles respond differently. Drivers have less time to identify and react to hazards. Collisions, when they do occur, tend to be more serious. Because highway driving presents special challenges, you must be prepared to adapt your use of IPDE to the specific problems you face on these roadways.

# Characteristics of Highway Driving

When driving on highways, you must be able to adjust your driving to a variety of traffic patterns, speeds, and road conditions.

## Less Congestion

The amount of traffic on highways varies according to the time of day and location. In rural areas, traffic may be very light at all times. Near large cities, there may be heavy traffic throughout the day. And, the traffic may become especially congested during rush hours. Highways that lead toward vacation and recreation areas often have more traffic on weekends and holidays. In general, however, highway driving is enjoyable because it takes you away from problems of heavy, slow-moving, or stop-and-go traffic and congested city streets.

Driving on highways poses other problems, though. Roads with little traffic can lull you into a false sense of security. You may find yourself forgetting about potential hazards. On long stretches of flat road you can become bored and sleepy. You may not be paying close attention to your surroundings. However, at any moment the driving situation can change. You may need to maneuver to prevent a collision.

# Higher Speeds

Because highways are generally less congested, the speed limits on highways are higher than on roads within a city. At high speeds, you need to use greater caution. As your speed increases, so do your chances of having a collision. Why is this so? Remember that your reaction distance and stopping distance increase along with your speed. Also, the distance you will cover before you can identify, predict, decide, and execute increases. Therefore, at higher speeds, you reach hazards more quickly. As your speed increases, you should look for wider and longer escape routes.

# Road Conditions

Highways may be narrow, two-lane roads or wide, multi-lane expressways. Highways also differ in their design and condition. Higher speeds make these differences important.

Well-designed highways avoid steep grades. Their curves are banked, and their shoulders are wide and well surfaced.

**Warning signs are often posted on highways to alert drivers to changes in speed or road conditions ahead.**

**To avoid potholes, you can pass around them to the left. If there were oncoming traffic, however, you could reduce your speed or pull off the road before reaching the potholes.**

Their lanes are wide, and there are enough lanes to carry the usual traffic. Driving at the posted speed on a well-designed highway is usually safe. But driving on poorly designed roads is not safe, even at moderate speeds. You should adapt your driving to highway conditions. If grades are steep and curves are not banked, reduce your speed.

Highway surfaces also vary widely. Most surfaces are paved, but the ones that are not are often hazardous. Some surfaces consist of loose gravel, which provides less traction. Before turning from a well-paved highway onto an unpaved road, reduce your speed.

Poorly paved surfaces can be as hazardous as unpaved surfaces. Especially hazardous are washboard surfaces and potholes. Roads with **washboard** surfaces have ridges that cross the roadway at right angles. They usually give a rough, slippery ride as the car bounces from ridge to ridge. As a result, you may lose control of your car. Watch the roadway ahead and identify the rough pavement in advance. If possible, reduce your speed well before you reach washboard surfaces.

**Potholes** occur in old or poorly maintained surfaces. Potholes can cause damage to tires and other parts of a car. In addition, they may cause you to lose control. Reduce your speed and try to avoid potholes. You may be able to steer around them. If you do, do so carefully.

# Using IPDE on the Highway

Identifying, predicting, deciding, and executing are essential to the driving task. Early recognition of highway hazards is important. The IPDE process will help you identify these hazards and predict problems. IPDE will also enable you to decide upon and execute the changes in speed and direction needed to deal with these hazards.

As speed increases, vehicle response time also increases. And some vehicle response capabilities decrease. Drivers also need more time and distance to respond to hazards at higher speeds.

Remember to keep at least a 2-second following distance and an 8- to 12-second visual lead on highways. You should be able to see beyond the distance you need to stop. If your stopping distance is greater than one half your sight distance, slow down.

# Special Hazards

When driving on highways, you must change your driving habits to meet highway conditions. Changes are necessary to deal with hazards when traveling at high speeds.

## ● Junctions

A **junction** is the place where two or more roads meet or intersect. Examples of junctions include T and Y intersections and crossroads.

At any junction, slow down enough to stop your car if necessary. Also select a swerving path. If you do not have room to stop, you may have to swerve to avoid a collision. On most highways, posted signs warn of a junction ahead.

**Although well marked, T intersections such as this can be dangerous. Slow down enough to stop if necessary.**

At particularly dangerous junctions where a stop is required, the road may have **rumble strips**. These are raised strips on the surface of the road that are closely spaced. They cause your car to vibrate and create a noise that warns you of a stop or hazard ahead. Always reduce your speed when going over rumble strips.

### ● Bridges

When approaching a bridge, slow down. Many bridges on two-lane highways, especially older roads, are narrow. Often there are no escape routes because of abutments or guardrails. Many drivers crowd the center line on a narrow bridge to make sure they clear the sides. On most bridges, however, two average-sized vehicles coming from opposite directions can cross at the same time.

Some bridges may only be wide enough for one vehicle to cross at a time. Usually a warning sign is posted well before a one-lane bridge. Before crossing such a bridge, slow down as you scan well ahead. If the way is clear, cross the bridge carefully. If it is not, wait until the oncoming traffic has crossed.

Remember that most bridges and overpasses remain wet or covered with ice and frost long after the rest of the highway is clear. The air under bridges and overpasses is often colder or warmer than the ground beneath the rest of the road. This causes the bridge surface to retain moisture longer. Therefore, reduce speed and proceed carefully.

### ● Hills and Mountain Roads

As you near the top of a hill, your view of the road ahead is blocked by the hillcrest. Try to maintain at least an 8-second visual lead. To provide a further margin of safety, do not crowd the center line. Ease up on the gas pedal as you near the hillcrest. Although the car will slow, it will have enough momentum to reach the crest. This gives you time to prepare for whatever traffic conditions are ahead.

When going downhill, you may not have to use the gas pedal at all. In fact, you may have to brake to keep the car from building up too much momentum. On very steep hills,

**What adjustments should a driver make when crossing a bridge or cresting a hill?**

avoid braking continuously. Continuous braking can cause the brakes to heat up and lose some of their effectiveness. Instead, shift to a lower gear and brake as necessary.

## ● Railroad Crossings

Warning signs are posted well ahead of where railroad tracks cross a road. When you see such a sign, slow down. As you do, look and listen carefully for an approaching train. Don't rely on a gate or flashing light to warn you. In many areas, gates are not used at crossings. Sometimes there are no flashing red lights to indicate a train is coming.

If the angle at which the tracks cross the road makes it difficult to see whether a train is coming, stop and check carefully before crossing. Even if a train has just passed, do not cross without first checking to see whether the way is clear. A second train may be close behind the first.

If your car should stall on the tracks, check for approaching trains. If one is nearing the crossing, you and all passengers should get out quickly. Run away from the car in the direction the train is coming from. If no train is coming, have the passengers get out. Then, try to start the car again. If it will not start, push it off the tracks. Be sure someone watches carefully for an approaching train.

**The pavement markings and signs alert drivers to the need to slow for a railroad crossing ahead.**

# Changing Lanes

Because speeds are higher on highways than they are in cities and towns, you need more time and space to make lane changes. Apply the IPDE process. Make sure that you can identify at least 12 seconds ahead. And, maintain at least a 2-second following distance.

Before changing lanes, be sure there is sufficient space between cars in the lane for you to move into. Once you are sure that there is enough time and space for you to complete the lane change, signal your intention to change lanes. Check both rearview mirrors. Glance over your shoulder to check your blind spot. When the path is clear, accelerate to move your car into the new lane. Then, match your speed to that of other traffic already in the lane. (Refer to Maneuver D in the In-Car Guide in the back of this book.)

# Passing

To pass on a two-lane two-way highway, you must enter and travel in the lane for oncoming traffic. For that reason, passing can be a difficult and dangerous maneuver.

When deciding to pass, there are several things you should take into account. Pass only on a straight section of road. Because it is more difficult to judge distances on curves, you may overestimate the space available for passing. Also, you cannot always see oncoming traffic on curves.

It is unwise to pass more than one vehicle at a time. Some of the vehicles ahead may be preparing to turn or leave the road soon. Others may pull out to pass vehicles ahead of them. If there are several cars ahead that you want to pass, do so one vehicle at a time. Also, do not pass a truck after it begins to descend a steep hill. The speed of a truck often increases rapidly on a downgrade.

Often you can avoid being passed by driving at the same speed as other traffic. But if someone is trying to pass you, never speed up. It is both illegal and dangerous to try to keep someone from passing. (Refer to Maneuver D in the In-Car Guide in the back of this book.)

Sometimes the way ahead is not clear. If you are being passed and you see a hazard ahead, you can pump your brakes to warn the other driver. If the driver begins to pass anyway, you should slow down  This reduces the distance the person passing will have to drive to clear your car. You should also select an escape route to the right. You may need one to avoid a collision.

**Because of limited visibility, passing on a curve is not only dangerous, but may also be illegal.**

# Driving on Expressways

**Expressways** are divided highways with at least two lanes going in each direction. Designed for safe, high-speed travel, expressways usually do not have steep hills. They have gentle, banked curves. Access to and from expressways is limited. They have no junctions or railroad crossings to interrupt traffic flow. Well-spaced entrance and exit ramps, minimum and maximum speed limits, and no traffic signals all help to keep traffic moving smoothly. Wide lanes, excellent shoulders, and extra-wide underpasses provide the driver with good escape routes.

# Special Characteristics

The main feature of expressways is uninterrupted travel. Traffic can move without interruption because of controlled access, separation of conflicting lanes of traffic, and minimum-maximum speed limits.

## ● Controlled Access

**Drivers entering an expressway should adjust their speed to match the speed of other cars already on the expressway.**

Most expressways are **controlled-access highways**. Controlled access helps prevent conflict. Vehicles are permitted to enter or exit the expressway only at specified (designated) entrances and exits. This helps to reduce conflicts that are common on other highways. Some expressway entrance ramps control access during rush hours by means of a red and green traffic signal.

## ● Conflicting Traffic Separated

Controlled-access highways protect drivers by dividing and separating them from opposing and cross traffic. Opposing lanes of traffic are separated by a **median strip** or **barrier**. Median strips and barriers reduce the possibility of head-on crashes by preventing vehicles from crossing into the oncoming traffic lanes. Median strips may be grass, shrubs, or trees. Barriers may be steel guard rails or concrete forms.

Controlled-access highways also eliminate the conflicts produced by cross traffic. Vehicles crossing the expressway do so by moving over or under the expressway on an overpass or underpass. This eliminates the need for stop signs and traffic signals. Many controlled-access highways are enclosed by fences. The fences reduce the dangers posed by pedestrians or animals on the road.

## ● Minimum-Maximum Speed Limits

Usually when driving on expressways, you must obey two speed limits — a **minimum** and **maximum** limit. These limits establish a range of acceptable speeds to promote a steady flow of traffic. It is important to travel at about the same speed as other vehicles on the expressway. Driving too slowly can block the flow of traffic and possibly cause a collision. Driving faster than other vehicles makes it necessary to continually pass. A driver traveling too fast may have to weave in and out of traffic to get around other vehicles. This is dangerous not only for the person driving too fast, but also for others on the road.

The minimum speed limit is most often 10 to 15 mph lower than the maximum speed. Of course, if weather, roadway, or traffic conditions are bad, the minimum speed limit is not enforced. You are expected to adjust your speed to conditions.

In most areas, the maximum speed limit is 55 mph. It is the highest legal speed limit allowed in the United States. In some places, however, the maximum speed limit on expressways is lower than 55 mph. Always follow the posted speed limits and adjust your speed as necessary for the conditions at hand.

**Driving conditions sometimes make it impossible to maintain the minimum speed limit on expressways.**

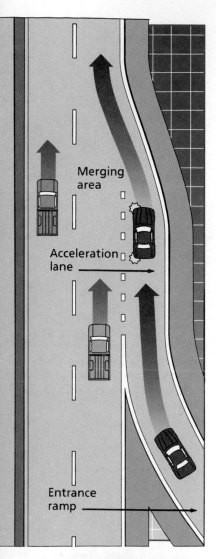

**Merging area**

**Acceleration lane**

**Entrance ramp**

**Follow the posted speed limit on an entrance ramp and use the acceleration lane to adjust your speed to expressway traffic.**

# Entering an Expressway

Entrances to expressways are clearly marked by guide signs. Before you use a ramp to enter an expressway, make sure it really is an entrance ramp. Do-not-enter and wrong-way signs are often placed on ramps to prevent drivers from using them incorrectly. As you enter the ramp, adjust your speed and position to avoid conflict with other vehicles on the ramp.

While on the ramp, look for a gap in traffic on the expressway that is large enough for you to move into. Next, begin to time your entry to that gap. Adjust your speed on the ramp so that you'll arrive at the expressway the same time the gap you have chosen opens up. Some expressways have **acceleration lanes** that merge traffic from the entrance ramp into the main expressway lanes. As you leave the entrance ramp, use the acceleration lane to adjust your speed to the speed of traffic on the expressway. As you move forward in the acceleration lane, make sure the gap on the expressway is still available. If it is, signal a lane change and speed up to merge smoothly into traffic. Once you are on the expressway, cancel your signal and establish a safe following distance. (Refer to Maneuver H in the In-Car Guide in the back of this book.)

# Lane Use

Most expressways have two or more lanes for traffic going in each direction. Once you are on the expressway, stay in the right lane until it is safe or desirable to move left. If the road has at least three lanes in each direction, use the right or center lane for travel. Leave the left lane open for high-speed traffic and those who wish to pass. Sometimes traffic is heavy in the right lane and many vehicles are entering and leaving the road. If so, use the center or left lane to avoid conflict.

On many expressways, trucks and vehicles towing trailers must stay in the right lanes. If you have to drive in a lane used by trucks, buses, and vehicles with trailers, avoid driv-

ing between two large vehicles. Try to change lanes as soon as possible. Until you can change lanes, however, increase your following distance to about four seconds. This extra margin of safety gives you a better view of the road ahead.

On expressways (or any other multilane road), you should not cross more than one lane at a time. After making a lane change, establish yourself in that lane before moving to another. Always signal a lane change and check the mirrors and your blind spot before moving into a new lane. (Refer to Maneuver D in the In-Car Guide in the back of this book.)

Often traffic on expressways bunches up into groups of vehicles or "packs" across several lanes. Drivers in packs are likely to adjust their position by frequent lane changes and speeding. Avoid driving with a pack of other vehicles. It is always best to drive between them so you do not have to give up following distance or a swerving path. When you see a pack coming from behind, move into the right lane, if possible, and allow the pack to pass.

**Maintain a safe following distance on expressways to avoid having to slow or change lanes quickly.**

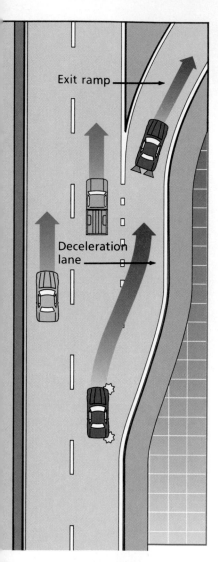

Exit ramp

Deceleration lane

**Begin to slow in the deceleration lane. Then, adjust your speed to the speed posted on the exit ramp.**

# Leaving an Expressway

Leaving an expressway safely requires planning. When you see the sign for your exit, move into the lane nearest your exit (usually the right lane). Use a turn signal to indicate that you are planning to leave the expressway. Maintain your speed until you are in the deceleration lane. Then reduce your speed immediately. The **deceleration lane** is a lane just off the main expressway that merges with the exit ramp. If there is no deceleration lane, reduce your speed as soon as you are on the exit ramp. Adjust your speed to the posted speed for the exit ramp. (Refer to Maneuver H in the In-Car Guide in the back of this book.)

After driving for some time at high speeds, you may become **velocitized** — unaware of how fast you are really going. When you slow down, you may think you have reduced your speed more than you actually have. For this reason, always check the speedometer when leaving an expressway. Be sure the speed you are driving at is safe and legal. After leaving the expressway, adjust your speed to the posted speeds and to the surface road conditions.

Never leave an expressway at high speed. There may be a stalled car, traffic, or roadway hazards on the ramp. Also, never make a last-second lane change to get onto an exit ramp. It is much safer to stay on the expressway and take the next exit.

# Driving to Conserve Fuel

In recent years, the costs of operating a motor vehicle have risen greatly. The greatest increase has been in the price of fuel. Fuel supplies are limited. To help conserve fuel, the federal government has set up fuel economy standards for all vehicles. However, as a driver, there are many things you can do to help conserve fuel.

The most efficient way to conserve fuel is through speed control. When you enter a road, accelerate moderately and smoothly to the speed of other traffic. Accelerating quickly wastes gas. Once your speed matches that of other highway traffic, try to maintain a smooth, steady speed. Avoid frequent lane changes and weaving in and out of traffic. Pass only where you can do so safely at a steady speed.

Anticipate changing conditions well ahead. Adjust your speed gradually as you approach slower cars and situations requiring you to slow or stop. Whenever possible, pass slower vehicles as soon as you encounter them. Avoid slowing to their pace and then speeding up to pass them.

By developing good driving habits, you can conserve fuel. You will also increase the life of your tires and brakes.

## Fuel Misers

To save fuel:

- Once you have reached highway speed, use light, steady pressure on the gas pedal to maintain speed.

- Do not weave in and out of traffic. Constant speed adjustments waste fuel.

- Join a carpool or vanpool to commute to work. If possible, use public transportation.

## Key Ideas

- Highway driving is characterized by less congestion and higher speeds.
- At higher speeds, your reaction distance and stopping distance increase.
- Unpaved and poorly paved surfaces pose handling problems for drivers.
- Maintain a 12-second visual lead and a 2-second (or more) following distance at highway speeds to identify hazards as early as possible.
- Passing and changing lanes require extra space and caution at highway speeds.
- Expressways provide the advantages of controlled access, divided roadways, good escape routes, minimum and maximum speeds, and no traffic lights.

• When leaving an expressway, remember that you are entering a roadway with much lower speed limits.

# Gauging Your Understanding

1. What kinds of special hazards exist on highways?

2. How can washboard roads and potholes affect the handling of your car?

3. List the reasons you should not pass on a curve.

4. On a three-lane expressway, when should you use the right lane? The center lane? The left lane?

5. What is the most efficient way to conserve fuel when driving on highways?

# In the Driver's Seat

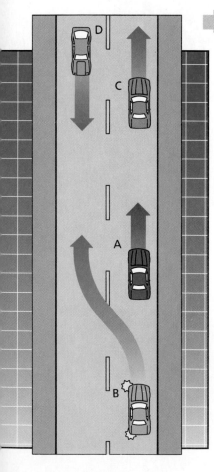

1. You are the driver of Car A. The driver of Car B does not see Car C directly ahead of you and begins to pass. You realize that there is not enough time or distance for Car B to pull into the lane ahead of you before meeting Car D. Identify the potential hazards. Predict what Car B might do. What can you do to minimize your risk? Predict what Car D might do.

2. You are driving on a controlled-access highway. As you approach an exit, you signal right and begin to enter the deceleration lane. As you do, you see a car backing onto the expressway from the exit ramp. What should you do? What hazards should you look for? If you started to turn off at the wrong exit, what would you do to correct your error?

## Special Projects

1. Stand at a safe location where you can observe traffic on a highway or expressway. Determine the following distance of 20 vehicles. How many drivers maintain a safe following distance? What risks do the others take?

2. Prepare a chart identifying special characteristics of highways or expressways in your area. Include such information as number of lanes, length and type of ramps, average distance between exits, road surfaces, and speed limits.

# ➡ Chapter Test 8

Name _____   Date _____

**Write "T" beside statements that are true and "F" beside those that are false.**

_____ **1.** At highway speeds you should have a 12-second visual lead.

_____ **2.** Passing is a simple, hazard-free maneuver.

_____ **3.** Banked curves are a feature of well-designed highways.

_____ **4.** Bridges usually provide good escape routes.

_____ **5.** Most drivers find it easier to judge distances on curves than on straightaways.

_____ **6.** You must usually obey a minimum speed limit on an expressway.

_____ **7.** On an expressway with three lanes going in each direction, you should use the left lane for travel.

_____ **8.** The most efficient way to conserve fuel is through speed control.

_____ **9.** Median strips and barriers are often the cause of head-on highway collisions.

**Write the letter of the best answer in the space provided.**

_____ **1.** When you must drive between two large vehicles, you should (a) decrease your following distance to about 2 seconds, (b) change lanes as soon as possible, (c) tap your brake to keep the vehicle behind from crowding you, (d) keep as far to the left of the lane as possible to see around the vehicles.

_____ **2.** An expressway differs from a highway in that it (a) has a large number of sharp curves and inclines, (b) has controlled access, (c) is controlled by traffic lights, (d) has more than one lane going in each direction.

_____ **3.** If your vehicle stalls on railroad tracks, the first thing you should do is (a) try to start the car, (b) get all passengers out of the vehicle, (c) push the car off the tracks, (d) leave the car and go for help.

_____ **4.** When passing a vehicle, a driver (a) may legally exceed the speed limit, (b) can safely pass on an upgrade, (c) can move partly into the passing lane, (d) should pass only on a straight section of road.

_____ **5.** A driving habit that wastes fuel is (a) staying in one lane, (b) tailgating, (c) maintaining a steady speed, (d) accelerating slowly.

_____ **6.** Crossroads and T roads are examples of (a) a highway, (b) an expressway, (c) a junction, (d) a kind of curve.

**155**

**Complete these sentences by writing the correct terms in the blanks.**

1. The lane used to slow down before getting on an exit ramp is known as the
   _____ lane.

2. To pick up speed before entering the main expressway lane, use the
   _____ lane.

3. Overpasses and underpasses eliminate the need for _____ on expressways.

4. It is _____ for the driver being passed to speed up while being
   passed.

5. After driving for some time at highway speeds, drivers often become
   _____, or unaware of how fast they are going.

6. Roads with _____ surfaces have ridges that cross the roadway at
   right angles.

7. Reaction distance and _____ distance increase along with speed.

8. Remember to keep a 2-second following distance and a(n) _____
   visual lead on highways.

9. Raised strips that create a noise to warn you of a stop ahead are called
   _____ strips.

10. On steep downgrades, _____ braking can cause the brakes to heat
    up and lose some of their effectiveness.

# Chapter 9

# Sharing the Road with Other Users

- **What adjustments do you think a driver must make when switching from driving a car to driving an RV?**
- **What advantages does a moped rider who is a licensed driver have over one who is not?**
- **What characteristics of large trucks might cause problems on some roads and in some areas?**

**Drivers must yield to pedestrians crossing in a crosswalk or with a "walk" light.**

If there were only cars on the road, driving would be a fairly easy task. Take away all the pedestrians, bicyclists, and motorcyclists, as well as the mopeds, vans, and trucks, and the roadway would not present many driving challenges. Safe driving, however, requires cooperation among all highway users. Each day there are more people and vehicles competing for space on the roadway. You need to learn the special characteristics and needs of other highway users and what to do to avoid conflicts with them.

# On Foot and on Bicycle

Care is essential when traveling on foot or on a bicycle. In most areas, safety laws have been written to help protect pedestrians and bicyclists. However, these laws have not eliminated the problems. Unfortunately, many people don't obey the laws. Thousands of pedestrians and cyclists are injured or killed each year.

## Pedestrians

Pedestrians are among the least protected and least trained highway users. Because many of them do not drive, they do not know how long it takes to stop a car. They may not understand or obey traffic rules and signals. Pedestrians often are not aware of how difficult it is for a driver to see them, especially at night.

The pedestrians at greatest risk are young children and the elderly. Children are likely to run into traffic without looking. The elderly often take a long time to decide when to cross a street and require extra time to do it. When it is raining, pedestrians may dash across the street without looking for traffic.

Skaters and joggers are a special hazard. As they try to maintain their pace, joggers sometimes run in front of vehicles. Skaters may slip and fall in your path.

As you drive, be aware of pedestrians in the area. Scan sidewalks, yards, and playgrounds for young children who may run into your path. Slow down when you see parked cars. Drive as far from them as you reasonably can to avoid car doors that may open suddenly. Also, establish a ground viewing habit to search for pedestrians about to step into the street. This habit may help prevent a collision.

Tap on your horn to alert pedestrians who appear to be headed into your path. A long blast is unnecessary and may scare people into doing the wrong thing.

Always yield to pedestrians in the street. However, do not motion for them to cross in front of you into a lane of moving traffic. Give a blind pedestrian extra space and time.

# Animals

Small animals, both domestic and wild, may run into the path of your car. If you can do so safely, swerve or slow down to avoid hitting them. Never risk your life — or the life of another person — in your attempt to avoid hitting a small animal. The best driving strategy is to watch for animals and expect them to run into the road at any time.

Hitting a large animal such as a horse or deer can damage your car and cause you serious injury. Be extra alert when you see a deer crossing sign. When you see an open range sign, be aware that there are no fences to keep livestock off the road in that area. Drive at a slower speed at night in areas where animals may appear on the road.

**Warning signs are often posted to remind drivers to scan carefully for animals.**

**What kinds of problems might bicycle riders present to drivers?**

# Bicycles

Bicycles have become a popular vehicle. Modern, lightweight ten-speed bicycles are an attractive alternative for some commuters, since riding a bicycle uses no gasoline, creates no pollution, and provides exercise.

Bicyclists' most common traffic violations are failing to yield the right of way and riding in the middle of the street. Some bicyclists ride too fast for road conditions and disregard traffic signs and signals. Others ride against the flow of traffic and make improper turns. Many cyclists weave between lanes of traffic and travel at speeds exceeding 20 mph. In addition, many cyclists do little to make themselves visible at night.

Roadway hazards such as railroad tracks, storm drains, puddles, and potholes may cause cyclists to swerve suddenly into your path. Carefully scan the roadway ahead of cyclists for these hazards. Be sure to give cyclists plenty of space to maneuver, particularly when you pass them.

When riding a bicycle, follow the rules of good driving. Obey traffic laws and signals. Ride with the flow of traffic, and use hand signals to show that you intend to change direction. Avoid riding in bad weather or at night. If you do ride at night, wear light colors and use headlights and reflectors to be sure you can be seen by drivers.

# Motorcycles and Mopeds

Operators of motorcycles and mopeds are usually more aware of traffic laws than bicyclists and pedestrians are. Even so, they can present special problems for drivers.

## Mopeds

Some operators unwisely ride mopeds in fast traffic even though their machines cannot keep up with the traffic. Riding uphill slows them down even more. Other moped operators may fail to give hand signals, since the rear brake requires use of the left hand. Therefore, they may turn or stop without warning. For these reasons, give mopeds extra space and follow no closer than three seconds.

You also need to watch for roadway hazards ahead that might cause the rider to swerve into your path. Many things that are hazards for bicyclists — potholes, storm drains, puddles — also cause problems for moped riders.

If you ride a moped, choose a quiet, open area to learn the controls and how the moped handles before you take it on the road. Obtain an operator's license if required.

**When making a right turn, always check to be sure a cyclist is not in your path.**

**Formal instruction is the best method of learning how to ride a motorcycle.**

Wear a helmet and protective clothing whenever you ride. Ride with the headlight on at all times. Never assume that other drivers see you.

# Motorcycles

Unlike mopeds, most motorcycles are powerful enough to keep up with other traffic. But like mopeds, they are more difficult for drivers to see than other vehicles. The headlight and taillights of new motorcycles light up whenever the engine is running. This feature helps to make motorcycles more visible to other highway users. Even with such safety measures, motorcycles are still harder to see than cars or trucks. Knowing this and some of the other problems that face motorcycle operators can help you share the road with them safely.

## ● Special Characteristics of Motorcycles

Operating a motorcycle requires greater skill and awareness than driving a car. Cyclists use their hands not only to steer, but also to operate the throttle (accelerator). The clutch, front brake, horn, turn signals, and light/dimmer switch are also hand-operated. The cyclist's feet are used for shifting gears and applying the rear brake, as well as for balancing the motorcycle when stopped.

Motorcycles differ from cars in the way they handle. Motorcyclists cannot stop as quickly as car drivers can. Motorcyclists often fail to use the front brake to full advantage in emergencies. Some may fail to use it at all. Failure to use both front and rear brakes result in increased stopping distances.

Swerving to avoid a hazard is more difficult on a motorcycle than in a car. Sharp curves can also cause problems. An inexperienced cyclist may make too wide a turn or fail to slow going into a curve. As a result, the motorcycle may tip over.

Some of the special roadway hazards motorcyclists face include angled railroad tracks, potholes, oil droppings (which create slippery spots when it rains), and manhole covers. Motorcyclists also have less visibility at night be-

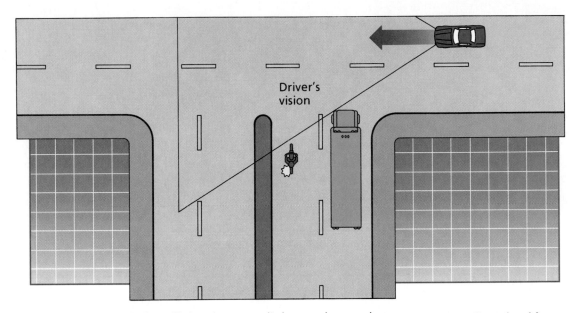

Driver's vision

cause a motorcycle headlight does not light up the road as well as car headlights.

Even with headlights lit, motorcycles can be difficult to see. Why? Most motorcycles are too small to command their full lane rights and are easily hidden by other vehicles. Many cyclists make the mistake of assuming that an oncoming, left-turning car sees them. This is often not true!

### ● Interacting with Motorcycles

Every time your view is blocked by another vehicle, imagine that a motorcyclist may be present. In that way you will always be prepared should a motorcycle enter your path suddenly.

As you prepare to turn left across a lane of oncoming traffic, be doubly certain that the way is clear. At night, a motorcycle headlight may blend into the headlights of the vehicle following it. Do not turn left until you have a clear view of oncoming traffic. When you turn right, get close enough to the curb to discourage a motorcyclist or a bicyclist from passing on your right. Check for motorcycles in your blind spot before you change lanes.

When you see a motorcycle with a turn signal on, do not assume that the cyclist intends to turn. The turn signals on

**Motorcyclists should never assume that other drivers see them. Often they are blocked from view by large vehicles.**

many motorcycles do not turn off automatically, like those in cars. An inattentive or inexperienced cyclist may forget to turn the signal off after making a turn.

To give a motorcyclist time and space to react to changing conditions, leave a 3-second interval between a motorcycle and your car. Maintaining this interval is especially important in heavy traffic, on poor roads, or when approaching a railroad crossing.

Sometimes cyclists travel in the left or right third of their lane to see or be seen more easily. Even if there is enough space in the lane for your car, you should never share a lane with a motorcyclist. When passing, go completely into the other lane just as you would when overtaking a car. Do not return to the travel lane until you are completely past the motorcycle.

## Motorcyclists' Responsibilities

Motorcyclists can do several things to improve their chances of avoiding collisions and to reduce their chances of being injured in traffic. They should dress properly when riding, learn to operate the cycle safely, and choose the safest lane position in traffic.

**Dress Intelligently.**   *Every* cyclist should wear a safety helmet, preferably with a full-coverage face shield. Helmets help protect against serious head, face, and eye injuries. Some states now have laws requiring cyclists to wear helmets. The cyclist should also wear heavy gloves and boots and easy-to-see protective clothing.

Light colors or reflective material make the helmet and clothing more visible at night. Also, reflective strips may be applied to the rear and sides of a motorcycle to make it more visible to drivers.

**Learn the Proper Way to Ride.**   If you decide to ride a motorcycle, learn how to ride correctly, preferably in a course approved by the Motorcycle Safety Foundation. Such courses enable you to learn, practice, and master skills essential to the safe operation of a motorcycle in traffic. They teach riding strategies that can keep you out of trouble when riding.

**Ride Safely.**   Prepare for every ride with an inspection of the motorcycle. A mechanical problem — such as a burned-out headlight — that may be minor for a motorist can have serious consequences for a cyclist.

Maintain a 3-second following distance when riding. This interval enables you to see roadway and traffic problems in time to respond properly. Maintaining a 3-second interval also makes you more visible at intersections and to oncoming traffic.

At night, slow down in order to adjust to the limitations of the headlight.

Until you are experienced, you should not carry passengers. When you do carry passengers, tell them to relax and keep their feet and hands positioned properly.

**Choose Proper Lane Position.**   Do not share a lane with cars. Nor should you pass other vehicles on the right unless you do so legally. When riding in a group, motorcyclists should ride in a staggered formation of no more than four.

**Reflectors make cyclists more visible at night to other drivers.**

165

**Motorcyclists should follow at a safe distance to give themselves more room to maneuver.**

Each cyclist should follow the cycle ahead by at least two seconds. Turns should be made in single file.

Ride in the left third of the lane when possible. In this position, you can see and be seen more easily. This position also forces overtaking vehicles to move fully into the passing lane.

Riding on wet roads is not advisable. When it is necessary to do so, it is best to ride in the left third of the lane in the wheel path of the vehicle ahead. This position provides better traction.

Do not rely on the view in your convex rearview mirrors when changing lanes. Although these mirrors reveal a wider scene to the rear, following vehicles appear farther away than they actually are. Always glance over your shoulder before changing lanes.

# Other Vehicles

In addition to sharing the road with pedestrians and cyclists, you must also share the road with small cars, trucks, and recreational vehicles (RVs).

## Small Cars

Every year there are more small cars on the road. Small cars have several advantages over large cars. They are usually less expensive to buy and are more economical to drive. It is easier to park a small car than a large one. In addition, small cars handle well and are easy to maneuver. Because they are lighter, they often have shorter stopping distances.

There are some disadvantages to driving a small car, however. What is gained in fuel economy may be partly offset by a loss of engine power, so accelerating can take longer. Because the driver sits lower in a small car, the view of the road is limited, especially if the road is hilly.

Despite these disadvantages, small cars are a safe and economical means of transportation. By staying within the speed limit, keeping at least a 2-second following distance, and maintaining an 8- to 12-second visual lead, the driver of a small car can avoid conflicts with other road users.

# Vans, Pickup Trucks, and Utility Vehicles

Drivers of vans, pickup trucks, and utility vehicles (four-wheel drive vehicles) sit higher than in a car. From this position, they can see the traffic and roadway more easily. Because they have a better view of the road ahead, drivers of these types of vehicles may tailgate cars in their eagerness to pass. If you are tailgated by a van or pickup truck, gradually slow down or move to the right to encourage the other driver to pass.

Because of their size, utility vehicles may block your view. Give them extra room and follow them at a greater distance in order to see around them more easily.

If you've ever ridden in one of these vehicles, you may have noticed that you feel that you are going slower than in a car traveling at the same speed. This feeling is a result of sitting higher. Also, because these vehicles have a higher center of gravity than cars, you feel the "lean" in a turn more than you do in a car. If you drive one, watch your speed and slow adequately for turns and curves. Be sure everyone buckles up. In a crash, utility vehicles have the highest occupant ejection rate of any vehicle. *Never* carry passengers in an open cargo area.

**Because of their size, vans may block your view of the road ahead.**

# Recreational Vehicles

**Recreational vehicles** (RVs) of all types are on the road. There are pickup campers and trailer combinations of many sizes. There are also many kinds of motor homes. Despite this variety, RVs have several features in common.

## ● Special Characteristics of RVs

To be affordable, most RVs are an engineering compromise. For example, pickup campers are a cross between a pickup truck and a motor home. This combination often results in difficult handling, even for an experienced driver.

Most campers are built with a wheelbase that is short in relation to the size of the coach. The result is a heavy, sway-prone rear end. They also tend to be top-heavy. Their higher center of gravity results in poor handling. Some drivers make their RVs even more unstable by placing cargo boxes or mopeds on the rear bumper. Others tow their small cars behind them.

When a car or a truck tows a travel trailer, stopping distances are increased. Quick lane changes are not possible in case of an emergency. Many drivers have difficulty passing when towing a trailer. They fail to consider the weight of the trailer and the extra length of the load. As a result, a driver towing a trailer may cut back in too soon after passing another vehicle.

If you tow a trailer, be sure to use an appropriate trailer hitch. When loading the trailer, place the heaviest objects

**Campers accelerate, brake, and steer differently from cars. Towing a small car can cause a camper to become more unstable.**

over the axles to reduce handling problems. On the road, establish a four-second following distance. If the trailer blocks your view to the rear, have special rearview mirrors attached to your vehicle.  Use extra caution when going downhill. Use controlled braking and downshifting to avoid excessive brake wear. When turning, remember that because of the added length of the trailer, you will need to make wider turns.

### ● Interacting with RVs

Always allow RVs ample space in traffic. Increase your following distance on curves and narrow roads and on windy days.

If an RV overtakes you, slow a little in case it returns to your lane early. If an RV begins to gain on you rapidly on a downgrade, be ready to escape onto the road shoulder.

When an RV is following you, allow yourself a 3- to 4-second following distance from the vehicle ahead of you. This way, if you must slow, you can do so gradually, giving the RV behind you more time to brake.

**Because trailers limit rear vision, extra trailer mirrors are advised and often required by law.**

## Large Trucks

Large trucks are essential to our economy. Truck drivers are dedicated to delivering their cargo on time without incident. Despite problems such as the size of their vehicles, bad weather, and occasional poor road conditions, truckers do a good job. As a car driver or a cyclist, you can safely interact with trucks if you know the problems truck drivers are faced with and respond properly.

### ● Special Characteristics of Large Trucks

Drivers of large trucks have an excellent view of the road ahead. This advantage is offset by long stopping distances. Also, large trucks do not accelerate quickly.

Truckers try to avoid losing their momentum, so they tend to go fast downhill to make it easier to go up the next hill. They may delay reducing their speed when they approach a lowered speed zone, especially if it is followed soon by a higher speed zone.

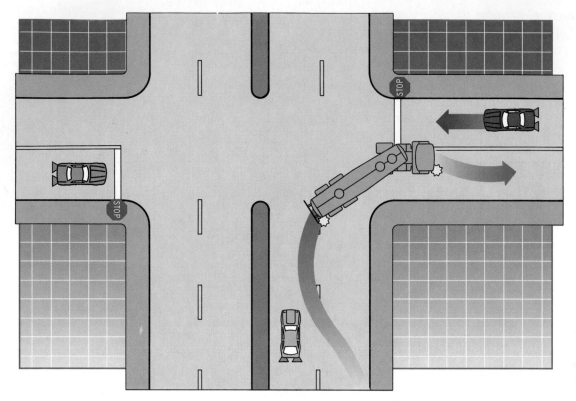

**Large trucks often need to move partially into other lanes to make a turn.**

Sometimes truckers are so destination-oriented that they speed or tailgate another vehicle. They may also **draft** another truck (follow closely to use the other truck's wind-breaking effect) to save fuel. This practice makes it difficult and sometimes dangerous for you to overtake a truck.

In cities, trucks stop frequently to make deliveries or to take on cargo. When stopped, they may block your lane. Because of their length, trucks may make wide turns from what would be considered the wrong lane if the maneuver were done in a car. Some trucks have a sign at the rear warning of wide turns.

### ● Interacting with Large Trucks

Because of their size, trucks often reduce other drivers' vision. Follow a truck at a greater distance so that you will be able to see around it more easily. When a large truck appears in your rearview mirror and begins to tailgate you,

slow down to encourage the trucker to pass you. On a multilane road, move into the middle or right lane so the truck can pass.

Never remain sandwiched between large trucks. Change lanes, speed up, slow down — do what you must to regain a large space cushion between you and the trucks.

**Because they sit up high, drivers of large trucks have an excellent view of the road ahead.**

## Safety Checks

- Keep your foot on the service brake while starting the engine.

- If you are being tailgated, change lanes or gradually reduce your speed.

- To ensure your safety and the safety of others in your vehicle, *always* use safety belts. The "buckle up" habit saves lives and sharply reduces the severity of injuries.

## Key Ideas

- Many pedestrians do not know it is difficult for you to see them (especially at night) or to stop for them.
- Look for roadway hazards that may cause a bicyclist to swerve into your path.
- Motorcycles are often difficult to see. Be especially alert for them when you turn left.

- Motorcyclists usually cannot swerve or stop their machines as quickly as cars, so give them extra space and follow them no closer than three seconds.
- Never share a lane with a motorcycle.
- Vans, pickups, utility vehicles, RVs, and large trucks may block your vision, so follow them at a greater distance.
- When you tow a trailer, double your following distance.
- Never become sandwiched between trucks.

# Gauging Your Understanding

**1.** What strategies can you use to avoid conflicts with pedestrians?

**2.** What kinds of errors do bicyclists often make?

**3.** Describe a properly dressed motorcyclist.

**4.** Why should you establish a longer following distance behind vans, RVs, and trucks?

**5.** What should you do when you encounter a large truck? When a large truck is following you?

# In the Driver's Seat

**1.** Study the illustration on page 163. Then answer the following questions.
   a. What hazards does the motorcyclist face?
   b. What hazards does the driver of the car face?

**2.** While driving on a two-lane, two-way road, you identify a bicyclist to your right just ahead of you. You know this section of the road is in bad shape with many potholes, especially near the side of the road. What can you predict the bicyclist will do? How should you proceed?

## Special Projects

**1.** Observe 5–10 motorcyclists. In what part of the lane is each traveling? Is that position appropriate? Is each cyclist dressed properly?

**2.** Ask a local traffic official or a police officer if there are any laws relating to bicyclists or moped drivers. Are these local or state laws? Are the laws enforced? Are they sufficient?

# ⇒ Chapter Test 9

Name _____ Date _____

**Write "T" beside statements that are true and "F" beside those that are false.**

_____   **1.** Most pedestrians recognize how difficult it is for drivers to see them.

_____   **2.** Blast your horn to alert pedestrians who may be heading into your path.

_____   **3.** One of the most common traffic violations of bicyclists is failing to yield the right of way.

_____   **4.** Bicyclists should use hand signals to show they intend to change direction.

_____   **5.** Moped riders may fail to give hand signals because the left hand is used to operate the rear brake.

_____   **6.** A motorcycle with its headlight on is as visible as another car to an oncoming driver.

_____   **7.** Motorcycles handle about the same as cars do.

_____   **8.** A driver should never share a lane with a motorcycle.

_____   **9.** Every cyclist should wear a protective safety helmet.

_____   **10.** Because of their size, it is legal for motorcycles to pass on the right at any time.

**Complete these sentences by writing the correct terms in the blanks.**

**1.** Whenever your view is blocked by another vehicle, assume that a _____ may be hidden by the vehicle.

**2.** A(n) _____ sign warns of the possible presence of livestock on the road.

**3.** Large trucks often _____ another truck to save fuel.

**4.** Never permit yourself to become _____ between large trucks.

**5.** When a car or truck tows a trailer, _____ distances are increased.

**Write the letter of the best answer in the space provided.**

_____   **1.** In good road, weather, and traffic conditions, motorcyclists should maintain a following distance of at least (a) 2 seconds, (b) 3 seconds, (c) 8 seconds, (d) 12 seconds.

_____ **2.** Bicycle riders should normally ride (a) with the flow of traffic, (b) on the left edge of the road, (c) on the sidewalk, (d) in the middle of a lane.

_____ **3.** A driver towing a trailer should maintain a following distance of at least (a) 2 seconds, (b) 3 seconds, (c) 4 seconds, (d) 6 seconds.

_____ **4.** The minimum following distance that a driver should follow a motorcycle at is (a) 2 seconds, (b) 3 seconds, (c) 4 seconds, (d) 5 seconds.

_____ **5.** Load a trailer so that the heaviest items are placed (a) near the hitch, (b) in the back of the trailer, (c) in the middle of the trailer, (d) over the axles.

_____ **6.** The highest occupant ejection rate in a crash is held by (a) large trucks, (b) utility vehicles, (c) motorcycles, (d) RVs.

_____ **7.** One way in which motorcycles differ from cars is that they (a) don't have turn signals, (b) cannot be stopped as quickly, (c) don't have headlights, (d) are not as fast.

_____ **8.** To improve their chances of avoiding collisions, motorcyclists can (a) avoid driving in traffic, (b) wear heavy, dark clothing, (c) ride only during daylight, (d) choose the safest lane position in traffic.

_____ **9.** Small cars (a) have longer than average stopping distances, (b) have a high roll-over record, (c) have slightly shorter than average stopping distances, (d) provide a good view of the road.

_____ **10.** Maintaining a 3-second interval between a motorcycle and your car is especially important (a) on open highways, (b) on narrow roads, (c) on poor roads, (d) at intersections.

# Careers in the HTS: Engineering

Highway, traffic, and automotive engineers help to shape the HTS.

## Highway Engineers

Highway engineers design or improve the nation's roads. These highway engineers not only study the system as it exists, but also plan for its future development. When a new road is needed, they suggest routes it might follow. To do so, they study present uses of the land. Then they consider what type of road would best fit the needs of people in the area.

Once a plan is accepted by the public, highway engineers see that the plan is carried out. They supervise the work of surveyors and construction crews.

## Traffic Engineers

Traffic engineers study the way traffic flows at various times of the day or year and resolve any problems that may exist. In their study of an area, they use spot maps, collision diagrams, speed charts, and collision records.

To reduce hazards, traffic engineers may ban parking on certain streets or decide

to make a street one way. Sometimes they suggest installation or removal of traffic controls.

Traffic engineers may also call for construction of pedestrian or bicycle over passes. Or they may try to clear an area of something that blocks a driver's view. Widening a road or removing sharp curves are some other recommendations a traffic engineer might make.

Traffic engineers often work with highway engineers, enforcement personnel, city planners, and public works departments to determine needs and solve problems.

## Automotive Engineers

Most automotive engineers work in private industry.

These men and women are responsible for designing motor vehicles. In doing so, they must meet federal safety, environmental, and fuel conservation requirements.

In developing a design, they must consider cost, the effect of natural laws on a vehicle, and the demands of consumers.

Some engineers work mainly on improving the appearance or comfort of the vehicle. Others seek ways of improving engine performance.

Before any new idea is accepted, it must be tried out. Some automotive engineers use computers to create alternative designs, and some build prototypes (models) and supervise their testing.

# 4 Driver Responsibilities

# Chapter 10

# Road Hazards and Vehicle Failures

- **Should all drivers be required to turn their headlights on any time the sun is not shining?**
- **What should you do first when a skid occurs?**
- **How can a safety belt help you in an emergency?**
- **Imagine that your left front tire just blew out — what should you do?**

Driving a motor vehicle under normal conditions is a challenge. However, there are times when driving becomes even more difficult. For example, a tire may suddenly blow out. Or during a snowstorm, you may have difficulty seeing.

You must act quickly to minimize the hazards caused by these or other situations. First, you must identify the hazards, then act to avoid them. To do so, you must remain alert and calm at all times. Using IPDE skills is especially important in such situations.

# Potential Problems

Any hazard or failure in the HTS can create a critical driving situation. Two of the most serious problems are limited visibility and loss of traction. If you are aware of what causes such problems, you will be better prepared to handle them when they occur.

## Visibility

Anything that reduces your vision also reduces your ability to safely maneuver your car. For this reason, seeing all parts of the HTS clearly is very important.

**Use over-the-shoulder checks and the outside rearview mirror more frequently when your view is blocked.**

### ● The Driver's View

How well you can see the roadway depends in part on what type of vehicle you drive. The size of a vehicle or its design sometimes results in large blind spots to the sides and rear. Before making a lane change or a turn in such a vehicle, it is especially important to check blind spots by looking over your shoulder.

Too, your view may be blocked by a passenger or items loaded in the car. If it is necessary to drive with a limited view, use shoulder checks and the outside rearview mirror more frequently.

Dirt also may limit your ability to see. A film of dirt is likely to reflect light and cause glare. For this reason, it is important to keep all windows clean both inside and out.

If a car's windows are dirty, its headlights and taillights may need cleaning too. Dirty lights do not light up the road as brightly as clean ones. This makes it more difficult for you to see and be seen at night. Whenever you clean the windows, also clean the lights.

**High-beam headlights improve visibility on poorly lit roads.**

## Lighting Conditions

Driving at night is more difficult because of reduced visibility. The lack of light may cause you to see only outlines of shapes and forms. Some parts of the HTS may be completely hidden from view. Also, glare from the headlights of oncoming traffic and roadside lights reduce visibility.

You can do several things to make up for lower visibility. Turn your headlights on early. Headlights help you see and be seen. Keep instrument panel lights low to avoid glare. Also, avoid looking directly into the headlights of oncoming vehicles. Instead, as a vehicle approaches, let your eyes follow the right edge of the roadway as far ahead as possible. This reduces your chance of being blinded by the headlight glare. Also, drive more slowly than you do during the day and increase following distance. This extra distance gives you more time to identify possible hazards.

**Wearing sunglasses helps reduce glare from bright sunlight.**

**In fog, headlights help make your vehicle more visible to other drivers.**

## ● Weather Conditions

The weather can also affect your ability to see. For example, bright sunlight — especially in the early morning and late afternoon — may temporarily blind you. To protect against glare during the day, wear sunglasses and use sun visors. Adjust the visors so that they cut off as little as possible of your view of traffic. Never wear sunglasses at night or when driving through long tunnels.

Fog, rain, snow, or dust may also cause glare. Wet surfaces and particles of dust or water in the air reflect light much as a mirror does. These weather conditions reduce visibility in other ways too. For instance, fog may be so thick that you can barely see objects two seconds ahead of you. Snow, ice, or dust can coat the windows making it difficult to see out of them. If this happens, stop as soon as you can do so safely and clean the windows.

When driving through fog, rain, snow, or dust, turn on the low-beam headlights. This not only helps you see better, but also helps drivers of oncoming vehicles to see you. Slow down and increase following distance to have more time to look for and react to traffic events.

# Traction

When traction is reduced, you lose some control of the car. For this reason, you must be aware of the conditions that may lead to traction loss.

## ● Wet Roads

Traction is not as good on a wet surface as a dry one. Roads are especially slippery during the first few minutes of a rain or snow storm. At that time the melted snow or rain mixes with oil and dirt on the road and forms a slick, oily film. Later, water may wash the film away. But by then, water may begin to build up on the road. Wet leaves on the road can also be very slippery and cause additional traction problems.

A combination of vehicle speed, tire pressure, and water buildup can lead to **hydroplaning**. Hydroplaning occurs when the tires begin to ride on a wedge of water that forms between the tires and the road surface. When this happens, you lose steering and braking control.

Whether or not a car hydroplanes depends on a number of factors. Properly inflated tires with good tread depth do a better job of cutting through the film of water than those that are worn out or not inflated properly. Too, the more water buildup on the road, the greater the chances of hydroplaning.

Hydroplaning is more likely to occur at high speeds. At speeds of less than 30 mph, tires will usually cut through the water to stay on the road surface. Between 30 and 50 mph, partial hydroplaning may occur. At speeds of more than 50 mph, the tires may ride almost completely on the water rather than on the pavement.

To improve traction on wet roads and prevent hydroplaning, slow down. Drive in the tracks of the vehicle ahead. Also, be sure that tires are properly inflated and have good tread. Still, hydroplaning may occur. If it does, do not use the brakes to slow down. Instead, slow down by releasing the accelerator. After the tires regain some contact with the road, brake gently to slow down even further.

**Reduce your speed on wet roads to prevent hydroplaning.**

**Tire chains work even better than snow tires to improve traction on snowy or icy roads.**

## Snow and Ice

Tires can usually push powdery snow aside. But as the snow melts, a car could hydroplane on the slush or wet surface. Also, the melted snow may refreeze and form a glaze that tires cannot grip. As the temperature rises, packed snow and ice on a road may become quite slick, especially before a stop sign or traffic signal. As a result, traction problems may increase.

Snow tires are one way of improving traction on loose or unpacked wet snow. The deeper grooves in the tread hold the road effectively. Tire chains work even better. In some areas, especially on mountain roads, drivers are required by law to use tire chains in snow conditions.

To control a vehicle on snow or ice you must accelerate, brake, and steer gently. Increase your following distance to allow plenty of room to stop and brake gently to maintain steering control.

You can reduce the chance of your car becoming stuck in the snow by trying to keep it moving and avoiding ruts. But if your car does get stuck, you might be able to free it by "rocking" it. Rocking involves moving the car quickly forward and backward. If this is done smoothly, a back-and-forth (rocking) motion is set up. Eventually the car may lift out of the rut. Success depends mainly on setting up a rhythmic rocking motion without spinning the wheels. However, unless you do this procedure carefully, you may damage your car's transmission.

## Gravel and Sand

Sand provides traction on a snow-covered road, but becomes a traction hazard on a dry road. Be especially wary of sand at junctions where it is most likely to build up. Quick takeoffs and hard braking on sand (or gravel) can cause your car to skid.

Gravel roads may have a buildup of gravel in the center of the road and small pockets of loose gravel in other areas. These can be especially hazardous. Gravel and sand can cause almost the same kind of traction problems as snow or ice. When driving on sand or gravel, make adjustments similar to those used when driving on snow or ice.

## ● Wind

High winds and wind gusts can push at a car, making it difficult to stay on the road. High, boxy vehicles or vehicles with trailers are affected most by side winds.

Winds are especially strong on bridges and between large buildings and rock ledges. A combination of wind gusts and slippery roads can be extremely dangerous. To avoid being pushed into another lane or off the road, slow down. Also, grip the wheel firmly with both hands and make steering adjustments as soon as the wind pushes your car.

**High winds can make it difficult for a driver to maintain vehicle control.**

# Other Emergencies

Every driver is likely to face an emergency situation at one time or another. Sometimes emergencies are caused by poor road conditions. More often they result from a mistake made by a driver or the failure of a vehicle to perform as expected.

**What might drivers in the right lane do to avoid conflict with cars entering the expressway?**

# Controlling the Vehicle

Through the use of the IPDE process you should be able to handle just about any emergency. But there are times when an error in judgment may require you to take extraordinary steps to avoid a collision.

To control your car in an emergency, you must remain behind the steering wheel. Wearing your safety belt helps you stay behind the wheel despite quick changes in speed or direction. Also, if passengers wear their belts, they will not be thrown against you or the controls.

## Brake and Accelerator Control

Under normal conditions, if you maintain a safe following distance you can gradually come to a smooth stop. But there are times when you will have very little space in which to brake. If you slam on the brakes, the wheels can lock and the car could go into a skid. To avoid this, use a technique known as **controlled braking**. It allows you to stop quickly without skidding. To do so, apply steady but progressively greater pressure on the brakes.

At times, you may have to avoid a collision by accelerating quickly. For example, if you are in the right lane of an expressway, you may have to accelerate to avoid being hit by a vehicle speeding down the entrance ramp.

## Swerving

There may be times when you do not have enough room to stop or accelerate to avoid a collision. In such cases you may be able to swerve into another lane. The best way to control steering in a swerve is to keep your hands in the 9 and 3 o'clock positions on the wheel.

Sometimes you must swerve off the roadway to avoid a hazard. You can usually return to the road as though making an ordinary lane change. If the shoulder is blocked, you may not have enough time for a gradual return to the roadway. In this case you must move back onto the highway quickly and accelerate to highway speed. (Refer to Maneuver I in the In-Car Guide in the back of this book.)

## ● Skids

A **skid** occurs when the car wheels slide rather than roll over the road. There are four basic types of skids: braking skids, power skids, cornering skids, and fast idle skids. When your car goes into a skid, you lose steering control. Skids frequently put a vehicle in the opposite lane of travel. You must take certain steps in each case to regain control of the car. (Refer to Maneuver I in the In-Car Guide in the back of this book.)

If you brake too hard, your car may go into a **braking skid**. One or all of the wheels may lock. Often one or both of the rear wheels lock, and the back end of the car slides to the left or right. To recover from a braking skid, first release the brake. Then, steer in the direction you want the front of the car to go. When the tires regain traction, straighten the wheels.

A **power skid** occurs when you accelerate suddenly or too hard. Power skids usually happen on slippery road surfaces or gravel. To correct a power skid, release the gas pedal and steer in the direction you want the front of the car to go. Steer as needed to straighten the car.

**Cornering skids** usually result from taking a turn or curve too fast. In a cornering skid, the car resists your attempts to steer and begins to slide. To recover from a cornering skid, release the gas pedal and steer in the direction you want the front of the car to go.

**Fast idle skids** occur when you try to stop your car when the engine is idling too fast. The fast idle causes the drive wheels to fight your braking effort. In turn, the braking effect to the non-drive wheels is so great that they skid. To correct a fast idle skid, shift to NEUTRAL and reduce your braking effort. Tap the accelerator pedal briskly to slow the idle speed.

## ● Counterskids

A **counterskid** may result from steering too sharply when trying to correct a skid. It may also be caused by failing to straighten the wheels quickly enough after recovering from a skid. To avoid this problem, steer only far

**To correct a skid, always steer in the direction you want the car to go.**

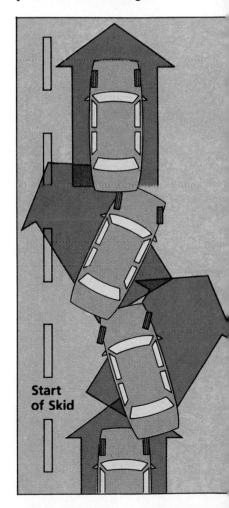

Start
of Skid

**This car skidded around the corner. What did the driver do wrong?**

enough to correct the skid. As soon as the car recovers from the skid, center steer to straighten the car in the lane.

While steering to recover from a skid, do not use the brakes or accelerator. Using either or both could cause the vehicle to go completely out of control. (Refer to Maneuver I in the In-Car Guide in the back of this book.)

## Handling Collisions

If a crash cannot be avoided, try to hit an object that "gives." While steering towards it, brake as much as possible. Before impact, grip the top of the steering wheel with both hands. Keep your arms in front of the wheel. This will help cushion you during the crash in case your shoulder belt is adjusted too loosely. Passengers in the rear seat should cradle their heads in their arms while leaning against the back of the front seat.

# Vehicle Equipment Failures

Driving emergencies are often caused by vehicle failures. Many of these emergencies can be avoided by keeping your car in good operating condition. But if your car does fail, get it off the road as soon as possible. Mark the car as disabled by putting the hood up, placing flares ahead of and behind it, using the emergency flashers, and tying a white cloth to the door handle or hood. Unless a telephone or service station is nearby, stay near the car but away from traffic. If the car is safely off the road, you may prefer to stay inside it with the doors locked.

## Tires

When a front tire blows out (or goes flat), the car pulls sharply in the direction of the blowout. When a rear tire blows out, the back end weaves. Regardless of which tire blows out, grip the wheel firmly at the 9 and 3 o'clock positions and release the gas pedal. When your car is under control, steer off the road onto solid, level ground. Once off the road, put the car in PARK (automatic) or REVERSE (standard). Set the parking brake. If a rear tire must be changed, block both front tires to keep the car from rolling. If a front tire must be replaced, block the rear tire on the opposite side of the car. Then follow these steps.

1. Get all necessary equipment out of the car and place it near the flat.
2. Using the tire iron, remove the hubcap and loosen the lug nuts.
3. Follow the instruction manual for your car to place and operate the jack. Jack the car up until the flat tire is about two inches off the ground.
4. Remove the lug nuts and place them in the hubcap to keep from losing them.
5. Remove the flat tire and put the spare tire in place.
6. Put the lug nuts back on and tighten them enough to hold the tire in place.

**If your vehicle does break down, get it well off the road to prevent a possible collision.**

**7.** Release the jack carefully and lower the car. Finish tightening the lug nuts and replace the hubcap.

**8.** Place the flat in the trunk and drive to a service station as soon as possible to have it repaired or replaced. If you have a compact spare tire, do not drive above 50 mph while it is on the car.

# Brakes

Complete service brake failure is unlikely in today's cars. New cars have a two-part brake system. Each controls two wheels. When one half fails, the other half can be used to bring the car to a stop. Even with total brake failure, sometimes you can pump the brake pedal and regain some braking power. If your brakes fail, shift to a lower gear to make use of engine braking. In an emergency you can use the parking brake for stopping. Pull the brake release lever out and hold it out. If the brake lever has a button release, hold the button in. Holding the lever or button keeps the rear wheels from locking. Then, apply the parking brake in a pumping, on-and-off action.

You may also be able to slow down by scraping the car against an embankment or the curbing. If you cannot stop by any other means, you will have to hit something. In such a case, choose something that will yield such as bushes or shrubbery, and prepare yourself for the crash. (Refer to Maneuver I in the In-Car Guide in the back of this book.)

Brakes sometimes fail (or partially fail) because they are wet. You can dry them by pressing the accelerator and the brake at the same time. The heat caused by friction will dry the brakes. You can also do this to keep the brakes from getting wet as you drive through deep water.

# Accelerator

If the accelerator pedal sticks, shift to NEUTRAL. Then, apply the brakes vigorously as you steer off the roadway. As soon as you get off the road, turn the ignition off. (Refer to Maneuver I in the In-Car Guide in the back of this book.)

# Steering

Steering failure is very unlikely. However, if you lose steering control, try to stop as quickly and safely as possible. Because you cannot control the direction in which the car moves, a collision is likely. Be prepared for it.

In a vehicle with power steering, power to the steering mechanism could fail. You will still be able to steer, but it will require a great deal of effort. Hold the wheel firmly and turn it with as much strength as possible.

# Engine

A stalled engine can usually be restarted by shifting to NEUTRAL and turning the ignition switch. A stalled car with a standard transmission may be moved by shifting to FIRST or REVERSE, releasing the clutch, and holding the ignition switch on. The battery power is usually enough to move the car off the road. If not, push the car off the road.

If the battery is dead, you may be able to start the car with the help of jumper (or booster) cables and another vehicle. To jump-start a car with a dead battery, follow these steps.

1. Position a working car so that the cables reach between the batteries of the two cars. Make sure the cars do not touch. Avoid any moving parts such as the fan and belts when attaching the cables.
2. Attach one end of the red booster cable to the working car's positive battery cable (indicated by a ''+'' on the battery). Attach the other end of the red booster cable to the positive terminal of the dead battery.
3. Next, attach one end of the black booster cable to the working car's negative battery terminal. Do not attach the other end of the black cable to the dead battery! If the battery has a serious malfunction, a spark could set off an explosion. Instead, attach the cable to a bolt on the engine compartment wall.
4. Start the engine of the working car. Then turn the ignition on to start the car with the dead battery.

**To prevent shock or a possible battery explosion, you must attach jumper cables correctly.**

**5.** Once the car has started, remove the cables in the reverse order that they were connected.

# Other Vehicle Failures

Many kinds of vehicle failures are unlikely to occur. Still you must be prepared to handle them. For example, an improperly latched hood could pop open. If this happens while driving, look under the hood or through the side windows. Steer off the road and stop. After you close the hood, make sure it will stay shut. If not, tie it down and have it repaired as soon as possible.

Another vehicle malfunction that requires quick driver action is headlight failure. Brake immediately and turn on your emergency flashers. Steer off the road and stop.

A fire under the hood is also unlikely. If it does happen, pull off the road immediately and stop. Have all passengers get out of the car and move well away from it. Before opening the hood, protect your hands with rags or gloves. Unlatch the hood and raise it slowly. Step back and keep your head below the hood while raising it.

Use a dry chemical extinguisher to put out the fire. Aim it at the base of the fire for best results. If an extinguisher is not available, use a blanket or coat to smother the fire. If the fire cannot be controlled, everyone should move as far away from the car as possible, because eventually the gas tank could explode.

# If Stranded

A vehicle breakdown or the weather could cause you to become stranded. Although most people will never be stranded, you should be prepared for the possibility. If your car does stop and cannot be restarted, mark it as disabled. Put flares in front of and behind the car to warn other drivers and to serve as a signal for help.

Unless you are sure you can find help nearby and reach it easily, do not leave your car. You and all passengers should stay inside the car. It provides shelter and is more easily seen than a person walking.

**In the event of a major fire, get as far away from the vehicle as possible and call the fire department.**

During the winter, keep blankets, a snow shovel, large plastic bags, flares, candles, matches, and nonperishable food in your car. Use the car heater for about 5 or 10 minutes every hour. But, use it only if a window is opened slightly for ventilation and the exhaust system is in good working condition. Shovel snow away from the tailpipe. Otherwise, carbon monoxide can leak into the car.

To help stay warm, wrap up in the blankets. Wrap the plastic bags around your feet and legs to insulate against the cold. Following these practices can help keep you comfortable until help arrives.

## Maintenance Tips

- Regular vehicle inspections can help to prevent expensive repairs. Have a mechanic inspect and service your car twice a year or every 6000 miles.

- Worn or damaged tires are dangerous. Check tires regularly for wear and replace when wear bars show.

- While accelerating, check to feel that the pedal moves up and down without hesitation or sticking. Have any problems corrected without delay.

- Replace windshield wiper blades as soon as they begin to leave streaks on the windshield.

## Key Ideas

- Any time your vision is blocked or reduced, your ability to maneuver safely is also reduced.
- A build-up of rain or slush combined with high speed can cause your car's tires to hydroplane.
- Snow tires help improve traction on loose snow, but tire chains work better.
- In an emergency, safety belts help keep you behind the wheel and prevent passengers from being thrown against you.
- To recover from a skid, release the gas pedal and the brake. Then steer in the direction you want the front of the car to go.
- When jump-starting a stalled car, do not attach the negative cable to the dead battery.

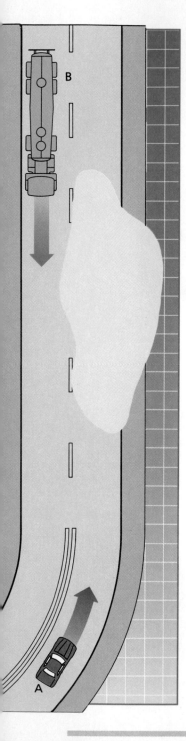

# Gauging Your Understanding

1. How can you make up for reduced visibility when driving at night? When driving in bright sunlight?

2. How can you prevent your car from hydroplaning?

3. What are the four major types of skids? What steering adjustments should you make for each?

4. If you must drive through deep water, how can you keep your car's brakes dry?

5. What should you do if your service brakes fail?

# In the Driver's Seat

1. As you drive down a dry, paved street, you start thinking about what else you have to do. You remember that you have to stop at the post office. You turn into the street without realizing that it is covered with packed snow. Your car starts to skid toward a row of parked cars. What should you do?

2. You are driving Car A at 50 mph on a crowned highway. The oncoming truck (B) is traveling 40 mph. A pool of water about 100 feet long is in your lane ahead. Should you drive through the water at your present speed? Why? Can you use the left lane to go around the water? Explain. What should you do after you go through the water?

## Special Projects

1. Survey two or three tire stores in your area. What kinds of road conditions can be handled by various kinds of tires? Make a list of adverse conditions and the tires that are recommended for those conditions.

2. With proper supervision, practice changing a tire on your family car or a friend's car.

3. With proper supervision, practice hooking up jumper cables between two cars.

# ⮞ Chapter Test 10

Name _____   Date _____

**Write "T" beside statements that are true and "F" beside those that are false.**

_____  **1.** If stranded in a snowstorm, you should usually stay with your vehicle.

_____  **2.** You can see better in dense fog when you use high-beam headlights.

_____  **3.** When a front tire blows out, the vehicle will pull sharply in the direction of the blowout.

_____  **4.** To avoid being blinded by headlights of oncoming cars, look as far ahead as possible at the right edge of the roadway.

_____  **5.** Sand improves traction on both wet and dry roads.

_____  **6.** To correct a skid, apply the brakes.

_____  **7.** A counterskid is caused by not steering enough to correct the initial skid.

_____  **8.** If the accelerator sticks, turn off the ignition immediately.

_____  **9.** On modern cars, complete brake failure is unlikely.

_____  **10.** In an emergency, you can use the parking brake to stop a car.

**Write the letter of the best answer in the space provided.**

_____  **1.** Hydroplaning may be caused by a combination of all of the following except (a) water buildup, (b) tire pressure, (c) brake pumping, (d) vehicle speed.

_____  **2.** For the best traction on snow or ice, a vehicle should be equipped with (a) tire chains, (b) a traction mat, (c) snow tires, (d) under-inflated tires.

_____  **3.** To minimize the glare caused by headlights at night you should (a) wear sunglasses, (b) use the visors, (c) look to the right edge of the roadway, (d) use parking lights.

_____  **4.** If you cannot avoid a collision, you should (a) steer toward an object that gives, (b) close your eyes, (c) put your arms down by your sides, (d) turn off the ignition.

_____  **5.** The roads are most slippery when a rainstorm has (a) just stopped, (b) been over for a while, (c) continued for a long time, (d) just started.

_____  **6.** Steering too sharply when correcting a skid may result in (a) hydroplaning, (b) a four-wheel skid, (c) a cornering skid, (d) a counterskid.

‒‒‒‒   **7.** If the brakes get wet, you can dry them by (a) pumping them, (b) using controlled braking, (c) applying the brake while in NEUTRAL, (d) pressing the accelerator and brake pedal at the same time while moving slowly.

## Complete these sentences by placing the correct terms in the blanks.

**1.** Gravel and sand can create almost the same traction problems as _____ and _____.

**2.** By holding the steering wheel in the _____ and _____ positions you can best control steering during a swerve.

**3.** If you cannot avoid a collision, grip the top of the _____ with both hands.

**4.** The technique that involves applying steady but progressively greater pressure on the brakes is called _____.

**5.** The four kinds of skids are _____, _____, _____, and _____ skids.

**6.** If you replace a flat tire with a compact spare tire, you should not drive faster than _____ mph.

**7.** While steering to correct a skid, do not use the _____ or _____.

**8.** When positioning cars to connect jumper cables, do not let the two cars _____.

Chapter 11   Driver Fitness and
Highway Safety

- **What disabilities would make you unable to drive?**
- **Young drivers have better reflexes than older drivers, yet they have more accidents. Why?**
- **In what ways can emotions affect your driving?**
- **How might common cold or allergy medications influence how you drive?**

**Roadside rest areas provide a place for tired drivers to stop and rest.**

Your ability to identify, predict, decide, and execute when driving is based on your physical and mental condition. Driving requires alertness and concentration. If you are tired, upset, or ill, you may not react quickly enough to an emergency. Taking certain medications or prescription drugs can make you drowsy and interfere with your driving. Before you get behind the wheel, make sure you are physically and mentally prepared to meet the demands of driving. By avoiding alcohol and other drugs that affect perception and behavior before you drive, you can help ensure the safety of all highway users.

## Physical Condition

Although driving is not a physically demanding task, there are some physical conditions that can reduce your driving ability. Even minor illnesses can interfere with your vision or concentration. If you become overtired, you cannot react as well to emergencies. Good driving requires that you be well rested and in generally good health.

# Coordination

Your nervous and muscular systems combine to determine how coordinated you are as a driver. Fortunately, driving does not require the same amount of physical coordination that is needed by highly skilled athletes. Driving does, however, require coordination of hands and feet to steer, accelerate, and brake.

Under most conditions, persons who have even modest coordination can become excellent drivers. A key to success is to avoid abusing substances that reduce your natural coordination. Avoid using alcohol or drugs when you drive. These substances almost always have a negative effect on driving ability.

When coordination is impaired by alcohol or drugs, reaction time is slowed. As a result, the driver may not be able to slow or swerve in time to avoid a hazard.

# Age

Age often works to the advantage of young drivers. With quick reaction time and good vision, teenage drivers have a physical advantage over older drivers. In spite of this advantage, beginning drivers are involved in far more than their share of highway collisions. Lack of experience and poor judgment often offset the age advantage. As a new driver, you should not assume that driving ability comes automatically. You can become a good driver only through concentration, experience, and practice.

Older drivers often lack the physical quickness that young people have. Aging can slow reflexes and reduce hearing and vision. As a result, some older drivers are not able to drive as well as they once could. Be considerate of all drivers, but be particularly alert when approaching older drivers and pedestrians.

Age does bring experience, however. Most older drivers are less likely to take risks. Because of their driving experience, they can often identify and avoid hazards that might present problems for younger drivers.

**More experienced drivers may take a less traveled route to avoid possible hazards.**

**Often a short stop at a roadside rest area is enough to help a driver avoid becoming overtired.**

# Fatigue

When you become **fatigued**, or overtired, your vision may become blurred, or you may begin to see double. Often you may not be aware of how tired you really are. You may doze off for a few seconds without realizing it. You could even fall asleep at the wheel.

A study of traffic statistics reveals that a large number of collisions occur at an hour when many drivers are likely to be fatigued. Driving home after a long day at work, you are certain to be tired. To reduce the chances of a collision, don't drive when you are overtired. If you are driving a long distance, stop and get out of the car on an hourly basis. Change drivers or stop to rest to reduce fatigue.

# Physical Disabilities

A temporary or a chronic illness can seriously affect driving ability. Such minor illnesses as a headache, cold, or the flu can affect your ability to think clearly. They may also cause dizziness, result in blurred vision, or increase reaction time. The medication you take for such illnesses may leave you feeling drowsy and inattentive.

If you have a temporary illness, you probably are not used to compensating for that illness. If possible, let someone else drive or take another form of transportation. If you must drive when ill, however, take a less demanding route. Increase your following distance and drive more slowly.

Chronic illnesses like epilepsy, diabetes, and some heart diseases can be medically controlled. People who have these diseases under control are able to drive. However, some chronic illnesses prevent a person from driving safely. For example, people suffering from diseases that affect muscle control are not issued driver's licenses.

Many drivers are disabled because of reduced use of arms or legs. Special controls and adjusted driving procedures can help compensate for these disabilities. For example, hand-operated gas and brake controls can enable a person without the use of legs to drive.

**Specially equipped vehicles such as this enable people who have limited use of arms and legs to drive in the HTS.**

Most states now provide special registration plates displaying the international logo for disabled persons. Parking spaces are reserved for cars carrying such plates in many shopping centers and parking lots. Respect these specially marked parking areas and park only in spaces not reserved for the disabled.

# Vision

Traffic safety research shows that drivers receive over 95 percent of traffic information through their eyes. Good vision is critically important to safe driving. When driving, you must be able to distinguish shapes and colors, judge distances, and adjust to changes in light.

You must see well enough to get the complete picture of the constantly changing traffic scene. You also need to be able to focus on specific events. There is a difference between looking and seeing. Often we see what we expect to see rather than what is really there. Scan the scene carefully. There may be more out there than you see at first.

## Visual Acuity and Field of Vision

**Visual acuity** is the measure of a person's ability to see things clearly. Each eye is checked and given a score. A rating of 20/20 means that a person can see at a distance of 20 feet what should be seen at 20 feet. A rating of 20/100 indicates that the individual can see at 20 feet what should be visible at 100 feet. Fortunately, corrective lenses are available to improve vision to at least minimum levels in most cases. Have your eyes checked to see if correction is necessary. If you do need glasses or contact lenses, wear them while driving. Take good care of your eyes. Have a thorough eye examination at least every two years.

**Peripheral vision** is a measure of side vision. Most people have a field of vision of about 170 degrees from side to side while looking straight ahead. However, only a small area in the center is actually seen clearly. Even though side vision may not be clear, it can still help you see hazards. If you have poor side vision, compensate by turning your head and scanning to the side.

## Color and Depth Perception

**Color perception**, or the ability to see color, is important to help identify traffic signs and other color-coded information. Have your color vision checked regularly. If your color vision is less than perfect, pay special attention to traffic signs and signals to be sure that you are obeying the law. Most warning and regulatory signs are recognizable by their shape as well as by their color. For example, an octagonal sign always means STOP.

**Depth perception** helps you determine how far away objects and hazards are. Your brain converts the two flat images from your eyes into a three-dimensional picture. If your ability to judge depth and distances is poor, compensate by driving more slowly.

## Night Vision

Driving at night presents an additional hazard — limited visibility. Other vehicles and pedestrians blend into the background and can suddenly appear as if out of nowhere.

**Side vision decreases as speed increases. Turn your head to scan to the side.**

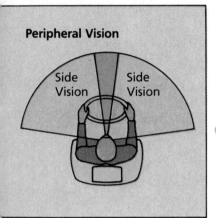

**Peripheral Vision**

Side Vision     Side Vision

Depth perception, color vision, and visual acuity are all reduced at night. Also, some people do not see as well in reduced light. Age reduces everyone's night vision.

Headlights light up objects directly in front of the vehicle, but their range is limited. Side lighting is poor at best. Dark-colored objects almost disappear, even within headlight range. To make up for the darkened areas on the roadway, reduce your speed at night.

On dark, stormy days or in rain or snow, it is often difficult to see ahead. To improve your visibility, turn on the headlights. In addition to helping you to see better, headlights also make your vehicle more visible to others. Improve the night vision of other drivers by turning on your lights long before it is completely dark.

Although headlights are essential to night driving, they do create the problem of glare. The sudden flash of bright headlights can temporarily blind you. Avoid looking directly into the headlights of oncoming vehicles.

As a pedestrian at night, always wear light-colored clothing. Light-colored clothing is far more visible to approaching drivers than dark clothing is at night. You should also stay out of the flow of traffic and use crosswalks when you must cross the roadway.

**Pedestrians wearing light-colored clothing are more visible at night to drivers.**

# Hearing

Hearing provides clues about approaching vehicles and other hazards. Always listen for traffic and maneuver to avoid conflicts. A siren or a horn can alert you to a hazard. An unusual noise may serve as an early warning of engine or other vehicle trouble.

If you play a radio or stereo system, keep the sound at a level that permits you to hear other highway users. If the weather is good, keep a window partially down so that you can hear approaching emergency vehicles.

A person with a partial or total hearing loss can still drive safely. Developing a particularly effective scanning routine when driving can help make up for such a disability. Hearing impaired drivers should glance to the sides frequently and use the rearview mirrors more than other drivers.

# Feeling

Road conditions are often "felt" rather than seen. Vibrations travel through the wheels and up through the steering column and body of the car. This feeling can help you to detect rough, slick, or frozen surfaces that will give you reason to slow down. Always keep both hands on the steering wheel so that you can feel any changes in road conditions or in the handling of the car.

A change in your car's condition can often be felt before serious problems develop. A blown-out tire can immediately be felt through the steering wheel. An engine that is misfiring can be felt as well as heard, especially at idle or very low speeds. Be on the alert with all of your senses.

# Mental Condition

When you get behind the wheel, your mental or emotional state is just as important as your physical condition. Because driving calls for a great deal of concentration and decision-making, anything that takes your mind off the driving task or makes you less alert can cause problems. It is up to you to make sure that you are mentally and physically prepared before you drive.

# Alertness

Being totally aware of what is going on around you is central to your safety. To be aware, you must be alert. Devote your total attention to the traffic environment around you and to those vehicles and pedestrians you encounter as you drive.

Alcohol and other drugs are responsible for over 50 percent of all injuries and fatalities in traffic collisions. The reason, in part, is that drivers become far less alert when under the influence of drugs. Avoid mixing drugs and driving. Even a common cold tablet can sharply reduce your alertness behind the wheel.

**By keeping both hands on the steering wheel you can "feel" sudden changes in road conditions.**

**To avoid carbon monoxide poisoning, never run a car's engine in a closed space.**

Many people are hospitalized each year because of carbon monoxide poisoning. **Carbon monoxide** is a gas that is given off as part of your vehicle's exhaust. This gas is colorless and odorless and is absorbed into the blood stream more quickly than oxygen. If it leaks into a car, it goes to work sedating the occupants without warning. In a short time, vehicle occupants become less alert, drowsy, and finally unconscious. Long exposure or exposure to a large amount of the gas can even lead to death.

To reduce the chance of being exposed to carbon monoxide, have the exhaust system checked periodically for leaks. If repairs are necessary, have them made immediately.

A leaky exhaust system is not the only way carbon monoxide can get into a car. It may also be pulled in through air vents or open back windows of station wagons and vans. Run your car's engine only in a well ventilated area. When delayed in slow-moving traffic or going through a long tunnel, turn off the heater, since carbon monoxide fumes can be drawn into the car. Never run the car in a closed garage. Also, never drive with the trunk of a car or the back window of a station wagon, van, or hatchback open.

If you are too occupied with conversation or listening to the radio when you drive, you are probably not concentrating on the driving task as much as you should be. Pay attention to the road, other highway users, and your driving. Your life depends on it.

If you smoke cigarettes while you drive, you are more likely to become involved in a collision than if you do not smoke. Gases such as carbon monoxide are produced in the cigarette burning process. These gases reduce oxygen flow to the brain. This reduction in oxygen dulls the senses and reduces alertness. In addition, smokers are often distracted by the very act of lighting or disposing of a cigarette. There is always the possibility of dropping a lighted cigarette on the floor or on your lap.

Many drivers lose their concentration on the road when they watch non-traffic events. Waving at friends or looking at the scenery can result in a loss of alertness. Don't allow yourself to be distracted by activity that is not related to the driving task.

# Awareness

**Never let distractions take your mind off the driving task or your eyes off the road.**

Driving in an unfamiliar area can cause serious problems. New situations, new hazards, or a new neighborhood can all act to make a driver less aware of the roadway. When you are away from familiar surroundings, reduce speed and be particularly aware of everything that is going on around you. Pay extra attention to traffic signs, signals, and markings. Driving often requires all of your concentration and ability. Being aware of highway conditions at all times is very important.

Driving a new or different vehicle can also cause temporary confusion. Even though controls, gauges, and instruments are similar on most vehicles, there are differences that require a brief period of study. For example, the location of the headlight controls varies from one car to another. Before you start the engine or attempt to enter traffic, review your vehicle's controls and identify the necessary equipment and safety devices. Once you are moving, confusion may well cause an emergency or a collision.

**Passengers may need to be reminded not to distract the driver from the driving task.**

**Traffic conditions can trigger a driver's emotions. What hazard does an upset driver pose to others?**

# Emotions

Of all human conditions, emotions are the most difficult to control or predict. All too often these emotions cause people to behave in ways that are not at all ordinary or reasonable. Events in their everyday lives cause people to change in ways that influence the way they drive. Fear, depression, or anger can all make people react to traffic conditions in irrational and bizarre ways. Happiness can cause the same problems if you allow your emotions to dominate your thinking.

Before you get in the car, determine whether you are emotionally fit to drive. If you are upset or excited, wait until the emotion is less strong. Once you are on the road, avoid heavily traveled routes and rush-hour traffic if possible. In that way, you will face fewer situations that could anger or upset you on the road.

Strong emotional feelings can make you less alert. If you become angry or resentful when another driver cuts you off or is driving too slowly ahead of you, you may become careless. If you are in a hurry and are worried about being late, you may take chances you would not normally take. If you find yourself driving dangerously to "get back" at a driver who has angered you, slow down and think about the driving task. Are you putting both yourself and other drivers in danger? If so, you should pull over and stop until you have calmed down. If possible, let someone else take over at the wheel until you feel ready to drive again.

Even if you are able to keep your own emotions under control when you are driving, you will have to face others who do not have the same control. Such drivers are hazards. Some do not pay attention to what is happening on the road. Others drive aggressively and take risks that endanger everyone. Give them plenty of room.

While you are driving, try to control your emotions. If you are unable to concentrate on the task at hand, don't drive. Get a ride or request help. Driving is so complex that it requires an even and level thought process. You must learn to control your emotions especially while driving in or walking near traffic.

## Fuel Misers

- Avoid stop-and-go driving when possible. Morning and evening rush hours are not the best times to start out on a trip.

- Drive only when necessary. Combine errands and eliminate unnecessary trips.

- Plan your route before driving. Travel the fewest number of miles possible.

- Watch traffic lights ahead to avoid unnecessary braking and accelerating.

## ▶ Key Ideas

- Physical and emotional fitness are critical to safe driving.
- Alcohol and other drugs have a negative influence on driver behavior.
- Illness, fatigue, and age all can reduce driving ability.
- In many cases, special controls are available to allow those with physical disabilites to drive.

- Good vision is the most important factor in avoiding hazardous situations.
- All of your senses, including hearing and feeling, should be used in driving.

# ⇨ Gauging Your Understanding

**1.** How does age affect driving ability?

**2.** What effects does fatigue have on drivers?

**3.** Describe several ways that drivers can compensate for physical disabilities.

**4.** How does visual acuity influence your ability to identify traffic hazards?

**5.** What are some of the hazards of driving at night?

**6.** What effect do your emotions have on your driving skills?

# ⇨ In the Driver's Seat

**1.** Following a long day at school and your evening job, you finally head for home. You feel fatigue creeping up on you as your vision, judgment, and senses are less than perfect. What can you do to minimize the temporary "disability" that you are experiencing?

**2.** While driving on a busy city street, you notice the car ahead is being driven by an older driver at a speed well below the posted speed limit. What predictions can you make? What actions should you take? What hazards can you anticipate?

## Special Projects

**1.** As you head for home today, look around at other highway users. What physical disabilities do you notice that might influence how they drive? Which disabilities are temporary, and which are permanent?

**2.** During the next week, keep a log of your driving. After a drive, record the emotions you experienced while on the road. How was your driving affected by your mental and emotional condition? How did you compensate? Were problems avoided? How?

# ⮕ Chapter Test 11

Name _____ Date _____

**Write "T" beside statements that are true and "F" beside those that are false.**

_____ **1.** Young drivers have a safer driving record than most other drivers.

_____ **2.** Alcohol and other drugs have a negative effect on driving ability.

_____ **3.** Visual acuity is a measure of a person's side vision.

_____ **4.** Strong emotional feelings can make you less alert when driving.

_____ **5.** Judging distances is easier when you drive at night.

_____ **6.** If a driver takes medication for a cold, the illness will no longer have an effect on that person's ability to drive.

_____ **7.** People who are physically disabled can drive safely.

**Complete these sentences by writing the correct terms in the blanks.**

**1.** _____ _____ is a colorless, odorless exhaust gas.

**2.** A deaf person can drive safely by developing an effective _____ routine.

**3.** _____ _____ is important to help identify traffic signs.

**4.** Side vision is referred to as _____ vision.

**5.** _____ _____ helps you tell how far away objects are.

**6.** It is important to control your _____ while driving.

**7.** Your vision may blur or you may see double when you are _____.

**Write the letter of the best answer in the space provided.**

_____ **1.** Carbon monoxide can cause (a) drowsiness, (b) death, (c) blurred vision, (d) all of the above.

_____ **2.** By driving more slowly, a driver may be able to make up in part for (a) color blindness, (b) highway hypnosis, (c) poor distance judgment, (d) a wide field of vision.

_____   **3.** The best way to overcome driving fatigue is (a) exercising, (b) taking frequent rest stops, (c) snacking, (d) napping.

_____   **4.** To reduce the chances of becoming poisoned by carbon monoxide, a driver should (a) open the back window, (b) smoke in a closed van, (c) drive a car with a defective muffler, (d) turn off the car engine when parked.

_____   **5.** Strong emotions can affect a driver (a) both mentally and physically, (b) neither physically nor mentally, (c) mentally only, (d) physically only.

_____   **6.** The advantage of youth is often offset by (a) poor vision, (b) lack of experience and poor judgment, (c) lack of coordination, (d) poor reflexes.

_____   **7.** Drivers receive over 95 percent of traffic information through (a) their hearing, (b) the steering wheel, (c) their eyes, (d) their emotions.

_____   **8.** Strong emotional feelings can (a) cause you to lose control of the car, (b) make you less alert, (c) make you more alert, (d) help you drive safely.

_____   **9.** Headlights are (a) essential on cloudy days, (b) helpful in heavy traffic, (c) essential at night, (d) helpful in seeing what is on the side of the road.

_____   **10.** If you must drive when you are ill, you should (a) take medication to help you, (b) drive more slowly, (c) drive fast so you get home quickly, (d) drive with the window open to keep you alert.

_____   **11.** At night, depth perception (a) is not important, (b) is improved, (c) helps compensate for poor visibility, (d) is reduced.

# Chapter 12 Alcohol, Other Drugs, and Driving

- **Many medications have side effects. What drugs should you avoid if you drive?**
- **What substances other than alcohol can affect your driving, even when taken in small amounts?**
- **What things can you do to help eliminate the problem of driving under the influence of alcohol?**

**Over 50 percent of all highway crashes result from the use of alcohol or other drugs.**

Every year, thousands of people are killed, injured, or permanently disfigured on our nation's highways. More than half of these fatal collisions involve drivers who are intoxicated, under the influence of drugs, or both.

Drugs, including alcohol, impair your ability to identify possible hazards, to use good judgment, and to control your car in traffic. Even a single drink can affect your ability to perform the steps in IPDE.

## Drug Use and Abuse

Alcohol and other drugs have been around for a long time. Not everyone drinks or takes drugs, yet many people do. Whether they do or not is largely an individual decision. Family values, religious beliefs, laws, and health considerations may affect the person's decision. With younger people, the desire to be part of the group may also encourage or discourage the use of alcohol or other drugs.

Although the decision to use alcohol or other drugs is a personal one, it usually affects more than just the individual. Studies have shown, for example, that the individual who smokes exposes others to the harmful effects of the smoke. The individual who drinks and then gets behind the wheel endangers the safety of others.

# Dangers of Using Drugs

There are many types of drugs, both legal and illegal. Most legal drugs are meant for use in treating and preventing various illnesses. Some — called **prescription drugs** — can be purchased legally only when prescribed by a doctor. Others can be obtained legally without a prescription. These are called **over-the-counter drugs**. Some drugs are illegal; that is, it is against the law to possess them.

When taken in moderate amounts and under the right circumstances, most legal drugs are relatively safe. For example, when taken as directed, most medications help, not harm, the user. But any drug, including alcohol, can be dangerous if it is abused.

Some of the major dangers associated with the use of drugs include:

1. **Physical harm.** Even drugs that are intended to prevent or treat an illness can be harmful to the body if taken in the wrong amounts. Other drugs can be harmful if used in combination with other medications, alcohol, or even certain food.
2. **Physical or emotional dependency.** When used regularly, some drugs can cause the user to become physically or emotionally dependent on them. One danger of drug use is that the user cannot predict or control this dependency on the drug.
3. **Side effects.** Many drugs have side effects. For example, the cold tablet that controls your sneezing may also make you sleepy. Although feeling sleepy is usually not harmful, it can be dangerous if you are driving.

# Cautions about Taking Drugs

To avoid the possible dangers of drug use, take only what is prescribed for you by your doctor. Carefully follow instructions about the amount and frequency of use. Ask your doctor or pharmacist about possible side effects. Don't experiment with drugs. And never take medication prescribed for someone else.

**Before taking any medication, be sure you know what possible effects it may have.**

# Drugs and the Driver

Medicines are not the only drugs Americans use. People who smoke use the drug nicotine. Do you ever drink coffee or cola? If so, you have taken the drug caffeine. Every drug has an effect on the user. And many drugs, even those considered ''safe,'' can affect the user's driving ability. Before you get behind the wheel of a car, you should know whether and how a drug may affect your ability to drive.

# Types of Drugs

Drugs are usually classified by the effect they have on the central nervous system. In general, there are three types of drugs: depressants, stimulants, and hallucinogens.

Drugs that slow down the central nervous system are called **depressants**. This category of drugs includes alcohol as well as barbiturates, morphine, codeine, and heroin.

Medications for colds, hay fever, and coughs contain depressants. So do sleeping pills and tranquilizers.

**Stimulants** speed up the central nervous system. Common stimulants include nicotine and caffeine. Caffeine is found in coffee, tea, some cola drinks, and drugs intended to fight sleep. Amphetamines, an ingredient in some diet pills, and cocaine are also stimulants.

**Hallucinogens** affect the senses and distort the user's perception and vision. Most hallucinogens, including marijuana, LSD, and PCP, are illegal.

# How Drugs Affect the Driver

Many drugs affect at least one of the major skills required in driving. Before you take any drug — even a cold tablet — you should know what effect it may have on your mental alertness, judgment, vision, concentration, and coordination. In general, you should avoid drugs entirely when you plan to drive.

**Drinking coffee while driving to stay awake can be distracting and dangerous.**

## Depressants

Depressants make a person drowsy and cloud thinking and judgment. Thus, these drugs affect a driver's ability to predict and decide.

Drivers taking depressants may find it hard to pay attention to their surroundings and to the task of driving. They are slow to see and identify traffic hazards. Reduced muscle coordination makes it difficult for them to change the car's speed and direction. So, even if they do identify a hazard, they may not react in time to avoid it. A collision is all too often the result.

## Stimulants

Stimulants often give a driver a false feeling of alertness and increased self-confidence. As self-confidence increases, a driver's willingness to take risks also increases. Some drivers feel wide awake when taking stimulants, and so they continue driving long after they should stop to rest. Tired drivers make poor decisions. Yet stimulants mask how tired they really are. Another danger is that the effects of stimulants wear off suddenly. Without any warning of drowsiness, the driver may fall asleep at the wheel.

## ● Hallucinogens

Hallucinogens, such as marijuana, can affect a driver's ability to judge space and time. They also cause people to see things that are not there. As a result, drivers taking hallucinogens may stop or swerve suddenly to avoid a hazard that does not exist. Even when they notice a hazardous situation, they may not recognize its danger.

Some people react to hallucinogens by concentrating or focusing on one thing. A driver using hallucinogens may therefore fail to scan the area to locate hazards.

# Alcohol and the Driver

Many people are surprised to learn that alcohol is a drug. After all, a person who has reached the drinking age can purchase alcohol legally in most stores and restaurants. Although alcohol is widely used in our society, it is still a drug. And, like any other drug, it can be abused.

Teenagers are among those who use and abuse alcohol. Even though it is not legal for them to drink, almost 90 percent of teenagers have at least one alcoholic drink while they are in high school. Studies show that about two thirds of high school students drink once a month. More than one fourth drink once a week. One of every five teenage drinkers is or will become a problem drinker.

The increase in teenage drinking is a matter of serious concern. One reason for this concern — but certainly not the only reason — is the relationship between drinking and traffic fatalities. Over 50 percent of the fatalities in highway crashes involve drinking drivers. And, teenagers are involved in one out of every five of these fatal crashes.

The fact is, drinking increases a driver's risk of having a collision. The more a person drinks, the more the risk increases. How does alcohol affect a driver's abilities?

# How Alcohol Affects the Body

Medically, alcohol is classified as a drug. In fact, it is used as the base of many medications such as cough syrup. Alcohol depresses, or slows, the central nervous system, including the brain. How does alcohol affect the way in which the brain functions?

The brain controls all mental and physical functions. One part of the brain controls manners, inhibitions, and decision-making ability. Another part of the brain controls muscle coordination, balance, reflexes, and consciousness. A third part of the brain controls breathing and heartbeat. All parts of the brain are affected by alcohol. As a result, various mental and physical functions are impaired.

When only a small amount of alcohol is consumed, the effects may not be obvious. Still, the drinker is affected. One of the first noticeable effects of drinking is loss of inhibitions. Feeling less inhibited, drinkers are likely to take more risks than usual. Alcohol also impairs judgment and decision-making skills. At the same time, however, alcohol increases self-confidence. The danger is this: Even small amounts of alcohol cause the drinker to feel *more* confident and capable at the very time he or she is actually *less* able to use good judgment and make sound decisions.

Alcohol also affects coordination. Even small amounts impair a drinker's ability to perform tasks that require eye-and-hand coordination, steadiness, and quick response.

As more alcohol is consumed, inhibitions, judgment, coordination and even speech become more and more impaired. In sufficient quantities, alcohol will cause a drinker to lose consciousness. It can even cause death.

**Alcohol impairs vision, coordination and decision-making ability and increases the risk of collision.**

## ● Individual Differences

It is difficult to determine exactly how alcohol will affect a person. People react differently at different times. Their mood or the occasion can make a difference. How fast they drink and how much food they have in their stomachs determine how they react to alcohol. Body chemistry, weight, and state of health also influence the effects of alcohol. Even the person's sex can make a difference. Females are usually affected sooner than males of the same body weight.

At first alcohol may appear to be a stimulant. This is because it depresses, or reduces, inhibitions. Often people who have been drinking appear to be more outgoing than usual. As they begin to feel more secure and confident, their judgment skills deteriorate. People who have been drinking take chances that they never would under normal circumstances. Behind the wheel, this can be deadly.

## How Alcohol Enters and Leaves the Body

Unlike food, which must be digested, alcohol is absorbed directly into the bloodstream. Once in the bloodstream, alcohol is absorbed by all body tissues. The amount of alcohol the tissues absorb depends on their fluid levels. Because the brain has a high fluid level, it absorbs more alcohol than other tissues.

The liver rids the body of alcohol mainly by breaking it down and oxidizing it — turning it into water and carbon dioxide. It takes the liver about one hour to oxidize a half to three quarters of an ounce of alcohol — the amount of alcohol contained in one standard drink. Any alcohol that the liver does not break down continues to circulate through the body. Despite popular beliefs, a person cannot "sober up" by drinking black coffee, taking a cold shower, or exercising. These remedies only make an individual feel less drowsy. But the alcohol will continue to affect physical and mental abilities until it is eliminated from the body. This takes time.

## Blood Alcohol Content (BAC)

The amount of alcohol in a person's bloodstream can be measured by a chemical analysis of the blood, urine, or breath. The amount of alcohol in the blood is expressed as a percent and is referred to as **blood alcohol content (BAC)**.

Many factors affect BAC. For example, when alcohol is mixed with a carbonated beverage (such as club soda or cola), it is absorbed into the bloodstream at a faster rate.

**Blood Alcohol Concentration Chart (BAC)**

| after hour | 1 drink | | | | 2 drinks | | | | 3 drinks | | | | 4 drinks | | | | 5 drinks | | | |
|---|---|---|---|---|---|---|---|---|---|---|---|---|---|---|---|---|---|---|---|---|
| weight | 4 | 3 | 2 | 1 | 4 | 3 | 2 | 1 | 4 | 3 | 2 | 1 | 4 | 3 | 2 | 1 | 4 | 3 | 2 | 1 |
| 80 | — | — | — | .02 | — | — | .05 | .08 | .07 | .10 | .10 | .10 | .12 | .12 | .15 | .15 | .17 | .17 | .19 | .20 |
| 100 | — | — | — | .02 | — | — | .04 | .06 | .05 | .07 | .08 | .09 | .09 | .10 | .12 | .13 | .13 | .14 | .16 | .17 |
| 120 | — | — | — | .02 | — | — | .03 | .04 | .03 | .04 | .06 | .08 | .06 | .08 | .09 | .11 | .09 | .11 | .13 | .14 |
| 140 | — | — | — | .01 | — | — | .02 | .04 | .02 | .03 | .05 | .06 | .04 | .06 | .08 | .09 | .07 | .09 | .10 | .12 |
| 160 | — | — | — | .01 | — | — | .02 | .03 | .01 | .02 | .04 | .05 | .03 | .04 | .06 | .08 | .06 | .07 | .09 | .10 |
| 180 | — | — | — | .01 | — | — | .01 | .03 | — | .02 | .03 | .04 | .02 | .04 | .05 | .07 | .04 | .06 | .07 | .09 |
| 200 | — | — | — | — | — | — | .01 | .02 | — | .01 | .03 | .04 | .01 | .03 | .04 | .06 | .03 | .04 | .06 | .08 |

Faster absorption causes the BAC to rise more quickly. Food in the stomach helps to slow the absorption of alcohol.

As the chart shows, BAC is also affected by the amount of alcohol consumed, the amount of time between drinks, and the drinker's body weight. For example, if a person weighs 100 pounds and has one drink in one hour, that person's BAC would be .02 percent at the end of one hour. If the person has two drinks in one hour, the BAC would rise to .06 percent. And, if the person has four drinks in one hour, it would rise to .13 percent — well above the legal definition of intoxication. A person is affected at a BAC of .01 percent and impaired over .02 percent.

Notice what happens when a person drinks more slowly. If the same person has one drink per hour over four hours, the BAC would be .09 percent, not .13 percent.

How much a person weighs also affects BAC. If someone weighs 180 pounds and drinks one drink per hour over four hours, the BAC would be .02 percent. The reason that heavier people can drink the same amount of alcohol and still have a lower BAC is that they have more body fluids.

Remember that females are affected by alcohol sooner than males of the same weight. For this reason, females should place themselves one weight category lighter when referring to the BAC chart.

**Remember that BAC charts only measure the amount of alcohol in the bloodstream—not a person's reaction to the alcohol.**

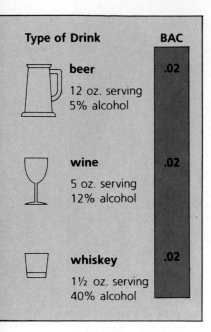

| Type of Drink | BAC |
|---|---|
| **beer**<br>12 oz. serving<br>5% alcohol | .02 |
| **wine**<br>5 oz. serving<br>12% alcohol | .02 |
| **whiskey**<br>1½ oz. serving<br>40% alcohol | .02 |

**Standard servings of beer, wine, and liquor contain the same amount of alcohol.**

Keep in mind that the effects of alcohol are the same no matter what type of alcoholic beverage a person drinks. Standard servings of beer, wine, and liquor all have about the same amount of alcohol. It is the alcohol in a drink that affects behavior, not the type of drink.

## ● Mixing Alcohol and Other Drugs

When alcohol is used with other drugs, several results are possible. First, the drug may tend to offset or delay the effects of the alcohol. Second, the alcohol and drug may work independently, so that neither is affected by the other. Third, the drug may have an additive effect. In this case, the effects of either the alcohol or the drug or both may be increased. The result of the combination can be hazardous or even deadly — especially when driving.

It is almost impossible to predict how the combination of alcohol and drugs will affect a person. Much depends on the drug; on the amount of alcohol consumed; and on the person's size, health, and even mood. The safest route is to never mix the two.

# How Alcohol Affects the Driver

When a driver drinks, the first loss of ability is judgment. Even with a BAC as low as .01 percent (one drink), judgment is impaired and the driver feels less inhibited. However, the driver doesn't recognize this loss of judgment because of increased self-confidence. Alcohol has a slow but increasing effect on the driver's vision, coordination, speech, and hearing. Side vision tends to narrow, and vision can become blurred. Eye movements usually slow and there is a tendency to stare too long at one place. Physical responses continue to slow. All of these affect a driver's ability to work through the IPDE process.

The less experienced a driver is, the sooner his or her judgment, decision-making skills, and physical abilities are impaired. The reason is that the skills most recently acquired, such as driving, are the first to be affected by alcohol. An experiment conducted with drivers under 25 years old showed that their ability to pay attention to and

| BAC and Driver Impairment | | |
|---|---|---|
| **BAC** | **Condition** | **Effects on Driving Ability** |
| .01–.02 | affected | Existing mood may be heightened. Bad driving habits are slightly pronounced. Inhibitions are reduced and judgment is affected. |
| .03–.05 | impaired | Inhibitions are further affected. Judgment is noticeably worse. Reaction time is slowed and sensitive car control is lessened. Risk-taking behavior increases. |
| .06–.10 | intoxicated | Exaggerated emotions and behavior emerge. Less concern is shown as inhibitions, self-criticism, and judgment are seriously affected. Coordination is significantly reduced. |
| .11–.15 | intoxicated | Physical and mental functions are seriously impaired. |

process information was impaired by a BAC of only .015 percent. Another study showed that sixteen- and seventeen-year-olds at a BAC of less than .05 percent are seven times more likely to have a collision than if they weren't drinking. This collision rate is matched by older, experienced drivers when they reach a BAC of .10 percent.

Several states recognize that younger drivers are more likely to be affected by alcohol than older drivers. For this reason, they have set varying BAC levels for determining whether a driver is impaired or intoxicated.

**Even one drink impairs a driver's judgment.**

# Laws to Prevent Driving While Intoxicated

Drivers who are impaired or intoxicated cause a large percentage of the deaths and injuries on the highway each year. For this reason, stricter DWI laws are now in effect. Furthermore, the number of arrests and convictions for DWI has grown significantly.

## ● Legal Drinking Age

Over the past 75 years, the life expectancy of every age group but one has improved. For 15- to 24-year-olds, the death rate is actually higher than it was 20 years ago. The

**Police often use breath tests to determine whether drivers are DWI.**

main reason for this increase is alcohol-related highway collisions. To reduce the number of highway fatalities, most states have raised the legal drinking age. The trend nationwide is to prohibit the purchase and consumption of alcohol by those under the age of 21.

## Implied Consent

Every state now has an **implied consent law** for drivers. According to this law, drivers stopped by the police for DWI consent (agree) either to take a chemical test for BAC or to give up their licenses. Although BAC can be determined by urine, blood, or breath tests, the one most commonly used is the breath test. Breath-testing devices are commonly used to measure the amount of alcohol in the breath as a person blows into a tube. If the results of the chemical test indicate that the driver is intoxicated, they can lead to a conviction for DWI (Driving While Intoxicated).

## Penalties for DWI

Drivers convicted of DWI generally have their licenses suspended for a specified period of time. They may also have to pay a fine or serve time in jail or both. It is also common for drivers convicted of DWI to have to attend a special school for drinking drivers.

The penalties for DWI are even more severe if the driver is involved in a collision while driving under the influence. If death results from the collision, the driver can be convicted of manslaughter or vehicular homicide.

In many parts of the United States and Canada, drivers convicted of drunk driving more than once may have their licenses revoked, usually for one year. Also, they generally have to serve time in jail. When a license is revoked (as opposed to suspended) the only way to be relicensed at the end of the period is to reapply and pass all the required licensing tests again.

# Your Responsibilities as an HTS User

The decision to drink, to smoke, or use other drugs is mainly a personal one. Each person must be guided by scientific facts, family values, religious beliefs, laws, and personal commitments. The responsibility for keeping unsafe drivers off the road, on the other hand, is a shared responsibility. Everyone has the responsibility for not driving after drinking or taking drugs. However, there are many other things you can do to ensure the safety of others. If you are a driver or a passenger, a party-goer or a host, you can do your part to reduce the hazard caused by drivers who drink.

## As a Driver

Not everyone chooses to drink, but many people do. The majority of those who do drink admit that they sometimes drive after drinking. Of course, the best advice is never to drink before driving. But drivers who do drink can take certain precautions to reduce the danger of alcohol.

First, in situations where drinks are served, drivers can control the amount of alcohol they drink. They can set a limit ahead of time — based on the BAC charts — and stick to it. Telling the host or their passengers about their limit is

**A person who has had too much to drink should not be allowed to drive.**

a good idea. Often others can help by not offering or pouring drinks for the driver.

Second, drivers can use good judgment by remembering how alcohol enters and leaves the body. By drinking slowly, they give the body time to rid itself of alcohol. By having their last drink several hours before they get in the car, they give their BAC time to fall to a "safe" level.

Third, drivers should remember that even a single drink can affect their judgment and ability to drive safely. Therefore, they should listen to friends who question whether they have had too much to drink. A nondrinking passenger or a sober friend is often willing to drive if only asked. Taxi cabs are another choice. Some communities have a Safe Rides program that can be called on for a ride home. If none of these options are available, the driver should simply stay put until the effects of the alcohol wear off.

## As a Passenger

As a passenger, you have a right to expect the driver to drive safely. If the driver has had too much to drink, your life is in danger. Don't get in the car. It's not easy to refuse to ride with a friend. But hurt feelings are better than broken bones — or worse injuries. Offer to drive. If the driver refuses, try to get a ride with someone else who has not been drinking. If that's not possible, call someone for a ride. If necessary, stay where you are until you can get home safely. Do whatever you must to protect your own life and health.

You should also do what you can to keep the drinker from driving. It may not be easy, but — if you care for your friend — you will get those keys!

## As a Party-Goer

Some people drink because they want to. Others drink because of pressure from other people. At parties, guests sometimes encourage each other to drink. For example, they may tease those who refuse to drink or who ask for a nonalcoholic beverage. Sometimes just by offering a drink to someone who has already refused one, they make the nondrinker feel uncomfortable. Some people don't mind the teasing, but others find it easier to give in to the pressure of friends.

At a party, guests can be responsible for each other by not encouraging drinking. Responsible guests don't "push" drinks. And they pay attention to their own drinking. Simply by not drinking or by limiting how much they drink, they often set the pace for other party-goers.

Guests can also help by keeping drinkers from driving. Don't worry that the drinker may be angry at the time.

## As a Host

The person hosting a party where alcohol is served is responsibile for the safety of guests — both during and after the party. There are several things the host can do to prevent guests from drinking too much and being a danger on the highways.

The host can plan activities that do not include drinking, such as dancing or playing electronic games. Serving food throughout the party discourages drinking on an empty stomach. Nonalcoholic beverages should be available in good supply as alternatives.

The host can help guests control the amount of alcohol they drink. The liquor supply can be kept out of sight so that guests can't help themselves. The host can limit the alcohol consumed by mixing less alcohol in the drinks. Of course, if someone has had too much to drink, the host should stop serving that person.

To be sure that the guests are in shape to drive home safely, no drinks should be served for at least one hour before the party is to end. The host should substitute soft drinks or coffee or tea for the alcohol, and serve more food. If any guest who is driving has had too much to drink, the host should arrange for a sober person to drive the car or give the drinker a ride home. If necessary, the host should invite the drinker to stay overnight rather than drive home.

**A host can prevent guests from becoming a danger on the highway by not pushing drinks and by planning non-drinking activities.**

# As a Responsible Person

"Friends don't let friends drive drunk" is a good slogan. There are three times that you can step in to keep friends — or members of your family — from driving when they have had too much to drink.

The first is before the party. If you know your friend or family member plans to drink, suggest that someone else do the driving. Or, get the person to agree to a realistic limit of drinks.

The second time you can intervene is during the party. See that the person limits the number of drinks and stops drinking early.

The third time you can intervene is before the person gets behind the wheel. This is your last chance, so be ready with help from others. Offer to call a cab, Safe Rides, a friend, or someone at home for a ride. If all else fails, take away the car keys.

**If necessary, have others help you get the keys away from a driver who has had too much to drink.**

Remember that keeping unsafe drivers off the road is everyone's responsibility. And every driver has the additional responsibility for driving safely. Still, there are drivers on the road who continue to drink and endanger your life and the lives of others. Your best protection against these drivers is your safety belt. Buckle up every time you get in a car. Wearing your safety belt increases your odds of surviving even if you are hit or forced off the road by an alcohol-impaired driver.

## Safety Checks

- Avoid driving late at night, particularly on weekends. At 2 a.m. on a Sunday, for example, chances are that one of the next three drivers you meet is overly tired or has had too much to drink.

- People see what they expect to see. That's why drivers are slow to recognize an oncoming car in their lane, for example. A visual lead of 8–12 seconds gives you the time you need to recognize and respond to the unexpected.

- To prevent fatigue on long trips, rotate drivers or stop for a rest every three hours. Do not rely on chemical stimulants to keep you alert.

## ➡ Key Ideas

- Alcohol and other drugs impair the driver's ability to use the IPDE process.
- Some of the dangers of drug use include physical harm, physical or emotional dependency, and side effects.
- Drugs are classified as depressants, stimulants, or hallucinogens, depending on the way they affect the central nervous system.
- The liver rids the body of alcohol at the rate of about one half an ounce of alcohol per hour.
- Many factors influence how a person reacts to alcohol. These include the occasion, the person's mood, sex, body chemistry, weight, and BAC (Blood Alcohol Content).
- BAC, the measure of how much alcohol is in the blood, is used to determine intoxication or impairment of a driver.
- Everyone is responsible for keeping unsafe drivers off the road.

# ⮕ Gauging Your Understanding

**1.** What are some of the things that may influence a person to use or avoid alcohol and other drugs?

**2.** Give two examples of each type of drug: depressants, stimulants, and hallucinogens.

**3.** Why would the same person react differently to the same amount of alcohol at different times?

**4.** How is alcohol absorbed into the body? How does the body rid itself of alcohol?

**5.** Which important driving skills used in the IPDE strategy are affected by alcohol?

**6.** List some of the things you can do as a guest at a party to prevent other guests from driving while alcohol-impaired.

# ⮕ In the Driver's Seat

**1.** Janet (100 pounds) and Sergie (160 pounds) drove to a party in Sergie's car. Sergie's friend George came alone. After an hour — and four beers — George (130 pounds) is very sociable. Janet has had one drink; Sergie has had two drinks. They are concerned because George wants to drive to Rosa's house (5 miles away) to give her a ride to the party. How should Janet and Sergie handle the situation? (Refer to the charts on pages 219 and 221.)

**2.** It's final exam week. As soon as your last test is over, you're going to celebrate with a few friends by attending a concert in a city two hours away. The driver of the car has been taking an over-the-counter drug to stay awake and study the last two nights. The driver claims to feel fine — not tired at all. Is it safe to ride with this person? What are some of the possible dangers? What can you suggest to ensure safe travel?

## Special Projects

**1.** Establish a Safe Rides program in your school. If there is one already in existence, find out how Safe Rides works.

**2.** Interview five people to determine how they handle drinking/driving situations as a driver and as a passenger.

# ➡️ Chapter Test 12

Name _____   Date _____

**Write "T" beside statements that are true and "F" beside those that are false.**

_____   **1.** Alcohol is a depressant.

_____   **2.** Drinking strong coffee after drinking alcohol helps a person to "sober up."

_____   **3.** Prescription drugs are safe to take when driving.

_____   **4.** Alcohol always affects a person the same way.

_____   **5.** Alcohol content in the bloodstream can be measured by blood tests and by breath tests.

_____   **6.** Alcohol is absorbed more quickly into the bloodstream when mixed with carbonated beverages.

_____   **7.** A driver's judgment is impaired after only one drink.

_____   **8.** The effects of wine or beer are less than the effects of liquor.

_____   **9.** The driving skills of inexperienced drivers are more likely to be affected by alcohol than the skills of experienced drivers.

_____   **10.** Every drug has an effect on the user.

**Write the letter of the best answer in the space provided.**

_____   **1.** Stimulants (a) distort perception, (b) give a false feeling of confidence, (c) should be taken by tired drivers, (d) make the driver more alert.

_____   **2.** Drivers taking depressants often (a) feel wide awake, (b) see things that are not there, (c) take unnecessary risks, (d) feel less confident.

_____   **3.** A drinking driver's first loss of ability is (a) coordination, (b) judgment, (c) perception, (d) vision.

_____   **4.** The most commonly used test to measure BAC is the (a) implied consent test, (b) analyzer test, (c) breath test, (d) blood test.

_____   **5.** The liver can rid the body of a half ounce of alcohol in (a) a minute, (b) an hour, (c) a day, (d) a week

_____   **6.** The amount of alcohol in a standard serving of beer is (a) less than in a shot of whiskey, (b) about the same as in a glass of wine, (c) more than in a shot of whiskey, (d) more than in a glass of wine.

——— **7.** The body rids itself of alcohol mostly through (a) digestion, (b) oxidation, (c) respiration, (d) perspiration.

——— **8.** If a person's BAC is .05 percent, that person is considered to be (a) affected, (b) impaired, (c) intoxicated, (d) unconscious.

——— **9.** An intoxicated person can sober up only by (a) letting time pass, (b) drinking coffee, (c) exercising, (d) showering.

——— **10.** If asked to submit to a test for BAC, a driver must do so or risk losing his or her license because of (a) financial responsibility laws, (b) implied-consent laws, (c) right-of-way laws, (d) alcohol-abuse laws.

——— **11.** An example of a drug classified as a stimulant is (a) caffeine, (b) codeine, (c) barbiturates, (d) marijuana.

**Match the items in Column B to the items in Column A by placing the correct letter in the space provided.**

### Column A

——— **1.** BAC of .02 percent

——— **2.** BAC of .05 percent

——— **3.** BAC of .10 percent

——— **4.** BAC of .15 percent

### Column B

**a.** Coordination is significantly reduced and exaggerated behavior emerges.

**b.** Physical and mental functions are seriously impaired.

**c.** Inhibitions are reduced and judgment is affected.

**d.** Reaction time is slowed and risk-taking behavior increases.

# Careers in the HTS: Emergency Services

A breakdown in one part of the HTS can cause problems in other parts as well. Limiting the effect of a breakdown is important to the smooth operation of the system.

## Traffic Control

A traffic tie-up is probably the most common HTS failure. A tie-up can be caused by a stalled vehicle, a collision, poor road or weather conditions, or unusually heavy traffic. When a tie-up occurs, a number of HTS helpers swing into action to clear it.

Highway service drivers move vehicles involved in a crash off the road. They then clean up the roadway so that broken glass or pieces of metal do not cause more trouble. They also provide aid to drivers of stalled vehicles. In these ways they help get traffic moving again.

Of course, the police are involved in helping the HTS work. So too are road maintenance and construction crews and traffic and highway engineers.

Radio and television reporters help drivers avoid tie-ups by telling them

where the traffic problems are. Often they can suggest alternate routes.

## Post-crash Services

Specially trained paramedics provide first-aid to the injured at the scene of a crash. Ambulance drivers take those who require additional medical attention to the hospital or trauma center.

People whose cars are heavily damaged in a crash may also need a towing

service. And later, they need to hire a mechanic who can fix their vehicles.

Insurance agents help settle the claims of those involved in the crash. They investigate collisions to determine cause and establish fault. They record and analyze data on collisions. These companies need the services of underwriters, investigators, and claim adjusters to perform these duties.

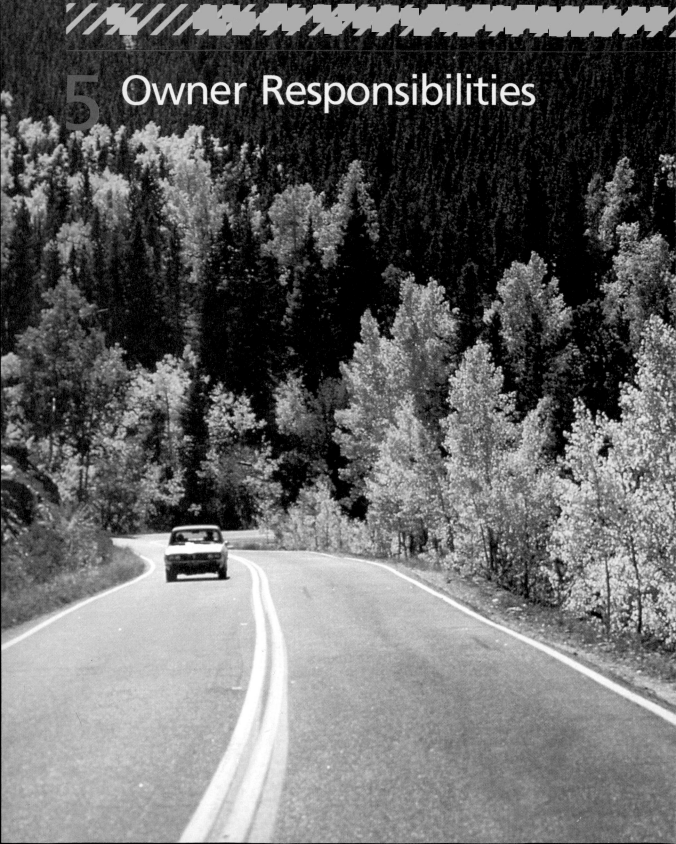

# Chapter 13  Owning a Motor Vehicle

- Some car owners trade in their cars and purchase new ones every two or three years. What are the advantages of this practice?
- Male drivers under age 25 usually pay higher car insurance premiums than others. Is this fair? Why or why not?

Driving a car is a big responsibility. As a driver, you are accountable for your own safety and also the safety of other highway users. When you own a car, you take on even more responsibilities.

You must be financially able to pay for, register, buy fuel for, and keep up your car. You must also have insurance coverage in case of a collision. Before you buy a car, determine whether you are capable of taking on these extra responsibilities.

# Deciding to Buy

In deciding what kind of vehicle to buy, you might ask such questions as: How will I use my vehicle? Do I drive mainly on expressways, highways, or city streets? How many passengers will I carry? How much cargo space do I need? What options do I want? How much can I afford to pay? The answers to these questions should help you find the right car.

# Shopping Around

One of the first decisions you must make as a prospective buyer is whether to purchase a new or used car. Many factors can influence your choice. One of these factors is the purchase price. A new car costs more than a used one of the same size with comparable features. However, a new car usually needs less maintenance.

## Buying a New Car

If you decide to buy a new car, you must determine what type of vehicle best meets your needs. To make that decision, check consumer and automotive magazines or pamphlets. These often provide information about vehicles and rate their performance. Note the fuel mileage ratings. A car that uses less fuel per mile driven usually costs less to drive.

Once you know what type of car you want, it is time to visit an automobile dealer. There you can test drive the car

you are interested in buying. This gives you a chance to see how the car handles and how comfortable it is.

## Selecting Options

After deciding on a particular model, you must determine how you would like the car equipped. For example, different sizes and types of engines may be available. In addition, you must usually select the kind of steering, brakes, tires, and transmission you would like to have.

Some options are not necessary, but may be desirable. They can add to a vehicle's resale or trade-in value. For example, a car with an air conditioner or a radio may be worth more. One with a rear-window defogger, automatic transmission, power steering, and power brakes will usually resell for a higher price than one without such options.

Visit several dealers who carry the model you want. Prices usually vary. Dealers are willing to bargain in order to make a sale.

**When buying a new car, visit several dealers to be sure you get the best buy.**

## ● Buying a Used Car

Shopping for a used car is a little more complicated. To avoid buying one with problems, check it over very carefully. In doing so, you should:

1. Examine the body of the car. Ripples or bubbles may indicate that there is rust beneath the paint. Look for evidence that the car has been in a crash. Check to see whether the paint under the hood matches the exterior paint. While the hood is up, check the hoses, belts, and fluid levels.

2. Inspect the tires for wear. Uneven wear may signal problems with the front end or the suspension system. Worn tires will need replacement. Don't forget to check the spare tire. While the trunk is open, also look for signs of a leak or rust.

3. Push down the front and rear ends of the car. If the end bounces more than once when pushed, the vehicle probably needs new shock absorbers.

4. Open and close the doors. Doors should work easily. Inspect windows for cracks or chips. Windows should roll up and down easily and close tightly.

5. See whether the interior is clean and the seats firm. Make sure that the windshield wipers and washer, the heater, and the defroster are all working. All lights and warning signals, as well as the radio and other optional equipment, should be operating properly.

6. Look at the control pedals. If they are badly worn, the car may have been used mainly for stop-and-go driving. Try the brake. If it gives way slowly after being pressed, the master brake cylinder may have to be replaced.

7. Start the engine. It should start easily and operate smoothly. Once it is warm, it should run evenly. If it does not, the ignition system parts may have to be replaced. Constant uneven running may be a sign that a costly valve job is needed.

8. If the car has power steering, there should be almost no play in the steering wheel while the engine is running. There should be no more than two inches of play before the wheels turn in a car with standard steering.

**9.** Move the car back and forth slowly to see how smoothly the transmission engages. Test the clutch in a vehicle with standard transmission. Make sure that the universal joints do not make a "clunking" noise when the car is moving. Have someone else accelerate the car so you can check exhaust emissions. If they are blue, the engine is burning oil. If they are black, the choke or carburetor may not be working properly. Check for oil or water on the pavement after you turn the car off.

**10.** Test drive the vehicle. The car should go almost straight when you let go of the steering wheel. The brakes should not pull to either side when applied. You should not have to press hard on the brake pedal to stop or slow down. If the wheels bounce at highway speeds, the tires may be out of balance. The car should not bounce or drift on a bumpy road. If it does, the suspension system may need repair. The car should also accelerate and shift gears smoothly.

If the car passes this inspection, take it to a vehicle diagnostic center. Or have a trusted mechanic look it over. He or she may find a problem you may not have noticed.

At this point you are in a position to decide whether to buy the car. Is the dealer willing to make needed repairs at no extra cost? If not, you must decide whether the car is worth fixing.

**Check a used car very carefully. Then have it looked at by a reputable mechanic or service center to be sure it is free of problems.**

**Car financing rates vary. Shop around for the lowest rates and be sure you know what all the charges are.**

# The Costs of Vehicle Ownership

As a car owner, you have certain obligations. If you take out a loan to pay for the car, you must make regular payments. You must also register the vehicle and meet a variety of other special requirements.

## ● Paying for a Vehicle

Many people borrow a portion of the money needed to buy a car. You cannot borrow the total purchase price. Most loans are limited to 80 percent of the price of the car. You must make up the difference. Loans are available from many sources. Some people arrange to finance their purchases through their car dealers. Others secure loans from their credit unions. This source usually costs the least. Many people borrow from savings and loan associations or banks.

Most lenders ask a borrower to offer something as **collateral** in case the loan is not repaid. Most people offer the vehicle itself as collateral. In such cases the lender holds the title to the vehicle until the loan is paid in full.

Shop around for a car loan, just as you would for the car itself. Lower interest rates cost you less. In discussing a loan, ask for a written statement of the annual rate of interest and total interest cost. The total cost of the loan depends on the interest rate, the amount of money borrowed, and how long it takes to repay the money. When talking about a loan, always ask for a list of any other charges besides interest.

## ● Other Expenses

Once you buy the car, you still face a variety of expenses. In most states you must pay a sales tax when you purchase the car. You must also buy car insurance and pay to register the vehicle. You must purchase fuel for the car as well as pay for routine maintenance and repairs. Parking and toll fees are still other costs, as is vehicle depreciation. **Depreciation** is the amount that the car decreases in value as it ages. Although depreciation is not money paid out of your pocket, it is still an expense.

You can easily figure out what it costs you per year to own a car by keeping careful records of all costs. Include the following expenses:

**Fuel and maintenance are other expenses to consider when purchasing a car.**

1. The year's depreciation of the vehicle according to its age.
2. Cost of insurance.
3. Amount paid for licenses, registration, taxes, and other fees.
4. Interest payments for that year.
5. Costs of maintenance and repairs.
6. Amount paid for fuel.
7. Parking and toll costs.

To find the cost per mile of running a car, divide the sum of all these costs by the number of miles the vehicle was driven in a year.

## Vehicle Warranties

When you buy a motor vehicle, you sign a sales contract. It details the dealer's responsibility to you as well as your rights as an owner. Before signing the contract be sure to read it carefully.

All new vehicles and many late-model used cars come with a warranty. A **warranty** is a written guarantee that the maker will repair or replace defective parts. The manufacturer pays for the repair as long as the warranty is in effect. Most warranties exclude parts that are guaranteed by their manufacturer — for example, the battery and tires. Also, most warranties do not cover the cost of any repair resulting from neglect or abuse of the vehicle.

Warranties are limited to a certain amount of time or the number of miles the vehicle is driven. For example, a first-owner warranty may cover a car for 12,000 miles or 12 months, whichever comes first. However, every vehicle has a 5-year or 50,000 mile warranty on all fuel emissions equipment. This warranty extends to future owners as well.

A number of vehicles have been recalled for repair of possible defects in the past few years. When buying a used car, contact the manufacturer's service representative to see if that model has been recalled. If it has been recalled, make sure the problem was corrected. If the problem was not corrected, the dealer should repair the car at no cost.

## Meeting State Requirements

Every motor vehicle must be registered in the state in which the owner lives. Registration plates show that the owner has met this requirement. Most dealers will register the vehicle for a buyer. If you purchase the car from a private seller, you must handle the registration.

When you purchase a vehicle, you apply for a **title** and pay the required fees. A title is proof of ownership. If you buy a vehicle from a private seller, *make sure the seller owns the car*. If a lender still has the title to the car, have the seller and the lender transfer the title and any outstanding loan payments to you. If such arrangements cannot be made, you should not buy the car.

# Insuring a Motor Vehicle

**Liability insurance covers damage done by a driver to another's property.**

Because most drivers cannot pay for the damage that results from a collision, they carry auto insurance. They pay a **premium**, or fee, to protect them from financial loss. In return, the insurance company issues a **policy** or written contract. The policy states how much it will pay and under what circumstances in case of a collision.

## Kinds of Insurance Coverage

Automobile insurance is available in two forms — insurance that protects the owner of the car, and insurance that protects others. The owner is protected by medical payments, collision, and comprehensive coverages. Medical payments insurance also protects others who ride in the owner's car. **Liability insurance** covers the losses that others suffer in a collision for which the owner is responsible.

**Comprehensive insurance protects owners of vehicles against losses caused by vandals.**

## Liability Insurance

Two kinds of liability coverage are standard. **Bodily injury liability** protects you against financial loss due to any injury you may cause another person. It covers injured pedestrians as well as an injured person in another vehicle. The minimum coverage is usually $10,000 for injuries to one person and $20,000 for injuries to two or more people.

**Property damage liability** pays for repairing or replacing other people's property. The minimum coverage available for property damage is usually $5,000.

Many collisions involve more than one person. Some cause more than $5,000 worth of damage to property. For these reasons, the minimum coverage available is usually not enough. If higher coverage is available, you should purchase at least ten times the minimum coverage.

## Collision Insurance

Damage to your own vehicle is covered by **collision insurance**. This insurance covers the cost of repairing or replacing your vehicle at its current market value. However, the company does not pay the full amount. Companies usually have a **deductible** of anywhere from $50 to $500. The deductible is the amount you have to pay. If you carry a $200 deductible and have a collision, you pay the first $200 of the bill. The insurance company pays the rest. The lower the deductible, the higher the cost of coverage.

## Comprehensive Coverage

**Comprehensive insurance** protects you from losses due to theft or vandalism. It also pays for damage caused by fire, flooding, or windstorms. As with collision coverage, you usually pay a deductible.

## No-Fault Insurance

Some states have adopted **no-fault insurance**. Through the no-fault plan, you and your passengers receive payment from your insurance company for injuries and damages. It is not necessary to determine who was at fault in the collision. The insurance company determines what the costs were to you and pays the claim directly. The advantages of this system are lower premiums and faster settlement of claims. Even with no-fault insurance, however, you can still sue another to determine who was at fault.

## ● Other Insurance Protection

All states have **financial responsibility laws**. These laws require that drivers prove they can pay for injuries and damages for which they are responsible. Most vehicle owners buy car insurance to meet this legal requirement.

Despite financial responsibility laws, a few people drive without insurance coverage. Some of them are not able to pay for injuries or damages themselves. For this reason most insured drivers carry **uninsured motorist insurance**. In many places this is a requirememt.

Regardless of who is responsible for a collision, **medical-payments insurance** covers your medical expenses and those of any passengers in your vehicle. Usually this coverage pays for any medical expense incurred for a year after the collision.

**Towing insurance** covers the cost of towing the vehicle or on-the-road repairs.

**A driver can purchase insurance to cover towing costs.**

**Insurance rates vary according to the area in which the insured lives and drives.**

# The Cost of Automobile Insurance

The costs of insurance policies differ according to kinds of coverage, the insurance company, and other factors. Statistics used as a basis for setting rates are gathered from collision data. Age, sex, state and county of residence, occupation, and marital status affect the cost of insurance. Anyone under 25 who is the principal driver of a vehicle pays the highest rates. Generally, an unmarried male under age 30 also pays high rates.

People who drive more than the average amount (about 10,000 miles) a year pay higher premiums. So do those who commute more than 15 miles one way each day. People living in high-population areas usually pay more than those in low density areas. The type of car you drive affects rates too. For example, sports models and expensive vehicles cost more to insure.

Your driving record also determines the cost of an insurance policy. Those with poor records pay more. Often drivers with good records can get special discounts. Those who have successfully finished a driver education course may get discounts. Discounts are also available to those who insure more than one vehicle.

# After a Collision

When involved in a collision, you are required by law to do several things. You must give aid to the injured, call the police, and give your name and address to the other drivers. In addition to these legal requirements, you should write down all available information about others involved in the collision as well as the names of witnesses. Draw a diagram of the collision and note the time of day and road and weather conditions. Record hazards that may have contributed to the collision. This information will be helpful when you report the collision to your insurance company.

If it is safe to do so, remove debris that might endanger others. If the car must be towed, read the towing contract carefully before signing it. You do not have to accept the towing service of the first truck on the scene. You can call another service. Report the accident to your insurance company as soon as possible. Most companies issue cards with a toll-free number that you can call. See a doctor if you believe you have been injured. Some injuries may not become noticeable for several days. If you don't see a doctor, your insurance company may not pay your claim.

**After a collision, get your vehicle out of the way of traffic so you can safely exchange information with the driver of the other vehicle.**

# Planning a Trip

Once you purchase a car and insure it properly, you may want to take a trip. You will find any trip more enjoyable if you plan it well. Before starting out on a routine trip or a long-distance journey, you should make certain preparations. First, be sure your car is in good operating condition. Then, decide what route to take and when to leave to reach your destination on time.

# Preparing Your Vehicle

You can avoid breakdowns on the roadway by keeping your car in good operating condition. Before a long trip, take the car to a service station to be checked and serviced.

Always start a trip with a full tank of fuel and plenty of window-washer fluid.

Be sure you carry the necessary emergency equipment in your car. You should have a spare tire, jack, and lug wrench. Keep a flashlight, flares, first-aid kit, and blanket in the passenger compartment. You might also carry an assortment of basic tools in the trunk for minor repairs.

## Packing the Car

To avoid last-minute delays, pack the luggage in the car the day before leaving. Make sure the weight is evenly distributed. In vehicles such as vans or cars with hatchbacks, luggage must be stored in the same compartment where people will be riding. Secure the luggage so that it does not hit someone during a sudden stop or maneuver. If possible, avoid loading the luggage so that it blocks the driver's view out the rear window.

## Choosing a Route

You must consider many questions when preparing a route plan. How quickly do I want to reach my destination? Do I want to take a longer, more scenic route? Do I want to enjoy interesting attractions on the way? Will I have to stop overnight? Where should I stop? Are there any problem roads I should avoid? How far should I go each day?

A travel agency or motor club can help you answer these and other questions. They may also help you draw up route plans. Motor clubs can prepare a plan that marks interesting areas along the way and also notes detours.

## Using a Road Map

To draw up and follow a route plan, you must be able to read a road map. A road map shows the location not only of cities, towns, and roadways, but also of parks, rivers, camping areas, airports, and other points of interest. Maps also show highways, service and rest areas, interchanges and toll gates, distance scales, and accumulated distances.

Maps use symbols to provide such information. To find out what the symbols mean, use the map **legend**, or key. For example, a small tent indicates a campsite. When you see a tent on the map, you know that camping is permitted in the area.

On the map itself, colors are often used for the names of places. The names of cities and towns appear in black. The larger the type used for the city name, the larger the city or town. The names of parks, universities, forest preserves, and other points of interest are often printed in red. The names of counties, rivers, and lakes may be printed in blue.

There are many kinds of road maps. City street maps, state highway maps, and county road maps are a few examples. Besides the folding road maps that are found at service stations and information centers, road atlases are also available. These atlases show the highways in each state and the major metropolitan areas. They are especially useful when traveling through more than one state.

**Reading a map while driving is dangerous. Pull off the road, or have a passenger read it for you.**

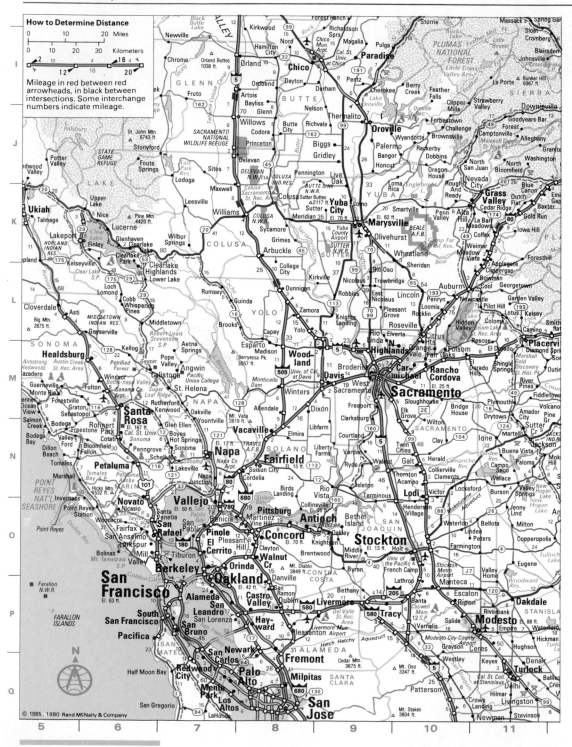

# Explanation of Map Symbols

## Roads and Related Symbols

Free Limited-Access Highways:
Under Construction

Toll Limited-Access Highways:
Under Construction

Other Four-Lane Divided Highways

Principal Highways

Other Through Highways

Interstate Highways

U.S. Highways

State and Provincial Highways

Secondary State, Provincial and County Highways

Cumulative miles (red) between arrows
Intermediate miles (black) between intersections
One mile or less not shown

Interchanges and Numbers
(For most states mileages between interchanges may be
determined by subtracting one number from the other.)

Rest Areas

Service Areas; Toll Booths

Waysides, Roadside Parks

## Parks, Recreation Areas, Points of Interest

U.S. and Canadian National, State and Provincial Parks:

with camping facilities

without camping facilities

Campsites

National Forests and Grasslands

Historic Sites and Monuments, Indian Reservations,
Military Installations, Points of Interest, Wildlife Refuges

**The map key, or legend, provides an explanation of the symbols used on the map. For example, the symbols used to differentiate the kinds of highways on the map are explained in the key.**

---

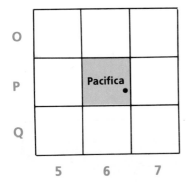

**A road map has a grid that has areas identified by a reference letter and number. The letter identifies the north-south boundaries, the number identifies the east-west boundaries. Look at the grid shown above. Pacifica is in area P-6. Then find the corresponding grid area on the road map and locate Pacifica.**

# California Index

Cities and towns 1980 census or latest estimates

# On the Way

Usually by starting a trip early in the day you can avoid heavy traffic. To avoid delays near large urban areas, arrange to drive through them before or after rush hour. You can get traffic information on local radio stations about the area. Often you can get advance notice of heavy traffic or construction areas so you that you can avoid such areas.

Never try to read a road map while driving. A passenger can help you by following the route plan and making adjustments in the plan as necessary. If you are alone and want to check the map, pull completely off the road and stop. It is even safer to stop at a rest or service area.

Driving is tiring. Always allow time for resting along the way. A long rest stop about every three hours is often better than more frequent short stops.

Eat lightly when traveling. Heavy meals can make you drowsy. If you are very tired, stop at a rest area and nap for a while. Or you might stop for the day and continue your trip the next day.

Avoid hurrying when traveling. A good trip plan allows extra time for unexpected stops or delays. If you are expected somewhere and are going to be late, call ahead. Do not try to make up for lost time by speeding or by staying on the road longer than planned.

## Fuel Misers

- Generally, a car with a small engine delivers better fuel economy than one with a large engine.

- A car with an automatic transmission usually uses more fuel than one with a standard transmission.

- Don't use a higher grade (and more expensive) fuel than your car requires.

- In some cases, choosing a longer travel route can be more economical. Driving on a smooth freeway uses less fuel than taking an older, shorter route with lots of traffic lights.

# ⟹ Key Ideas

- When shopping for a car, consider how much you can afford, what options or features you want, and whether a new or used car would be best.
- Thoroughly inspect and test drive any car before you decide to buy it.
- Check a used car carefully for defects. Take it to a mechanic or diagnostic center for inspection.
- Financing for the purchase of a car is available from credit unions, banks, and savings and loan associations. Compare interest rates to determine the best deal.
- Car ownership costs include depreciation, insurance costs, interest payments, fuel, maintenance and repair costs, and parking and toll fees.
- Read all contracts and check the vehicle warranty before completing the purchase.
- Insurance coverage protects drivers from financial losses resulting from an accident. Such coverage may be required by state law.
- Liability insurance covers you for injury to other people or to another's property. Collision insurance covers damage to your own vehicle. Comprehensive coverage protects you from losses not caused by a collision.
- Traveling by car requires planning. Take care to map out your route, pack your car properly, and decide on your objective.
- Do not continue to drive when tired.

# ⟹ Gauging Your Understanding

1. When shopping for a new car, what should you consider in deciding what model to buy and what features and options it will include?

2. What are some common sources for new-car loans? What information do you need in order to choose the most economical loan plan?

3. List some of the things you should check on a used car before you buy.

4. What is the difference between collision insurance and comprehensive insurance?

5. What factors do insurance companies consider in setting insurance premium rates?

**6.** In what ways can you qualify for a discount on your car insurance rates?

**7.** When involved in a collision, what steps are you required by law to take?

## ➡ In the Driver's Seat

**1.** Use the road map, map key, and index on pages 248-249 to complete the following activities.
   a. Look up Sacramento and Stockton in the map index. In what grids on the map are they located? Find both cities on the map. Map out two routes on major roads between them.
   b. Name the national forests located in this section of California. How did you find them? Is camping permitted in any of them? How do you know?
   c. Find Healdsburg and Petaluma in the index and then locate them on the map. What is the accumulated mileage between them on Route 101? Multiply the mileage by 1.6 to find the distance in kilometers.
   d. What interstate highways provide access to Sacramento?

**2.** You are driving to a vacation resort several hundred miles from your home. Using a map, you carefully plan the most direct route to get there. While you are driving, a local radio station announces that the highway you are on has just been closed a few miles ahead because of a collision. It will probably be closed for a few hours. What should you do? What information do you need to make a wise decision?

## Special Projects

**1.** A recall number has been established for consumers. Call this number (1-800-424-9393) and ask if there have been any recalls on your family car or the driver education car. Be ready to supply all necessary information about the car, including make, model, and year.

**2.** Visit a bank, a credit union, and a car dealer finance office and ask about car loans. Get information from each on payment schedules and interest rates and finance charges. Compare these figures and decide which source offers the best deal in a car loan.

# ➡ Chapter Test 13

Name _____ Date _____

**Write "T" beside statements that are true and "F" beside those that are false.**

_____ **1.** A driver can usually obtain a loan for the total purchase price of a vehicle.

_____ **2.** A title is proof of ownership of a vehicle.

_____ **3.** Discounts on insurance premiums are sometimes available to those who insure more than one vehicle.

_____ **4.** When inspecting a used car, check for rust only inside the trunk.

_____ **5.** The premium paid for collision and comprehensive insurance will be lower if a driver has a $500 deductible rather than a $100 deductible.

_____ **6.** A person covered by a no-fault insurance plan does not need liability insurance.

_____ **7.** A driver should never buy a used car without test driving it.

_____ **8.** Insurance premiums are often lower for safe drivers.

**Write the letter of the best answer in the space provided.**

_____ **1.** Blue exhaust may mean a vehicle has (a) a faulty choke, (b) a diesel engine, (c) an engine burning oil, (d) a properly operating engine.

_____ **2.** The amount a vehicle decreases in value as it ages is known as (a) collateral, (b) depreciation, (c) interest, (d) liability.

_____ **3.** A deductible clause refers to the (a) discounted premium, (b) no-fault insurance plan, (c) cost of liability insurance, (d) amount a driver must pay for a collision.

_____ **4.** The manufacturer's guarantee is known as a (a) vehicle warranty, (b) vehicle registration, (c) dealer's contract, (d) car title.

_____ **5.** If exhaust emissions are black, a vehicle probably has (a) a faulty choke, (b) a diesel engine, (c) an engine burning oil, (d) a properly operating engine.

_____ **6.** Every vehicle has a 5-year or 50,000 mile warranty on (a) the battery, (b) fuel emissions equipment, (c) the tires, (d) neglected or abused parts.

_____ **7.** On a long-distance trip a driver should avoid (a) eating light meals, (b) taking long rest stops, (c) drinking alcohol, (d) allowing extra time for unplanned stops.

_____ **8.** Symbols used on a map are explained in the (a) map index, (b) distance scale, (c) interstate number key, (d) map legend.

_____ **9.** If the odometer reading is low but the control pedals are badly worn, a vehicle was probably used for (a) expressway driving, (b) stop-and-go driving, (c) rural highway driving, (d) cross-country trips.

_____ **10.** When involved in a collision, you must (a) call the relatives of anyone injured, (b) stay in your car until the police arrive, (c) aid anyone who is injured, (d) take photographs of the collision scene.

**Match the items in Column B to the items in Column A by placing the correct letter in the space provided.**

**Column A**

_____ **1.** Bodily injury liability

_____ **2.** Property damage liability

_____ **3.** Medical-payments insurance

_____ **4.** Comprehensive insurance

_____ **5.** Collision insurance

_____ **6.** Uninsured-motorist insurance

_____ **7.** Towing insurance

**Column B**

**a.** Covers damage to your own vehicle.

**b.** Covers damage to your car caused by a driver who failed to show financial responsibility.

**c.** Covers injuries to passengers in your car.

**d.** Covers injuries to pedestrians caused by a driver.

**e.** Covers on-the-road repairs.

**f.** Covers damage to a vehicle caused by lightning.

**g.** Covers damage to a parked car caused by a driver.

# Chapter 14 Maintaining Your Vehicle

- Some drivers wait until something breaks down to have their cars serviced. Why is this dangerous?
- Why do some states require an annual inspection of all motor vehicles?
- How can the way you drive affect what will wear out or break down in your car?

**Checking exhaust emissions has become an important part of many vehicle inspections.**

When you own a car, you are responsible for keeping it in good operating condition. A car that is maintained at maximum efficiency uses less fuel which, in turn, saves money. In addition, it is less likely to have a major breakdown. Therefore, a well-maintained car is safer to drive.

## Vehicle Inspection

Inspecting your car to make sure everything is working does not require any special mechanical knowledge. There are a number of simple checks you can make before you get in the car or when you stop for fuel. These quick inspections can alert you to a possibly dangerous problem. If you identify such problems early, you may avoid a costly breakdown later. However, you should have the car checked out by a mechanic at least once a year, even if a regular safety inspection is not required in your area.

# State and City Inspections

Some states and cities require owners to have their vehicles inspected once or twice a year. Such inspections usually include all of the exterior lights, horn, glass, windshield wipers, tires, steering, wheel alignment, suspension system, and brakes. In recent years, a concern for air quality has led to vehicle exhaust emissions inspections as well.

If your car does not pass an inspection, usually you have a few days to get it repaired and re-inspected. If you fail to have the car inspected, your registration may be suspended.

# At the Service Station

Once you get into the car and start the engine, check all the gauges and controls to be sure they are operating properly. If your fuel gauge shows less than half a tank, plan to stop and fill up.

Stopping for fuel gives you an opportunity to check under the hood of your car. Raise the hood to check the oil. Remove the oil dipstick and wipe it off with a rag. Re-insert the dipstick and remove it once more. If the oil level registers below the "Add 1 quart" line, you should add a quart of oil. Do not add more oil than is needed, however.

Also check the fluid levels in the radiator, windshield washer container, and battery (most new batteries are sealed, however, and never need to have water added).

Inspect hoses for cracks or leaks. Check the tension of the fan belt and power steering belt. Make sure the windshield wiper blades are in good condition. Check tires for proper inflation and signs of wear.

When you fill the fuel tank, be sure that you use the right grade and kind of fuel. Using the wrong type of fuel can cause your car to run poorly and cost you more money. Most new cars use unleaded gas. These vehicles have the printed warning "unleaded gas only" near the fuel cap and on the instrument panel. If you are not certain what kind of fuel your car uses, check the owner's manual.

**The oil dipstick measures the amount of oil in the engine.**

# Choosing a Mechanic

**A good driver not only knows driving strategies, but understands some of the mechanics of a vehicle also.**

You can learn to do some of the preventive maintenance yourself. By doing simple jobs such as changing the oil, you can save money. However, there are some jobs that are best left to a specialist. These are jobs that may require specialized training and special tools or equipment.

Often, new car warranties require you to have certain services on the car performed by the dealer to protect the warranty. Other services may be performed elsewhere. After the warranty expires, you may have all services performed any place you choose. You may decide to bring the car to a dealer, garage, service station, or independent mechanic.

Whatever you decide, it is important to find someone you can trust. Ask friends and relatives where they have their cars serviced and whether they have been satisfied with the work. If their experiences have been good, you may want to take your car to the same place.

Before you have any work done on your car, ask for an estimate of repair costs. Also ask about the warranty. Make it clear that any work not included in the estimate should not be done without your permission. Ask that any old parts that are removed and replaced be saved and returned to you for inspection. These precautions may save you from paying for unnecessary repairs.

# Preventive Maintenance

Keeping your car at the best possible performance level takes time and organization. Developing a preventive maintenance schedule will help take care of most things before they become problems.

Based on recommendations in the owner's manual of your car, set up a routine maintenance schedule. Record what kind of work is done and when it is done — whether you do the work yourself or have a mechanic do it.

# Brakes

Brakes, like other equipment, wear out. However, how you use the brakes can affect how quickly they wear. For example, constant hard braking or riding the brakes causes wear. To reduce brake wear, apply steady pressure to the brake pedal. Keep your foot off the pedal when not braking. When driving down a steep hill, shift to a lower gear rather than using only the brakes.

Changes in braking power are usually gradual. You may be completely unaware of a problem developing with the brakes. Therefore, have the entire brake system inspected at least once a year. Check other parts of the brake system more often. For example, check the fluid level in the master brake cylinder every time you have the oil changed. The front brakes usually wear out more quickly than the rear brakes and should be checked more often.

If the brakes squeal or the car pulls to one side when you press the service brake, the brake system may need adjustment or repair. Pedal action that is spongy or hard usually indicates a problem as well. If the brake pedal goes right to the floor, or if you must pump the pedal repeatedly to stop the car, the brakes are in need of repair.

**Vehicles are equipped with a dual master-brake cylinder, which reduces the chance of losing total braking power.**

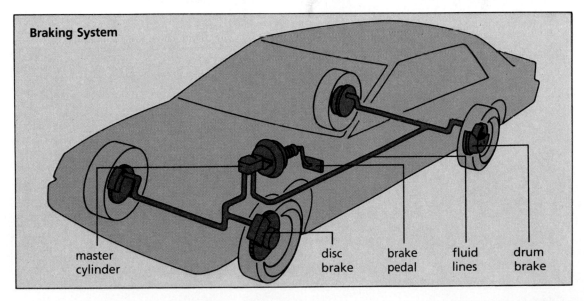

**Braking System**

master cylinder     disc brake     brake pedal     fluid lines     drum brake

# Tires

When buying tires, take into account tire-tread width, load capacity, wheel size, and type of construction.

Tires are constructed with protective cord layers underneath the outer material. These layers, or **plies**, of cord strips strengthen the tire. In a **bias ply tire**, the cord layers crisscross at a slight angle. These tires ride well at low speeds. But heat created by high speeds and sharp turns can weaken them.

In addition to plies, **belted tires** are circled by additional cord strips. Belted tires are stronger than regular bias ply tires.

The plies of **radial tires** run straight across the tire. Radial tires also have belts that circle the tires. Because of their construction, the walls of radial tires are more flexible than those of bias tires.

Keep in mind that you should never use radial tires and bias tires on the same vehicle. Mixing the two kinds of tires can result in serious handling problems. Because they wear longer, radial tires are usually a better choice.

**Note how the plies are layered on each type of tire. How do radial tires differ from bias ply and belted tires?**

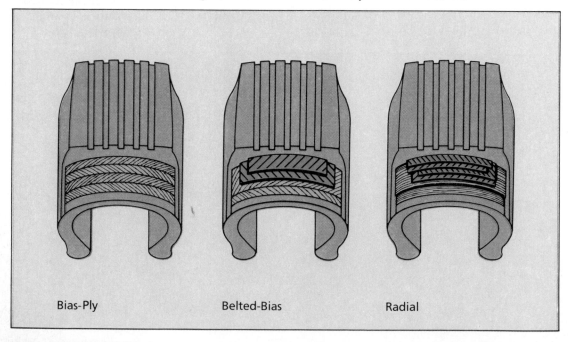

Bias-Ply          Belted-Bias          Radial

Check tire air pressure regularly, but only when the tires are cold. Tires heat up from friction with the road after you drive the car even a short distance. Because heat causes the air in the tires to expand, a pressure reading taken right after driving is not accurate. Do not let air out of warm tires to get a normal reading. Wait for the tires to cool before checking the pressure.

Tire-tread wear often indicates problems in tire inflation or wheel alignment. A tire with more wear at the outer edges than in the middle is underinflated. A tire with more wear in the middle than at the edges is overinflated. If one side of the tire tread is worn more than the other, the wheels probably need to be realigned and balanced. Regularly check the tires for bald spots, cracks, or bulges that could weaken them.

**Wear bars** appear on the tire when tread depth is only about $\frac{1}{16}$ inch (0.16 cm) deep. When wear bars show, the tire must be replaced. It is illegal to drive on tires that are badly worn. When you buy replacement tires, always buy the size and type of tire recommended for your vehicle. Refer to your owner's manual if you are not sure of what tire to buy.

**These patterns show tires that were over-inflated (left), under-inflated (center), and with wear bars (right).**

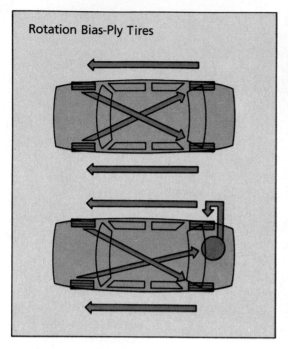

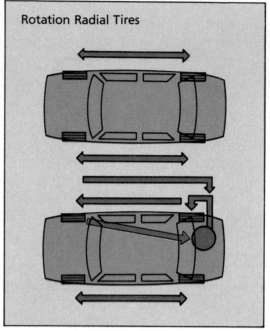

**Rotating tires can increase their life. However, radial and bias tire rotation patterns differ.**

To help lengthen tire life, rotate the tires. Follow the recommended schedule in the owner's manual. The manual should also show how to rotate them depending on the type of tire. Most manufacturers suggest that radial tires not be rotated from one side of the vehicle to the other.

# Steering and Suspension

Low tire pressure and badly aligned wheels can cause a car to steer hard or wander and pull from side to side. Such handling difficulties more likely indicate problems in the steering or suspension systems. Parts of the steering system may need to be tightened. New springs or shock absorbers may be needed. Other problems in the steering and suspension systems may cause the vehicle to shake at high speeds, the front wheels to "shimmy" (vibrate), or the steering wheel to have too much play. A squealing noise when the car is turned may indicate a loose power steering belt. Scraping sounds from the wheels may mean the wheel bearings need replacing.

# Lights and Other Safety Devices

**To be effective, headlights must be properly aligned so they shine where needed.**

Keep head and taillights clean at all times. Check them regularly to make sure they are working. You can easily replace burned-out bulbs or blown fuses. The fuses are usually located under the instrument panel. Keep a few spare fuses in the car. Problems with loose or broken wiring usually must be taken care of by a mechanic.

Check headlight alignment at least once a year. Even if the aim is only slightly off, the beam will not shine where needed. Not only is your night vision reduced, but other drivers may be blinded by your beam.

Keep mirrors clean and properly adjusted. If windshield wipers streak the windows, replace the blades. If the wipers do not stay in contact with the windshield, the wiper arms may also need replacing.

Use an antifreeze solution made just for this purpose in the windshield washer container, especially in the winter. This fluid is less likely to freeze than plain water.

# Under the Hood

Regular engine tune-ups and inspection of fan and other drive belts can help prevent serious engine problems. Check the tension of all belts and tighten any that are loose. Replace frayed or cracked belts.

## ● The Engine Coolant System

**The cooling system helps reduce the heat created by the engine.**

Keep an eye on the fluid level in the radiator. If the level is constantly low, there may be leaks in the radiator or hoses. Flush the cooling system and replace the antifreeze and water about every 2 years or 30,000 miles. Be sure there is enough antifreeze in the solution to keep it from freezing. If the coolant freezes, serious damage to the cooling system and engine could result.

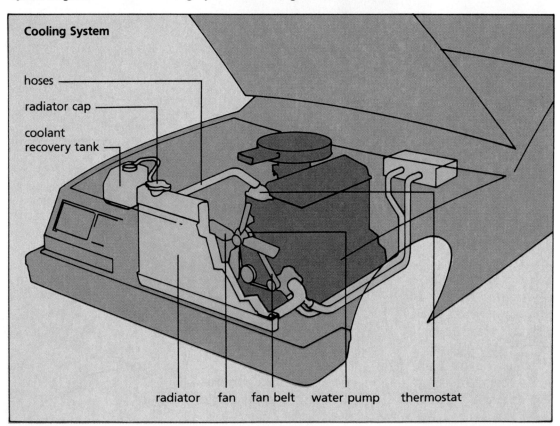

**Cooling System**

hoses

radiator cap

coolant recovery tank

radiator    fan    fan belt    water pump    thermostat

Leaves, insects, and dirt on the radiator can hamper the flow of air needed for cooling the radiator. Spraying water through the radiator from the engine side should remove such debris.

The temperature gauge or light on the instrument panel alerts you to an overheated engine. In heavy stop-and-go driving, you can reduce minor overheating by shifting to NEUTRAL and pressing the accelerator. This causes the engine to run faster, which, in turn, causes the water pump to run faster. The increased flow of coolant through the radiator should cool the engine. In older cars, this action also increases the speed of the fan. As a result, the radiator cools more rapidly.

If the overheating problem is more serious, pull well off the road and out of traffic before trying to determine the cause. If steam is coming from under the hood, do not open it until the steam has stopped. Loosen — but do not remove — the radiator cap. Cover the cap with a thick rag when loosening it so your hands are not burned. While waiting to remove the cap, inspect for a broken fan belt or leaking hoses.

If there is not enough antifreeze in the cooling system, the radiator can freeze in cold weather. Since the coolant cannot pass from the engine through the radiator, overheating will result.

If the coolant level is low, start the engine and add more. The engine should be running while the coolant is being added. This procedure prevents cracking of components from a sudden temperature change in the hot radiator. In warm weather, water alone can be used if antifreeze is not available.

## The Engine Lubricating System

The **lubricating system**, which circulates oil through the engine, helps clean the internal parts of the engine. It also prevents wear of parts and excessive heat from friction. The owner's manual should suggest the intervals at which the oil and oil filter should be replaced. Change the oil more frequently than recommended if you use the car mostly for short trips, on dusty roads, or in temperature extremes.

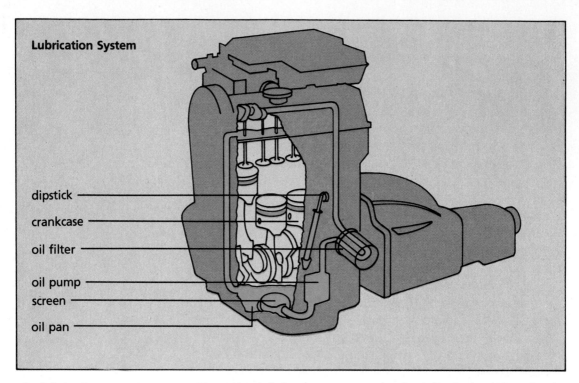

**Lubrication System**

dipstick

crankcase

oil filter

oil pump

screen

oil pan

**The lubricating system helps reduce the amount of friction between moving parts.**

Have the lubricating system checked for leaks. Also check the power steering fluid and automatic transmission fluid levels. Many cars eventually require other lubrication as well. Check the owner's manual for a recommended lubrication schedule.

## ● Battery and Wiring

Most new batteries are sealed and never need to have water added. The fluid level in older batteries should be checked occasionally. Some of the fluid is lost through evaporation. A low fluid level may cause a battery to wear down. A "dead" battery — one that has lost its charge — sometimes can be recharged.

Inspect the battery cables for cracks and torn insulation. The clamps at the battery terminals should be tight and free of corrosion. To slow the buildup of corrosion, smear petroleum jelly on the terminals. When cleaning battery caps and terminals, be careful not to get battery acid on your clothes, skin, or eyes. Smoking near the battery is

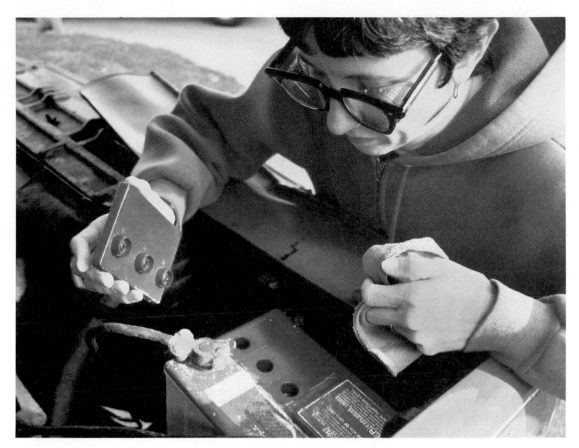

extremely dangerous. Fumes from the battery can ignite and explode violently.

High engine temperature causes ignition wiring and vacuum hoses to wear out eventually. Have them inspected regularly and replace them as needed.

**The battery is the power source that provides the energy to start the engine.**

# Drive Train

Automatic transmission fluid should be changed about every 25,000 miles. When you check the level of the automatic transmission fluid, the engine should be running. If you add fluid, however, the engine should be off. An automatic transmission may also require occasional adjustments.

Have the entire drive train inspected regularly. Other preventive maintenance on the system must be performed less

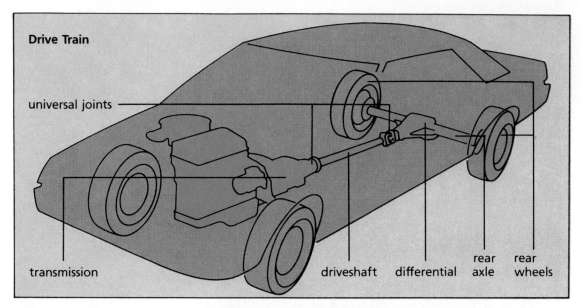

**Drive Train**

universal joints

transmission

driveshaft   differential   rear axle   rear wheels

**The power train is the system that transmits power from the engine to the drive wheels.**

frequently. Refer to your owner's manual for the recommended schedule. Have the driveshaft, wheel bearings, and universal joints checked at appropriate times.

## Clean Inside and Out

Keeping a car clean makes it look good and can help prolong the life of the paint and trim. Wash and wax the car body regularly. Spray water beneath the car to help prevent corrosion from road dust and salt. Wash the windows inside and out with a household cleaner and water.

Vacuum the interior of the car and, if necessary, wipe down the upholstery and interior walls with a damp rag.

## Fuel Economy

In recent years, the costs of operating a car have risen. People have become increasingly aware of the need for fuel conservation. The federal government has set up fuel economy standards for vehicles. There are many things you can do yourself to save fuel and reduce costs.

# Vehicle Choice and Maintenance

The kind of car you drive and the kind of accessories on that vehicle affect its fuel economy. Some cars use less fuel than others. When buying a car, ask to see its **Environmental Protection Agency (EPA)** fuel ratings. These ratings show the average amount of fuel that kind of car uses in normal driving in city traffic and on the highways.

Properly inflated and balanced tires also save fuel, because they rotate with less effort. Check tire pressure at least once a month. Have a mechanic check wheel alignment. Wheels that are not properly aligned use more fuel. Snow tires may also reduce fuel economy — remove them as soon as the risk of snow is over.

Always make sure your car is well maintained. Tune-ups can help keep the engine in good running condition. A well-tuned engine uses fuel more efficiently than one not maintained.

# Driving Habits

From the time you start the car to the time you turn it off, you can save fuel by following certain practices. When the engine is cold, set the choke by pressing the accelerator to the floor and releasing it slowly. When turning the ignition switch, you may not have to use the accelerator.

To pick up speed, accelerate gradually. Sudden "jack-rabbit" starts waste gas. After you reach the desired speed, you can ease up on the accelerator slightly and still maintain that speed. Drive smoothly at an even speed without continually pressing and releasing the gas pedal. You can save fuel by easing up on the accelerator and letting your speed drop slightly when going uphill.

By anticipating a stop ahead, you can often slow down by taking your foot off the accelerator. In that way, you also reduce the need to use the brakes.

Avoid frequent lane changes and weaving in and out of traffic. More fuel is used by these maneuvers than by staying in one lane. Avoid tailgating. Tailgating is not only

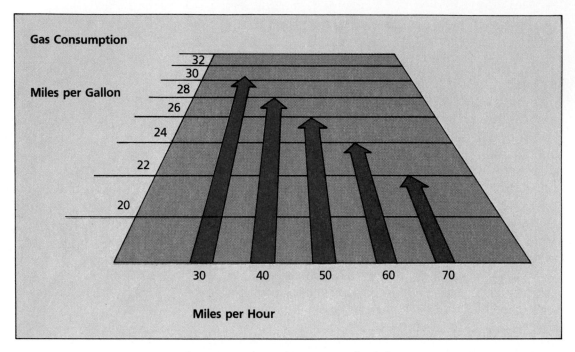

**Gas Consumption**

**Miles per Gallon**

32
30
28
26
24
22
20

30    40    50    60    70

**Miles per Hour**

**Gas mileage decreases as speed increases.**

dangerous but also wastes fuel, because constant speed adjustments are needed.

Use accessories such as the air conditioner as little as possible. Turn the car off if you are going to be stopped for longer than a minute. More fuel is burned by idling than by restarting the car.

The most efficient way to save fuel is through speed control. Studies have shown that the best fuel economy is achieved at about 35 to 40 mph. Traveling at 60 mph requires 15–20 percent more fuel than traveling at 50 mph.

# Calculating Miles Per Gallon

You can easily figure out your car's mileage. Determining how many miles you can travel per gallon of gas gives you an idea of how well the car is running and how efficiently you are driving. Follow these steps to calculate miles per gallon:

**1.** Fill the fuel tank. Record the mileage reading on the odometer.

**2.** Drive the car as you normally would until the tank is about half empty. Fill the tank again, recording both the odometer reading and the number of gallons it takes to fill the tank.

**3.** Subtract the first odometer reading from the second one. This tells you how many miles you have driven.

**4.** Divide the number of miles driven by the number of gallons used. This gives you the miles per gallon rating. Study the following example:

| | |
|---|---|
| Second odometer reading | 24,500 |
| First odometer reading | − 24,250 |
| Miles driven | $\dfrac{250}{10} = 25$ mpg |
| Gallons used | |

Your car's mileage varies according to the type of driving you do. For example, you get poorer mileage in city driving than on the highway. Therefore, you should check the mileage several times and average the results.

## Maintenance Tips

- Watch your mileage. A decrease could signal a mechanical problem such as a stuck choke or a faulty carburetor.

- Regularly check for leaks under your car. Radiator coolant is usually watery green or watery red. Transmission fluid is oily red. Motor oil is usually dark brown or nearly black.

- Both master brake cylinders should be full of brake fluid. If you have to add fluid frequently, have a mechanic check the brake system.

## Key Ideas

- A quick inspection of your vehicle before you drive or when you stop for fuel can help you avoid costly breakdowns.
- Many maintenance and repair tasks must be done by a mechanic, since these tasks require specialized training and special tools or equipment.
- Developing a preventive maintenance schedule helps ensure safe and economical driving.
- Changes in a vehicle's braking ability signal that repairs to the brake system are needed.

- Tires are available in three basic designs: bias ply, belted, and radial.
- To prevent overheating and engine damage, check the engine coolant and lubricating systems regularly.
- The type of vehicle you buy and the way you drive it determine how good your fuel economy will be.

# Gauging Your Understanding

1. What under-the-hood checks should you make when you stop for fuel?

2. How can you reduce brake wear?

3. List some of the symptoms of possible brake trouble.

4. How do radial tires compare with bias ply or belted tires?

5. What suggestions would you give a friend who complained of poor gas mileage?

# In the Driver's Seat

1. Eduardo's car failed the state inspection. The radial tires on the rear were worn down to the wear bars. Eduardo has a week to replace the tires and have the car reinspected. However, he is short of money. Freda offered to sell him a pair of used belted tires for only $25. This is a lot less than the radial tires he priced at the tire store. What should Eduardo do? Why?

2. You are driving in the middle lane on the expressway. Suddenly the needle on the temperature gauge swings to HOT. What should you do?

## Special Projects

1. Perform a thorough inspection of your family car or a friend's car. Check all fluid levels, as well as the lights, horn, wipers, etc. What possible problems do you find? What should be done to correct these problems?

2. Phone two or three repair shops. Ask what it would cost to have four brakes reworked. Explain that the front are disc and the rear are drum brakes. Ask what kind of warranty you would receive on the work.

# ➡️ Chapter Test 14

Name _____   Date _____

**Write "T" beside statements that are true and "F" beside those that are false.**

_____   **1.** A car maintained at maximum efficiency uses more fuel.

_____   **2.** Add oil only when the dipstick shows no oil.

_____   **3.** How you use the brakes affects how quickly they wear.

_____   **4.** Check tire pressure after you have driven a few miles.

_____   **5.** Dead batteries can sometimes be recharged.

_____   **6.** The engine should be turned off when you add coolant.

_____   **7.** Antifreeze is needed in the cooling system all year long.

_____   **8.** Air should be let out of a warm tire to achieve a normal pressure reading.

_____   **9.** To avoid having to add oil on a long trip, add an extra quart to the engine before you start out.

_____   **10.** Radial tires should be rotated to opposite sides of a vehicle.

**Write the letter of the best answer in the space provided.**

_____   **1.** Tires that are more worn on the edges than in the middle are probably (a) misaligned, (b) underinflated, (c) overinflated, (d) out of balance.

_____   **2.** If one side of the tire tread is worn more than the other, (a) the tires need to be replaced, (b) the wheels need to be aligned, (c) the tires need to be inflated, (d) the tires need to be rotated.

_____   **3.** When tires show wear bars, (a) the tires must be inflated, (b) it is illegal to drive on the tires, (c) the tires must be rotated, (d) tire pressure should be checked.

_____   **4.** When the engine is running, check the (a) engine oil level, (b) transmission fluid level, (c) master brake fluid level, (d) battery fluid level.

_____   **5.** When adding transmission fluid to a vehicle, be sure that the (a) engine is running, (b) transmission is in NEUTRAL, (c) transmission is in PARK, (d) engine is not running.

_____   **6.** The engine should always be running when fluid is added to (a) a hot radiator, (b) the windshield-washer fluid container, (c) the battery, (d) the automatic transmission.

**Complete these sentences by writing the correct terms in the blanks.**

**1.** The _____ system circulates oil through the engine.

**2.** Sudden _____ starts waste fuel.

**3.** Always get a(n) _____ of repairs before having your vehicle worked on.

**4.** The _____ shows the average amount of fuel a car uses in normal driving.

**5.** Regular vehicle _____ can alert you to possibly dangerous problems.

**6.** Developing a _____ _____ schedule for your car can help you take care of most things before they become problems.

**7.** New car _____ often require you to have some services performed by the dealer.

**8.** To help lengthen tire life, _____ the tires at regular intervals.

**9.** Check headlight _____ at least once a year to be sure the beam shines where needed.

# Careers in the HTS: Maintenance and Repair

There are many maintenance jobs and minor repairs you can perform to keep your vehicle running smoothly and safely. However, when your car has a serious problem or breakdown, usually you must turn to a qualified mechanic or other repair specialist.

There are many career opportunities in the field of automotive maintenance and repair. Many of these jobs require special training and experience.

## Mechanical Repairs

Some shops specialize in engine diagnostics and tune ups. Other shops may handle special vehicle systems. For example, there are service centers that repair only transmissions or brakes. Still other shops specialize in muffler and exhaust system repair. Service centers that perform front end and suspension work often handle wheel balancing and alignment, as well as tire rotation and replacement.

Many garages and service centers also have towing and road services available.

## Body Repair

The body or frame of a vehicle may be badly damaged in a collision. Even a minor crash can result in damage to the fenders or other body parts. Body repair shops specialize in repairing the damage caused by collisions or rust.

Those who work in body shops repair and paint damaged parts of the outside of a vehicle. Their work often requires special training in the use of cutting and welding tools.

## Sales

Mechanics and other repair specialists use a wide assortment of parts, tools, and equipment. Many jobs exist in the sales of these items to both repair shops and "do-it-yourself" vehicle owners.

Many people also sell used and reconditioned parts. They buy old and damaged vehicles and remove any parts that are still useable. They sell these parts for less than what new parts cost.

# Glossary

**Absolute speed limit** The maximum or minimum posted speed at which one may drive under normal conditions. p. 65

**Acceleration** An increase in vehicle speed. p. 39

**Acceleration lane** A lane used by drivers entering an expressway to pick up speed so they can merge with expressway traffic. p. 150

**Accelerator** The foot control that regulates the amount of fuel going to the engine. p. 22

**Accessory position** A position on the ignition switch that can be used to run the electrical system without starting the engine. p. 21

**Air bag** A passive restraint device that inflates in the event of a collision and prevents occupants from striking the dashboard. p. 28

**Alternator** A device that produces the electricity to recharge the battery and operate electrical equipment in a running vehicle. p. 21

**Alternator gauge** A light or gauge that warns a driver if the battery is not being properly charged. p. 21

**Antifreeze** A chemical solution used with or instead of water in the vehicle's radiator to prevent freezing. p. 265

**Automatic transmission** A system in which a vehicle automatically shifts through the forward gears as it is accelerated. p. 23

**Backup lights** White lights at the rear of a vehicle that shine when the transmission is put in REVERSE. p. 26

**Banked curve** A roadway that slopes down from one edge to the other. p. 89

**Basic driving rules** Certain rules of the road that apply in all parts of the United States and Canada. p. 63

**Basic speed limit** Any speed below the absolute limit that is safe for existing road, weather, or traffic conditions. p. 66

**Battery** A set of cells that stores and emits electrical charges and provides electricity for a vehicle. p. 266.

**Belted tires** Tires constructed with a combination of cord layers crisscrossed at a slight angle and cord strips circling the tire. p. 260

**Bias ply tires** Tires constructed with protective cord layers, or plies, crisscrossed underneath the outer material. p. 260

**Blind spots** Areas to the sides and rear of a vehicle that a driver cannot see in the rearview mirrors. p. 31

**Blood-alcohol content (BAC)** The percentage of alcohol in a person's bloodstream. p. 218

**Bodily injury liability insurance** Insurance that protects the driver against financial loss due to injuries caused to another person in a collision. p. 242

**Brake lights** Red warning lights on the rear of a vehicle that are activated by pressing the service brake pedal. p. 26

**Braking distance** The distance a vehicle travels from the time the brake pedal is depressed to the time the vehicle comes to a complete stop. p. 90

**Braking skid** A skid, caused by sudden hard braking, in which one or all wheels lock and the back end of the car slides to the left or right. p. 185

**Braking system** An automotive system that is used to slow or stop a moving vehicle. p. 188

**Carbon monoxide**   A poisonous gas emitted through an automobile's exhaust system.   p. 204

**Center of gravity**   The point around which the weight of a vehicle is balanced.   p. 85

**Centering**   Looking ahead to where your vehicle will be in about eight seconds. p. 99

**Centrifugal force**   The force that tends to push a vehicle out of a curve or turn on to a straight path.   p. 88

**Choke**   The device that regulates the flow of air to the carburetor.   p. 32

**Clutch**   The device in a standard-transmission vehicle that disengages the engine power from the drive wheels so that gears can be shifted.   p. 25

**Collateral**   Property presented as security for a loan.   p. 238

**Collision**   A crash between motor vehicles or between a motor vehicle and another object.   p. 245

**Collision insurance**   Insurance protection that covers damages to one's own vehicle resulting from a crash.   p. 242

**Color perception**   The ability to see color.   p. 200

**Comprehensive insurance**   Insurance protection that covers one's vehicle in the event that it is stolen or damaged by vandalism, storms, or fire.   p. 242

**Compromising hazards**   Risking involvement with one hazard to avoid a more serious hazard.   p. 107

**Controlled-access highway**   A highway that vehicles can enter or exit only at designated entrances and exits.   p. 148

**Controlled braking**   A braking technique that involves applying steady but progressively greater pressure to the service brake pedal to stop quickly without skidding.   p. 184

**Controlled intersection**   An intersection that is regulated by traffic lights or stop signs at all approaches.   p. 126

**Cornering skid**   A skid that results from taking a turn or curve too fast.   p. 185

**Counterskid**   A skid that results from oversteering to correct a skid or from failing to straighten the wheels quickly enough after recovering from a skid. p. 185

**Crosswalk lines**   White lines that guide pedestrians across intersections.   p. 75

**Crowned road**   A roadway that slopes down from the middle to each side.   p. 89

**Dashboard**   A panel under the windshield of a vehicle containing indicators, gauges, compartments, and sometimes hand controls.   p. 18

**Deceleration**   A decrease in vehicle speed.   p. 152

**Deceleration lane**   A lane on an expressway used by drivers to decrease vehicle speed before getting on an exit ramp.   p. 152

**Decide**   The third step in the IPDE process in which a driver determines what course of action to take.   p. 102

**Deductible**   The amount of money a driver must pay before collision or comprehensive insurance will cover the remaining cost to repair or replace a motor vehicle.   p. 242

**Depreciation**   The value a motor vehicle loses as it ages.   p. 238

**Depressants**   Drugs that slow down the central nervous system.   p. 214

**Depth perception**   The three-dimensional perception of distances between objects.   p. 200

**Detour**   A temporary alternate route.   p. 67

**Diagonal parking spaces**   Parking spaces arranged side by side at an angle to the curb or side of the road.   p. 51

**Diesel fuel**   A heavy oil used as a fuel in some motor vehicles.   p. 20

**Differential**   Gears that send the turning force of the drive shaft to the drive axle of a vehicle.   p. 268

**Dimmer switch**   A switch that is used to select low- or high-beam headlights.   p. 25

**Directional signals**   Lights on a motor vehicle or hand signals used to indicate left and right turns and stops.   p. 26

**Disc brakes**   A braking system that creates stopping friction by pressing both sides of a round disc.   p. 259

**Downshift**   The process of shifting from one transmission gear to a lower gear. p. 43

**Driver's license**   State-issued permit legally granting a person the right to operate a motor vehicle in the HTS.   p. 9

**Drive shaft**   A metal bar that transfers turning power to the differential from the transmission.   p. 268

**Drive train**   The system that transfers the engine power to the drive wheels; it consists of the crankshaft, transmission, driveshaft, universal joints, and differential.   p. 267

**Driving While Intoxicated (DWI)**   Operating a vehicle while under the influence of alcohol.   p. 77

**Drugs**   Chemical mixtures that have a physical and sometimes psychological effect on those who use them.   p. 212

**Drum brakes**   A braking system that creates stopping friction by the rubbing of brake shoes against the inside of a drum.   p. 259

**DWI**   Abbreviation for driving while intoxicated.   p. 222

**Edge lines**   Solid white lines that mark the outside edge of a road.   p. 74

**Emergency flashers**   A device that flashes all four signals on and off.   p. 26

**Emergency vehicle**   A police car, fire truck, or ambulance, which is given the right of way when its lights are flashing and siren is blaring.   p. 133

**Energy of motion**   The energy produced by a moving object; also known as kinetic energy.   p. 87

**Engine braking**   Easing up on the gas pedal or shifting to a lower gear to allow the power of the engine to slow the vehicle.   p. 188

**Entrance ramp**   A roadway that serves as a controlled-access point leading to a highway or expressway.   p. 147

**EPA rating**   The rating of a car's gas mileage by the Environmental Protection Agency.   p. 269

**Escape route**   Path available for swerving to avoid a hazard.   p. 147

**Execute**   The final step in the IPDE process in which a driver uses vehicle controls and equipment to change speed, change direction, warn other drivers, or perform a combination of these maneuvers.   p. 102

**Exhaust emissions**   Waste gases, formed from the incomplete burning of fuel, that are expelled from the engine through the exhaust system.   p. 204

**Exhaust system**   The pipes and other parts of the automotive system that carry waste gases from the engine and reduce the noise of the explosions in the engine cylinders.   p. 204

**Exit ramp**   A roadway that is used for leaving a controlled-access expressway or highway.   p. 148

**Expressway**   A controlled-access, divided highway designed for high-volume, high-speed traffic.   p. 147

**Fan belt**   A flexible band driven by the crankshaft that turns the radiator fan and drives the alternator.   p. 264

**Fast-idle skid**   A skid that occurs when a driver tries to stop a vehicle when the engine is idling too fast.   p. 185

**Fatigue**   Physical or mental exhaustion. p. 198

**Field of vision**   The total range of space that one can see without moving one's eyes.   p. 201

**Financial responsibility laws**   A legal requirement that all drivers must be able to prove ability to pay damages resulting from collisions for which they are responsible.   p. 78

**Flashing signals**   Flashing lights used at intersections where traffic is not very heavy or steady.   p. 92

**Following distance**   The amount of space a driver allows between his or her vehicle and the one ahead.   p. 108

**Force of impact**   The amount of power with which objects collide with one another. It varies with the objects' speeds and weights.   p. 91

**Friction**   The force that resists the motion of one surface against another.   p. 86

**Friction point**   The clutch position at which engine power and the transmission engage. A vehicle in gear will begin to move when the clutch is released higher than this point.   p. 41

**Fuel gauge**   The indicator on the instrument panel that shows how much gasoline or other fuel is in the tank.   p. 20

**Fuel tank**   The container in which gasoline or other fuel is stored.   p. 20

**Gauge**   An instrument with a graduated scale or dial that indicates quantity or amounts.   p. 20

**Gears**   Cogged wheels that work to transmit power. Usually used in reference to transmission gears, which determine speed and direction.   p. 24

**Gear selector lever**   A projecting bar used to change from one gear to another in an automatic transmission vehicle.   p. 23

**Gearshift lever**   A projecting bar used to change from one gear to another in a standard-transmission vehicle.   p. 24

**Good Samaritan law**   A law designed to protect people who give first aid at the scene of a collision from a possible lawsuit.   p. 78

**Gravity**   The force that pulls objects toward the center of the earth.   p. 84

**Ground viewing**   Identifying the direction other cars are headed by determining the direction their wheels are turned.   p. 101

**Guide signs**   Signs along a roadway that provide information about location, direction, availability or services, or points of interest.   p. 70

**Hallucinogen**   A drug that affects the senses and distorts the user's perception and vision.   p. 215

**Hand-over-hand steering**   Method of turning the steering wheel by crossing one hand over the other.   p. 44

**Hand signals**   Arm motions or positions that alert other drivers that one is slowing, stopping, or turning right or left.   p. 63

**Headlights**   Lights mounted on the front of a vehicle for use at night or in reduced lighting conditions.   p. 25

**Head restraint**   A padded device, sometimes adjustable, extending above the front seat-back; designed to reduce whiplash or neck injuries.   p. 28

**High beams**   A headlight setting that projects light farther ahead of a vehicle than lowbeams.   p. 25

**Highway transportation system (HTS)**   The network of roadway environments, people who use the roadways, and the vehicles they use.   p. 4

**Hydroplaning**   The riding of wheels on top of a layer of water rather than on the road surface.   p. 181

**Identify**   The first step of the driving strategy IPDE. It is the process of searching for and recognizing any part of the HTS that may affect a driver.   p. 98

**Idle**   The rate at which the engine runs when the accelerator is not used.   p. 24

**Ignition switch**   The switch, usually located on the steering column, that is turned by a key to activate the vehicle's electrical system and start the engine.   p. 21

**Ignition system**   The automotive system used to start a vehicle and to send an electrical charge to the spark plugs.   p. 21

**Immediate path of travel**   The distance a moving vehicle can cover in four seconds.   p. 108

**Implied-consent law**   Legal requirement that drivers submit to a BAC test when asked to do so or lose their licenses to drive.   p. 222

**Inertia**   The tendency of a moving object to continue in a straight line unless acted upon by an outside force.   p. 87

**Instruction permit**   A state-issued, temporary, restricted license that allows a person to use the roadways when learning how to drive.   p. 9

**Instrument panel**   The panel directly in front of the driver on which are located various indicators, gauges, and controls. p. 18

**Intersection**   The place at which two or more streets cross one another.   p. 125

**Interval rule**   The principle stating that you should maintain at least a 2-second following distance.   p. 108

**IPDE**   Abbreviation for *identify, predict, decide, execute* — a driving strategy for gathering, interpreting, and acting on traffic information.   p. 98

**Jumper cables**   Cables used to carry an electrical charge from the battery of a working vehicle to the dead battery of another vehicle.   p. 189

**Junction**   The area where two or more roadways meet.   p. 143

**Kinetic energy**   Energy of motion.   p. 87

**KPH or km/h**   Abbreviations for kilometers per hour — that is, number of kilometers traveled in one hour.   p. 19

**Lane-use signals**   Signals that show which lanes are open to traffic.   p. 72

**Lateral access**   Areas such as intersections where pedestrians or vehicles can enter your driving path.   p. 113

**Legend**   Key explaining the symbols and markings used on a road map.   p. 247

**Liability insurance**   Insurance coverage that protects a driver from financial loss due to injuries or damage he or she may have caused others or their property. p. 241

**Low beams**   The normal setting for headlights.   p. 25

**Lubricating system**   The automotive system that keeps parts of the engine oiled to help prevent damage or overheating caused by friction.   p. 265

**Maintenance**   The checkups, service, and repairs needed to keep one's vehicle in good operating condition.   p. 256

**Master-brake cylinder**   Unit in hydraulic braking system in which fluid is stored and from which it is forced through the system to the wheel cylinders.   p. 259

**Median strip**   An area on a highway that separates opposing lanes of traffic.   p. 149

**Medical payments insurance**   Insurance that covers the cost of hospitalization and treatments for passengers who are injured in a collision.   p. 243

**Merging**   The gradual blending together of vehicles in traffic.   p. 150

**Minimal insurance coverage**   The least amount of automobile insurance made available to drivers.   p. 242

**Minimizing hazards**   Reducing chances of becoming involved in a collision by adjusting speed, changing lane position, or both.   p. 104

**Minimum-maximum speed limits**   The slowest and fastest posted speeds at which you can legally drive under normal conditions.   p. 149

**MPH**   Abbreviation for miles per hour; that is, the number of miles traveled in one hour.   p. 65

**Multilane roads**   Roads with two or more lanes in each direction.   p. 129

**Neutral**   The gear in which no power is transmitted to the drive wheels.   p. 23

**Night blindness**   Inability to see well at night.   p. 201

**Night vision**   One's visual acuity, depth perception, and glare recovery after dusk and before dawn.   p. 200

**No-fault insurance**   An insurance plan that requires insurance companies to pay personal injury claims to those insured by them regardless of which driver was at fault in a collision.   p. 242

**No-passing lines**   Solid yellow lines that separate lanes of opposing traffic.   p. 74

**Odometer**   Indicator that measures total distance a vehicle has been driven.   p. 19

**Oil filter**   Device that cleans dirt from the oil in the engine's lubricating system. p. 265

**Oil-pressure gauge**   Gauge or light that shows the pressure at which the oil pump is forcing oil to the moving parts of the engine.   p. 21

**Oil pump**   Pump that moves oil from the oil pan to parts of the engine needing oil. p. 266

**One-way street**   A street on which all traffic moves in the same direction.   p. 130

**Overpass**   A bridge that carries one roadway over another; also a bridge that carries railway tracks over a street or highway.   p. 149

**Oversteering**   Steering more than necessary when changing lanes, avoiding a hazard, or correcting a skid.   p. 39

**Over-the-counter drug**   Drug that can be legally obtained without a prescription. p. 213

**Owner's manual**   A booklet giving the vehicle owner detailed information about the vehicle and instructions for its operation.   p. 20

**Parallel parking spaces**   Parking spaces arranged parallel to the curb or side of the road.   p. 52

**Parking brake**   A manually set brake used when the car is parked to keep it from rolling.   p. 23

**Parking lights**   Lights that come on in the front of a vehicle when the light switch is pulled out halfway or turned partially. p. 26

**Partially controlled intersections**   Intersections where at least one approach is regulated by a stop or yield sign. p. 127

**Passive restraints**   Safety devices that help prevent occupants from striking the dashboard or windshield in a collision; they operate without requiring any action by either driver or passengers.   p. 28

**Passive safety belts**   Lap and shoulder restraints that automatically connect from the door to the seat when the door is closed.   p. 93

**Pavement markings**   Yellow or white markings painted onto the road surface that help to regulate traffic, define lanes, and warn of possible dangers.   p. 73

**Pedestrian** Anyone walking in the HTS. p. 3

**Pedestrian signals** Signals that guide pedestrians across traffic paths. p. 72

**Perception time** The time it takes to identify, predict, and decide. p. 90.

**Peripheral vision** Side vision; the outer edges of one's field of vision. p. 200

**Perpendicular parking spaces** Parking spaces arranged side by side at right angles to the curb or side of the road. p. 51

**Policy** A contract between a vehicle owner and an insurance company that states the amount and kind of insurance coverage provided. p. 241

**Posted speed limit** The maximum speed limit considered safe for the road and traffic conditions; shown on a road sign. p. 65

**Power skid** A skid that results from sudden or hard acceleration. p. 185

**Power steering** A device that uses some form of power — such as electricity, liquids, compressed air, or a vacuum — to help the driver turn the steering wheel. p. 38

**Predict** The second step of the IPDE process in which a driver evaluates how and if a situation may affect him or her. p. 101

**Premium** The payment made by a vehicle owner to the insurance company for its policy. p. 241

**Prescription drugs** Drugs that can be purchased legally only when prescribed by a doctor. p. 213

**Preventive maintenance** Inspection and servicing of vehicle systems to prevent costly repairs or breakdowns. p. 258

**Prohibitory signs** Signs that tell you what you cannot do. They consist of a black symbol crossed by a red bar and enclosed in a circle. p. 68

**Pumping the brake** Applying pressure on the brake pedal, then releasing it, and repeating the action. p. 147

**Radial tires** Tires constructed with plies running straight across the tire from one side to the other and encircled by belts of nylon or steel material. p. 260

**Radiator** Container where water is stored and cooled before it circulates around the engine. p. 264

**Ramps** Those portions of a roadway, usually banked, that are used for entering or exiting an expressway. p. 148

**Reaction distance** Distance a vehicle travels during reaction time. p. 90

**Reaction time** Time that elapses between the moment a hazard is identified and the moment a driver acts. p. 90

**Recreational vehicles (RV's)** Vehicles, such as campers or motor homes, used for traveling and recreational activities. p. 167

**Registered vehicle** A vehicle that has been officially licensed by the state in which the vehicle owner resides. p. 240

**Regulatory signs** Traffic signs that tell what a driver must or must not do under penalty of the law. p. 68

**Reverse gear** Gear that allows the vehicle to move backward. p. 23

**Revocation of license** Cancellation by the state of a legal permit to drive a vehicle. p. 223

**Right of way** The right to go first. Traffic rules indicate who has the legal right of way. p. 63

**Risk** A potential danger. p. 114

**Risk-takers** Drivers who deliberately expose themselves to hazards and endanger other highway users. p. 114

**Roadway markings** Markings on pavement separating lanes of travel or indicating what a driver may do. p. 73

**Rocking a vehicle**   Alternately moving a vehicle backward and then forward several times in succession so as to drive out of snow, mud, or sand.   p. 182

**Route marker**   A sign indicating the number of a highway; the shape and color of the sign depend on the kind of highway.   p. 70

**Rumble strip**   A section of rippled concrete that alerts drivers to slow or stop.   p. 144

**Safety belt**   A belt anchored to the vehicle frame. It prevents the passengers from being thrown against parts of the interior of the vehicle or being thrown from the vehicle in the event of a collision.   p. 28

**Safety helmet**   A protective head covering worn by motorcyclists and bicycle riders.   p. 164

**Scanning**   Examining the immediate area around your vehicle for possible hazards.   p. 101

**Separating hazards**   Dealing with multiple hazards one at a time.   p. 105

**Service brake**   The foot control located to the left of the accelerator that slows or stops the vehicle.   p. 22

**Shock absorbers**   Devices that absorb the bouncing action of the wheels.   p. 262

**Side vision**   The ability to see objects to the side while looking straight ahead.   p. 200

**Skidding**   Loss of traction between automobile tires and the road surface.   p. 185

**Space cushion**   The traffic-free zone that a driver should maintain around his or her vehicle.   p. 109

**Speedometer**   A gauge that indicates how fast a vehicle is traveling.   p. 19

**Standard transmission**   A system in which gears are selected manually by using the gearshift lever and the clutch pedal.   p. 24

**Stimulants**   Drugs such as caffeine that speed up the central nervous system. p. 215

**Stop lines**   Solid white strips across lanes controlled by a signal or stop sign.   p. 75

**Stopping distance**   The total distance required to stop a vehicle. Perception distance plus reaction distance plus braking distance equals total stopping distance.   p. 110

**Strategy**   A plan for driving that prepares a driver for changing conditions.   p. 98

**Suspension of license**   Withdrawal by the state of a person's license for a given period of time.   p. 77

**Swerving path time**   The amount of time it takes to steer a car off the immediate travel path — usually two seconds.   p. 111

**Tailgating**   Following too closely behind another vehicle.   p. 109

**Taillights**   Red lights on the rear of a vehicle. They turn on when the headlights or parking lights are turned on.   p. 25

**Temperature gauge**   The gauge or light that warns you if the engine temperature goes above a safe level.   p. 20

**Thermostat**   A device that controls the temperature of the engine by controlling the flow of the cooling liquid through the radiator.   p. 264

**Title**   Legal proof of vehicle ownership.   p. 240

**Towing**   Pulling of one vehicle by another.   p. 243

**Towing insurance**   Optional vehicle insurance that covers the cost of towing or on-the-road repairs.   p. 243

**Traction**   The contact between the tire and road surface; the adhesive or holding quality of friction.   p. 86

**Traffic**   The flow of all motor vehicles and pedestrians along the streets and the highways.   p. 82

**Traffic-activated signals**   System in which traffic signals automatically give the green light to vehicles that trigger a sensor.   p. 127

**Traffic-control devices**   The signs, signals, and markings used in the highway transportation system.   p. 66

**Traffic-signal lights**   Traffic controls that usually are located at intersections to regulate traffic flow.   p. 71

**Transmission**   A mechanism with gears that transfers power from the engine to the drive shaft which, in turn, carries it to the axle shafts.   p. 23

**Tread**   The raised pattern on the face of a tire that enables the tire to grip the road.   p. 261

**Trip odometer**   An odometer that can be reset to zero; used to determine the distance driven over a particular period.   p. 19

**Turn signals**   Lights on a motor vehicle or hand signals used to indicate left or right turns.   p. 26

**Twelve-second visual lead**   The technique of centering one's vision on the highway to where his or her vehicle will be in 12 seconds in order to identify hazards.   p. 167

**Two-second interval**   The minimum following distance for vehicles under ideal conditions.   p. 108

**Uncontrolled intersection**   An intersection that has no signs or signals regulating it.   p. 128

**Uniform Motor Vehicle Code**   Vehicle laws recommended by a national committee and used in part by all states.   p. 67

**Uninsured motorist insurance**   Protection from certain financial losses resulting from a collision caused by a driver who does not have insurance protection.   p. 243

**Universal joints**   Connections that move so that power may be transmitted from one shaft to another.   p. 268

**Utility vehicle**   A four-wheel drive vehicle.   p. 167

**U-turn**   A complete turn-around without having to back.   p. 48

**Velocitization**   The sensation of moving more slowly than one actually is, usually experienced when exiting a highway or expressway.   p. 152

**Visual acuity**   The measure of a person's ability to see clearly.   p. 200

**Visual lead time**   The time and space a driver has available for identifying and reacting to a traffic situation.   p. 99

**Warning signs**   Traffic signs that alert drivers to potential hazards ahead.   p. 69

**Warranty**   A written guarantee that a maker will replace or repair defective parts for a certain amount of time or number of miles a vehicle is used.   p. 240

**Washboard surface**   A road surface with ridges crossing the road at right angles.   p. 142

**Water pump**   Pump that circulates water through the radiator and the engine block.   p. 265

**Wear bars**   Tread-wear indicators built into tires that appear when tread depth is about 1/16 inch.   p. 261

**Wheel alignment**   Mechanical lining up of a vehicle's front wheels.   p. 262

**Wheel bearings**   Devices that reduce friction of motion in the wheels.   p. 268

**Y-turn**   A turn made by turning left as sharply as possible until the front wheel approaches the opposite curb, backing the car, straightening it, and then proceeding forward.   p. 48

# In-Car Guide

## Outside Checks

☐ **1. Check around the front, rear, and sides of the car for possible hazards.**

☐ **2. Inspect the lights and body of the car for any damage. Be sure the lights are clean.**

☐ **3. Be sure the tires are properly inflated.**

☐ **4. Look for leaking fluids under the car.**

☐ **5. Check for any broken glass on or around the car.**

☐ **6. Be sure the windows are clear.**

☐ **7. Check for pedestrians and animals under or around the car.**

☑ Check each item that you performed competently. Work to improve on the other items.

# Inside Checks

☐ **1.** Lock the doors.

☐ **2.** Adjust the seat properly. Adjust the head restraint (if it is adjustable) so that it supports the middle of the back of your head.

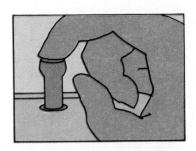
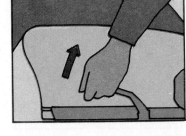

☐ **3.** Adjust both the inside and outside rearview mirrors.

☐ **4.** Fasten and tighten your safety belt. Be sure any passengers have fastened theirs.

☐ **5.** Locate the driving controls you will be using (steering wheel, gear selector, accelerator, brake, clutch, parking brake).

☐ **6.** Locate the safety and communication devices you may be using (turn signal lever, headlight switch, windshield wiper/washer switch, horn, dimmer switch, emergency flashers).

☞ Check each item that you performed competently. Work to improve on the other items.

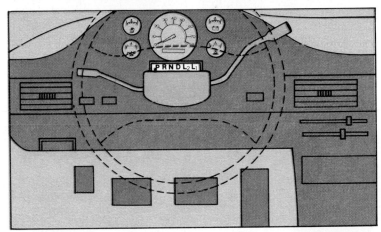

## Starting the Engine

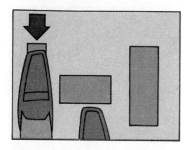

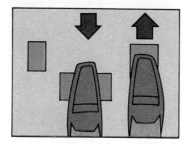
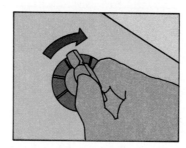

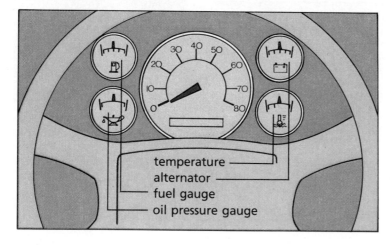

temperature
alternator
fuel gauge
oil pressure gauge

☐ **1.** Be sure that the parking brake is set.

☐ **2.** Check to see that the car is in PARK. In a standard-shift car, use NEUTRAL and press in the clutch.

☐ **3.** If the engine is cold, press the accelerator to the floor and release it to set the automatic choke.

☐ **4.** Move your foot to cover the service brake pedal.

☐ **5.** Turn the key in the ignition switch to start the car. Release the key as soon as the engine starts.

☐ **6.** Check the gauges on the instrument panel to be sure all systems are working properly (fuel gauge, temperature gauge, oil pressure gauge, alternator gauge).

☑ Check each item that you performed competently. Work to improve on the other items.

## Steering

☐ **1.** Place your hands on the steering wheel. Place your right hand between 2 and 3 o'clock and your left hand between 9 and 10 o'clock.

☐ **2.** To turn left, pull the wheel down with your left hand and turn the wheel to the left with your right hand. Release your left hand when it nears the 7 o'clock position.

☐ **3.** Continue to turn the wheel to the left with your right hand. At the same time, cross your left hand over the right and grasp the wheel with it.

☐ **4.** Take your right hand off the wheel. Continue turning the wheel to the left with your left hand.

☐ **5.** When you have turned the wheel enough to make the turn, move both hands to a good control position. Hold the wheel until the car is about two thirds of the way through the turn.

☐ **6.** Release your grip slightly and let the wheel slip slowly through your hands until the wheel is centered.

☑ Check each item that you performed competently. Work to improve on the other items.

## Moving the Car Forward

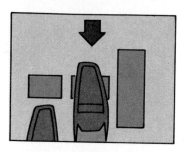

☐ **1.** Firmly press the service brake pedal and shift to DRIVE. In a standard shift, press in the clutch, press the service brake pedal, and shift from NEUTRAL to FIRST.

☐ **2.** Release the parking brake.

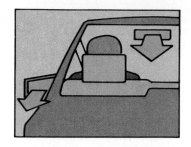

☐ **3.** Check the mirrors for approaching traffic. Glance back over your shoulder to check your blind spot.

☐ **4.** Signal your intent to pull away from the curb.

☐ **5.** Just before you begin to move forward, glance over your shoulder again. If no traffic is approaching, look forward into your intended path.

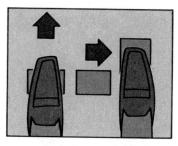

☐ **6.** Release the brake pedal and press down slowly on the gas pedal. In a standard shift, let up on the clutch until you reach the friction point.

☐ **7.** Gently press on the gas pedal to move into the proper lane. In a standard shift, continue to let the clutch up slowly.

☞ Check each item that you performed competently. Work to improve on the other items.

## Starting on a Hill

### Automatic

☐ **1. Press the service brake pedal with your left foot.**

☐ **2. At the same time, press the gas pedal with your right foot.**

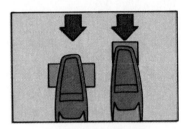

☐ **3. Gradually apply more pressure to the accelerator as you start to release the brake pedal.**

**take your foot completely off the brake. Continue to accelerate.**

☑ Check each item that you performed competently. Work to improve on the other items.

☐ **4. When the car begins to move forward,**

Note
Alternate method: Set the parking brake. Accelerate until you feel the engine pulling against the brake. Release the parking brake and continue to accelerate.

### Standard Shift

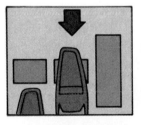 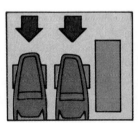 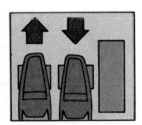 

☐ **1. Press the service brake pedal with your right foot.**

☐ **2. Press in the clutch with your left foot and shift to FIRST.**

☐ **3. Let up the clutch until it reaches the friction point. Hold it at this point.**

☐ **4. Take your foot off the brake and press the accelerator.**

☐ **5. Let up the clutch slowly as you accelerate.**

☑ Check each item that you performed competently. Work to improve on the other items.

Note
Alternate method: Set the parking brake. Let the clutch up until it reaches the friction point and press the accelerator slowly. Continue to let the clutch up as you accelerate, then release the parking brake.

## Slowing and Stopping

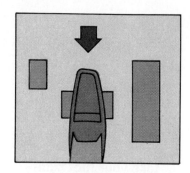
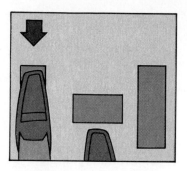

☐ **1. Check the mirrors for traffic and glance over your shoulder to check your blind spot.**

☐ **2. Take your foot off the accelerator to slow gradually before you apply the brakes.**

☐ **3. Use your turn signal to indicate that you are pulling over.**

☐ **4. Press the service brake gently but firmly. In a standard shift, also press in and hold down the clutch with your left foot.**

☐ **5. Just before you actually stop, decrease the pressure on the brake slightly for a fraction of a second. Then, reapply pressure firmly to the brake pedal.**

☐ **6. When you have stopped, shift to PARK. In a standard shift, use REVERSE. Then, set the parking brake, turn off the ignition, and take the keys.**

☑ Check each item that you performed competently. Work to improve on the other items.

## In a Straight Path

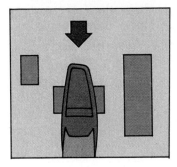

☐ **1.** Place your foot on the service brake.

☐ **2.** Shift to REVERSE and release the parking brake.

☐ **3.** Before backing, be sure to look over both shoulders for pedestrians, obstacles, and other vehicles in your path.

☐ **4.** Turn to the right in the seat and look back over your right shoulder. To help maintain this position, you may want to put your right arm across the top of the seat or behind the head restraint to support yourself.

☐ **5.** Put your left hand at the top of the steering wheel (12 o'clock). Keep in mind that with only one hand on the wheel, it is difficult to make major steering adjustments.

☐ **6.** Remove most of the pressure from the service brake, but keep the brake covered. If necessary, press the accelerator slightly to begin moving.

☐ **7.** As soon as the car begins moving, remove your foot from the gas pedal and cover the brake. Often you can control speed in REVERSE with the brake, rather than the gas.

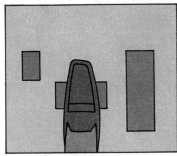

☐ **8.** Continue to look back until you reach the desired point. Then, brake gently to stop the car smoothly.

☑ Check each item that you performed competently. Work to improve on the other items.

## To the Right

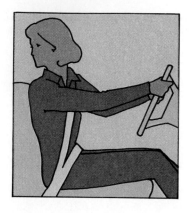

☐ **1. Turn in the seat and look over your right shoulder.**

☐ **2. Pull the steering wheel down to the right with your left hand. Use the hand-over-hand steering method for sharp turns.**

☐ **3. As you back, glance ahead occasionally to** check the front and sides to be sure your car is clearing all obstacles.

☐ **4. As you begin to stop, "shuffle" the steering wheel to straighten the wheels.**

☑ Check each item that you performed competently. Work to improve on the other items.

## To the Left

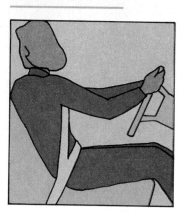

☐ **1. Turn in the seat and look over your left shoulder.**

☐ **2. Pull the steering wheel down to the left with your right hand. Use the hand-over-hand steering method for sharp turns.**

☐ **3. As you back, glance ahead occasionally to check the front and sides to be sure your car is clearing all obstacles.**

☐ **4. As you begin to stop, "shuffle" the steering wheel to straighten the wheels.**

☑ Check each item that you performed competently. Work to improve on the other items.

# Changing Lanes

## To the Left

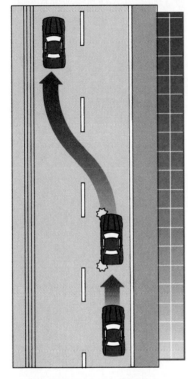

☐ **1.** Check for traffic in the inside rearview mirror.

☐ **2.** Look for traffic in the outside rearview mirror.

☐ **3.** Check over your left shoulder for vehicles in your blind spot.

☐ **4.** When the way is clear, signal to move left.

☐ **5.** Move gradually into the left lane. Center your vehicle in the lane, and maintain your speed.

☐ **6.** If necessary, cancel your turn signal after you complete the lane change.

☞ Check each item that you performed competently. Work to improve on the other items.

## To the Right

☐ **1.** Check for traffic in the inside rearview mirror.

☐ **2.** Look over your right shoulder for vehicles in your blind spot.

☐ **3.** When the way is clear, signal to move right.

☐ **4.** Move gradually into the right lane. Center your vehicle in the lane, and maintain your speed.

☐ **5.** If necessary, cancel your turn signal after you complete the lane change.

☞ Check each item that you performed competently. Work to improve on the other items.

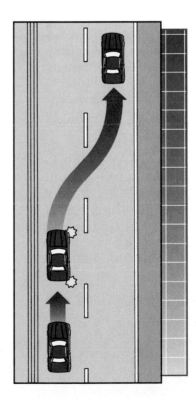

# Passing

☐ **1.** Be sure it is legal to pass and make certain the way ahead is clear.

☐ **2.** Check both mirrors to be certain you are not being passed. Glance over your left shoulder to check your blind spot.

☐ **3.** Signal left, and check ahead again to be sure the way is clear.

☐ **4.** Speed up at least 10 mph faster than the car you are passing. Move smoothly into the passing lane.

☐ **5.** Recheck the space ahead.

☐ **6.** Check your inside mirror. When both headlights of the car you have just passed are visible in the mirror, signal right and check your blind spot.

☐ **7.** Move smoothly into the right lane.

☐ **8.** Cancel your signal and adjust your speed if necessary.

☑ Check each item that you performed competently. Work to improve on the other items.

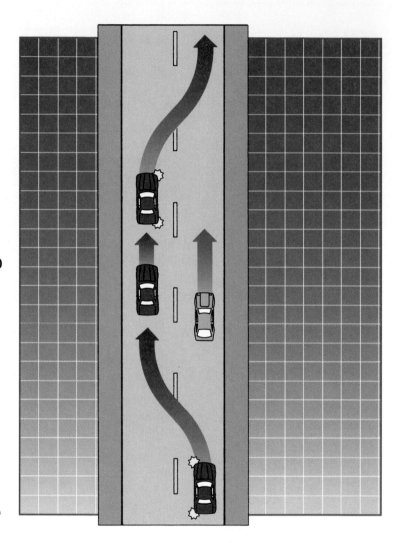

## Right Turn

☐ **1.** Be sure the planned turn is legal.

☐ **2.** Signal for the turn at least 100 feet before the turn.

☐ **3.** Check for traffic in the inside rearview mirror and over your right shoulder.

☐ **4.** Move to the proper lane position.

☐ **5.** Check the intersection for vehicles and pedestrians. Look ahead, left, right, ahead, left, right.

☐ **6.** Ease up on the gas pedal, and brake just before the turn.

☐ **7.** Ease your foot off the brake. At the corner, turn the wheel using the hand-over-hand method. Yield to other vehicles and pedestrians.

☐ **8.** Look well up the street into which you are turning.

☐ **9.** When you are half-way around the turn, straighten the steering wheel as you press the gas pedal gently. Use

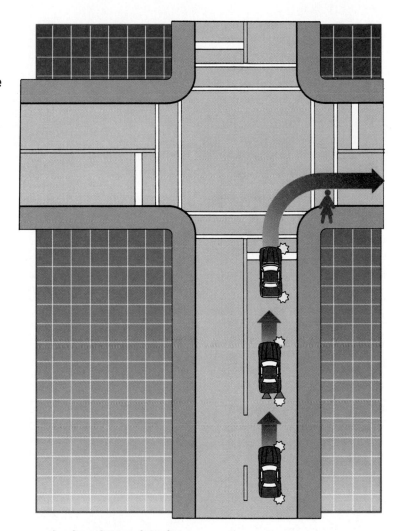

the hand-over-hand technique, if necessary, to unwind the wheel.

☑ Check each item that you performed competently. Work to improve on the other items.

# Left Turn

□ **1.** Be sure the planned turn is legal.

□ **2.** Signal the turn at least 100 feet before the turn.

□ **3.** Check for traffic in the inside rearview mirror and over your left shoulder.

□ **4.** Move to the proper lane position.

□ **5.** Check the intersection for vehicles and pedestrians. Look left, right, ahead, left, right, ahead, left.

□ **6.** Ease up on the gas pedal and brake just before the turn. However, keep the wheels straight.

□ **7.** Ease your foot off the brake. At the corner, turn the wheel using the hand-over-hand method. Yield to other vehicles and pedestrians.

□ **8.** Check for vehicles in the oncoming lane to your right. Then look out the left window down the street into which you are turning.

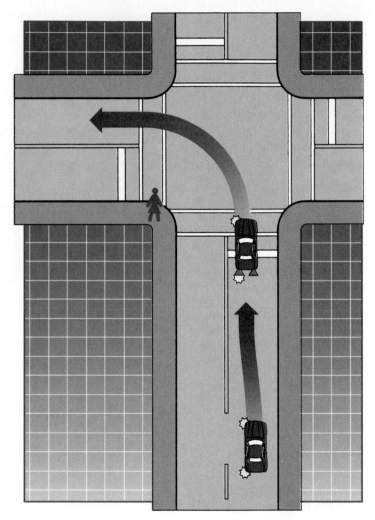

□ **9.** Straighten the steering wheel as you press the gas pedal gently. Use the hand-over-hand technique, if necessary, to unwind the wheel.

☑ Check each item that you performed competently. Work to improve on the other items.

# U-turn

☐ **1. Check for traffic in your rearview mirrors and glance over your right shoulder to check your blind spot.**

☐ **2. Signal a right turn.**

☐ **3. Pull over to the side of the road and stop close to the curb or roadside.**

☐ **4. Check for oncoming traffic and signal a left turn.**

☐ **5. Glance over your left shoulder to check for approaching traffic. Check ahead again.**

☐ **6. Accelerate gently while rapidly turning the steering wheel to the left. Use the hand-over-hand method to turn the wheel sharply.**

☐ **7. As you complete the turn, straighten the wheels and drive on, checking behind for traffic.**

☑ Check each item that you performed competently. Work to improve on the other items.

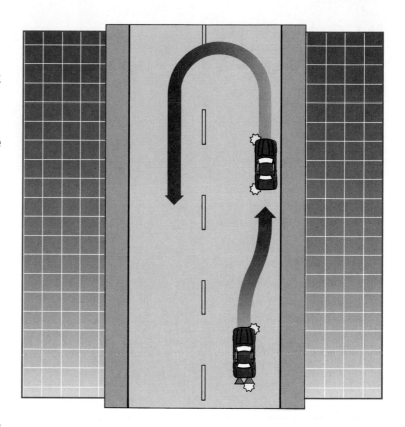

# Y-turn

☐ **1.** Check the rearview mirror. Glance over your right shoulder, and signal right.

☐ **2.** Pull over to the right and stop close to the curb or roadside.

☐ **3.** Glance over your shoulder to check for traffic. When the way is clear, signal for a left turn. Check ahead.

☐ **4.** Accelerate gently while rapidly turning the wheel to the left.

☐ **5.** When the front of the car is close to the curb, turn the wheel rapidly to the right. Stop before you touch the curb.

☐ **6.** Shift to REVERSE. Check for traffic, and begin to back slowly. Look primarily over your right shoulder as you turn rapidly to the right.

☐ **7.** When you have backed far enough for your right front wheel to clear the curb as you drive ahead, turn the wheel rapidly to the left and stop.

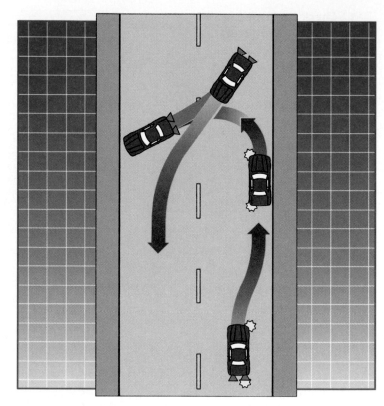

☐ **8.** Shift to DRIVE, check for traffic, and proceed.

☑ Check each item that you performed competently. Work to improve on the other items.

# Backing into an Alley

☐ **1.** Check for vehicles in the inside rearview mirror.

☐ **2.** Signal to move right. Check over your right shoulder.

☐ **3.** Stop the car about half a car length beyond the alley or driveway. The car should be about two feet from the curb.

☐ **4.** Check to see that there is no traffic behind you and shift into REVERSE.

☐ **5.** Turn the wheel to the right using hand-over-hand steering. Look to the rear primarily over your right shoulder.

☐ **6.** Stop your car when it is completely in the alley. The front wheels should be straight or slightly to the left. Shift into DRIVE.

☐ **7.** Signal to move left. Check to the left and right for approaching traffic.

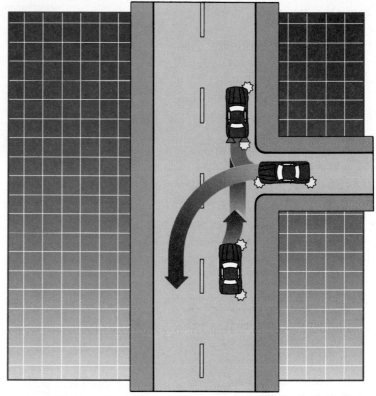

☐ **8.** Proceed into the proper lane.

☑ Check each item that you performed competently. Work to improve on the other items.

## Backing Out of an Alley

### On the Right

☐ **1.** Check for traffic in the rearview mirrors and over your shoulder. Signal a right turn.

☐ **2.** Turn into the middle of the alley. Stop when your car is completely off the street.

☐ **3.** Check to see that no traffic is approaching and shift to RE-VERSE. Signal left and begin backing slowly out of the alley.

☐ **4.** If there is a sidewalk, stop to check for pedestrians. Stop at the street to look for approaching traffic.

☐ **5.** Continue to back slowly into the street, rapidly turning the wheel to the left. Look to the rear primarily over your left shoulder. Glance at the front and sides of your car to be sure it is clearing all objects.

☐ **6.** Look over your right shoulder to position the car properly in the intended lane.

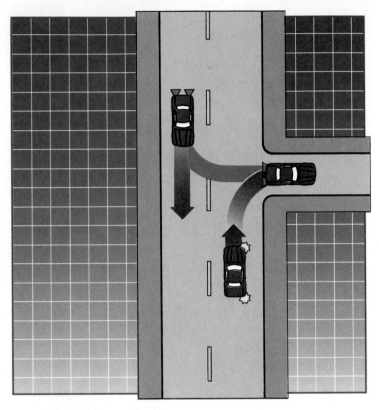

☐ **7.** Straighten the car by moving the steering wheel to the right. Stop and shift to DRIVE.

☐ **8.** Gradually accelerate into the lane of traffic.

☑ Check each item that you performed competently. Work to improve on the other items.

# Backing Out of an Alley

## On the Left

☐ **1.** Signal for a left turn and flash your brake lights to indicate that you are slowing. Check over your left shoulder to be sure no one is passing you.

☐ **2.** Turn left into the alley when it is safe to do so. Stop when your car is clear of the street.

☐ **3.** Keep your foot on the brake and shift to REVERSE. Check to see that no traffic is approaching.

☐ **4.** Begin to back slowly as you turn the steering wheel quickly to the right. If there is a sidewalk, stop to check for pedestrians. Stop at the street to check for approaching traffic.

☐ **5.** Continue to back slowly into the street, turning the wheel rapidly to the right. Look to the rear primarily over your right shoulder while backing. Check to see if the

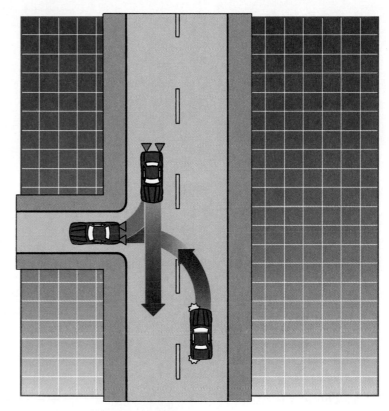

front of the car is clear of the alley.

☐ **6.** Straighten the car by turning the steering wheel to the left. Stop the car and shift to DRIVE, then proceed.

☑ Check each item that you performed competently. Work to improve on the other items.

## Entering a Diagonal Space

☐ **1. Check for traffic in the rearview mirror. Look over your right shoulder to check your blind spot. Tap your brake pedal once or twice to warn other drivers that you are slowing.**

☐ **2. Signal a right turn.**

☐ **3. When you can see into your parking space, turn the steering wheel sharply to the right using hand-over-hand steering.**

☐ **4. Enter the space slowly, checking your left front bumper and right rear fender to be sure they clear other vehicles.**

☐ **5. Center the car in the space and straighten the wheels.**

☐ **6. Stop before you touch the curb, shift to PARK, and set the parking brake. In a standard shift, use REVERSE.**

☞ Check each item that you performed competently. Work to improve on the other items.

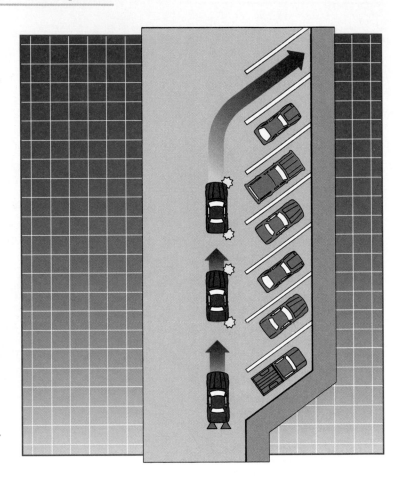

# Leaving a Diagonal Space

☐ **1.** Be sure the wheels are straight. Check to see that no traffic is approaching and shift into REVERSE.

☐ **2.** Back slowly, keeping your foot on the brake to control your speed. When your steering wheel is even with the back of the car to your right, turn the steering wheel sharply to the right using hand-over-hand steering.

☐ **3.** Continue to back, looking primarily over your right shoulder for approaching traffic. Glance at your left front bumper and right rear fender occasionally to be sure they clear other vehicles.

☐ **4.** When you have backed into the travel lane, straighten the wheels by steering to the left and stop.

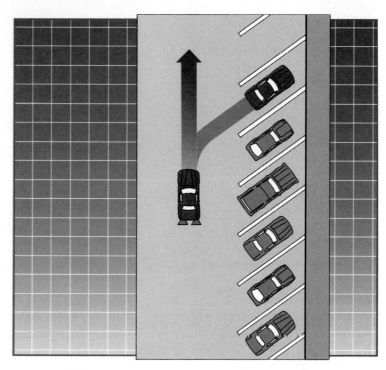

☐ **5.** Shift to DRIVE, check for traffic, and proceed.

☑ Check each item that you performed competently. Work to improve on the other items.

## Entering a Perpendicular Space

☐ **1. Check for traffic in the rearview mirror. Check your blind spot. Tap your brake pedal once or twice to warn other drivers that you are slowing.**

☐ **2. Signal a right turn.**

☐ **3. When you can see into your parking space, turn the steering wheel sharply to the right using hand-over-hand steering.**

☐ **4. Enter the space slowly, checking your left front bumper and right rear fender to be sure they clear other vehicles.**

☐ **5. Center the car in the space and straighten the wheels.**

☐ **6. Stop before you touch the curb, shift to PARK, and set the parking brake. In a standard shift, use REVERSE.**

☑ Check each item that you performed competently. Work to improve on the other items.

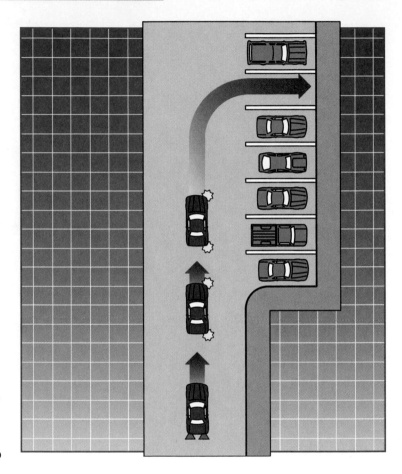

# Leaving a Perpendicular Space

☐ **1. Be sure the wheels are straight. Check to see that no traffic is approaching and shift into REVERSE.**

☐ **2. Back slowly, keeping your foot lightly on the brake. When your steering wheel is even with the back of the car on your right, turn the steering wheel sharply to the right using hand-over-hand steering.**

☐ **3. Continue to back, looking primarily over your right shoulder for approaching traffic or other parked cars. Glance at your left front bumper and right rear fender occasionally to be sure they clear other vehicles.**

☐ **4. When you have backed into the travel lane, straighten the wheels by steering to the left and stop.**

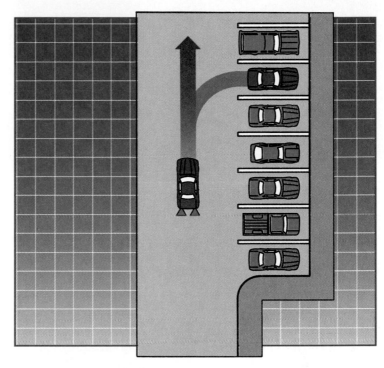

☐ **5. Shift to DRIVE, check for traffic, and proceed.**

☑ Check each item that you performed competently. Work to improve on the other items.

# Entering a Parallel Space

☐ **1.** Check for traffic in the rearview mirror and over your shoulder. Then signal a right turn.

☐ **2.** Drive past the space. Stop when your car is alongside the car parked ahead of the space you have chosen. The side of your car should be about 2 feet from the side of this car.

☐ **3.** Check to see that no traffic is approaching, then shift into RE-VERSE. Keep the brake covered.

☐ **4.** Turn the steering wheel to the right using hand-over-hand steering while you back slowly into the space.

☐ **5.** When the front seat of your car is even with the rear bumper of the car ahead, begin turning to the left. Glance ahead to be sure the front of your car clears the car ahead, but look mainly behind you.

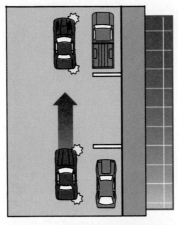

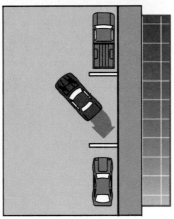

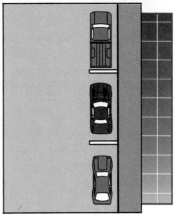

☐ **6.** When your car is parallel to the curb, turn the steering wheel rapidly to the right to straighten the wheels. Stop before you touch the curb.

☐ **7.** Shift to DRIVE and center your car in the space. Then shift to PARK (in a standard shift use REVERSE), and set the parking brake.

☑ Check each item that you performed competently. Work to improve on the other items.

# Leaving a Parallel Space

☐ **1. Shift to REVERSE. Release the parking brake, and back slowly while turning the steering wheel slightly to the right. Look behind you while backing.**

☐ **2. Turn the steering wheel rapidly to the left and stop before you touch the car behind you.**

☐ **3. Shift to DRIVE, check over your left shoulder for traffic, and signal a left turn.**

☐ **4. Continue to turn left as you move forward. Be sure your front bumper clears the car ahead.**

☐ **5. When your car has cleared the rear of the car ahead, turn the wheel to the right to center the car in the travel lane and accelerate to move with the traffic.**

☑ Check each item that you performed competently. Work to improve on the other items.

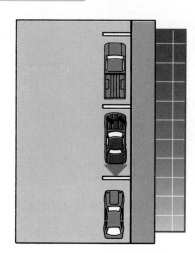
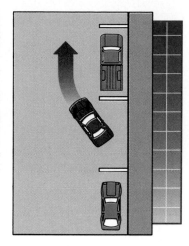

## Uphill

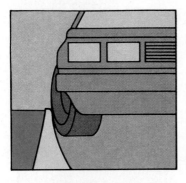 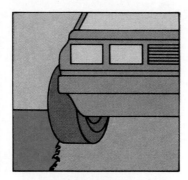

☐ **1. Stop your car about 6 inches from the curb or side of the road.**

☐ **2. As the car slowly rolls back, turn the steering wheel so that the back of the front** **tire closest to the curb touches the curb. If there is no curb, turn the steering wheel so the wheels face the side of the road.**

☐ **3. Shift to PARK (use FIRST in a standard shift) and set the parking brake.**

☞ Check each item that you performed competently. Work to improve on the other items.

## Downhill

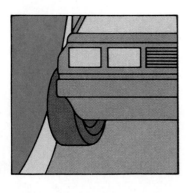

☐ **1. Stop your car about 6 inches from the curb or side of the road.**

☐ **2. As the car slowly rolls forward, turn the wheel sharply toward the curb or the side of the road.**

☐ **3. Shift to PARK (use FIRST or REVERSE in a standard shift) and set the parking brake.**

☞ Check each item that you performed competently. Work to improve on the other items.

# Shifting Forward

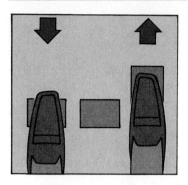

☐ **1. Press the clutch pedal to the floor. At the same time, let up on the gas pedal.**

☐ **2. Move the gearshift lever through the neutral position to the next higher gear.**

**Note**
The speeds at which you will need to shift vary with different cars. Generally, however, shift from FIRST to SECOND at about 15 mph; from SECOND to THIRD at about 20–30 mph; from THIRD to FOURTH at about 30–35 mph; and from FOURTH to FIFTH at about 40–50 mph.

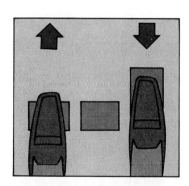

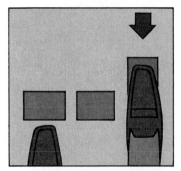

☐ **3. Press down gently on the accelerator as you gradually let up on the clutch.**

☐ **4. Continue to accelerate as you completely release the clutch.**

☑ Check each item that you performed competently. Work to improve on the other items.

## Downshifting

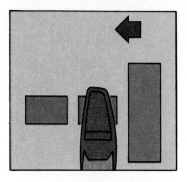

☐ **1.** Take your foot off the accelerator.

☐ **2.** Press the brake pedal to slow the car if necessary.

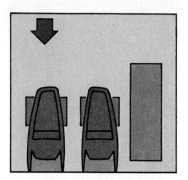

☐ **3.** When you feel the engine begin to labor, press the clutch in.

☐ **4.** Shift to the next lowest gear. (For example, from THIRD to SECOND).

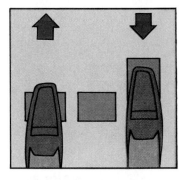

☐ **5.** Let the clutch up gradually as you adjust foot pressure on the gas pedal to reach your desired speed.

☞ Check each item that you performed competently. Work to improve on the other items.

# Entering an Expressway

☐ **1.** Enter the entrance ramp at the suggested speed. If there are other vehicles on the ramp, adjust your speed to match that of the other vehicles.

☐ **2.** When you can see traffic on the expressway, search for a gap large enough for you to move into without interfering with other vehicles. Begin to time your entry to the gap.

☐ **3.** Use the acceleration lane to adjust your speed to match the speed of traffic already on the expressway.

☐ **4.** Check to be sure the gap you chose is still available. If it is, signal to move left, and accelerate to merge smoothly into the traffic.

☐ **5.** Once you are on the expressway, cancel your signal and establish a safe following distance. Remain in the right lane until it is safe to move left.

☑ Check each item that you performed competently. Work to improve on the other items.

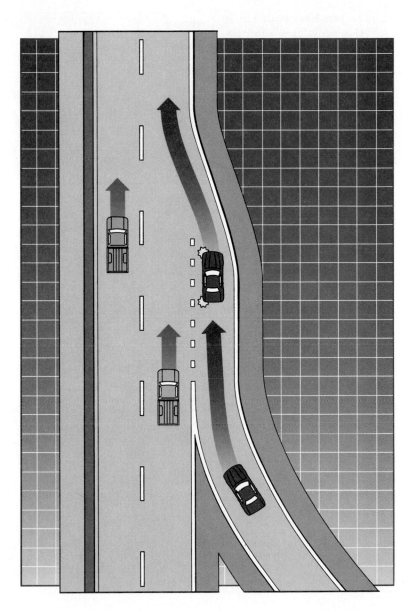

# Exiting an Expressway

☐ **1. Position your car in the right lane well before your planned exit.**

☐ **2. Before you reach your exit, signal right.**

☐ **3. Maintain expressway speed.**

☐ **4. Reduce your speed as soon as you are in the deceleration lane. If there is no deceleration lane, begin to reduce your speed as soon as you are on the exit ramp. Cancel your signal.**

☐ **5. After you leave the expressway, adjust your speed to the posted speeds of the surface roads.**

☑ Check each item that you performed competently. Work to improve on the other items.

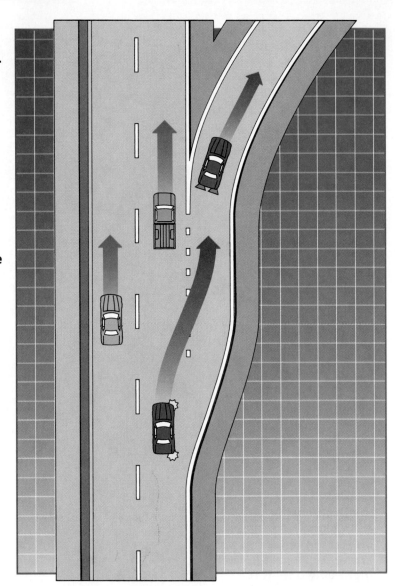

## Accelerator Sticks

 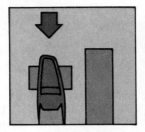  

☐ 1. Try to raise the gas pedal by sliding your foot under the pedal and lifting it.

☐ 2. If that doesn't work, shift to NEUTRAL.

☐ 3. Press the brake pedal to stop the car.

☐ 4. Steer to the side of the road.

☐ 5. Turn off the ignition.

☐ 6. Set the parking brake.

☑ Check each item that you performed competently. Work to improve on the other items.

## Service Brakes Fail

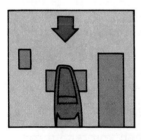 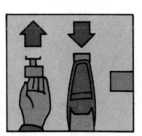  

☐ 1. Quickly pump the brake pedal.

☐ 2. Gradually apply the parking brake while you hold the release lever out to keep the rear wheels from locking. If you have a hand brake, press the re-lease lever as you pull the lever up gradually.

☐ 3. Downshift to slow the engine.

☐ 4. If you cannot stop, honk your horn or flash your lights to warn other drivers.

☐ 5. Steer your car off the road toward something that will yield (such as bushes). Choose a path that minimizes the chances of colliding with other vehicles or people.

☑ Check each item that you performed competently. Work to improve on the other items.

## Steering to Correct a Skid

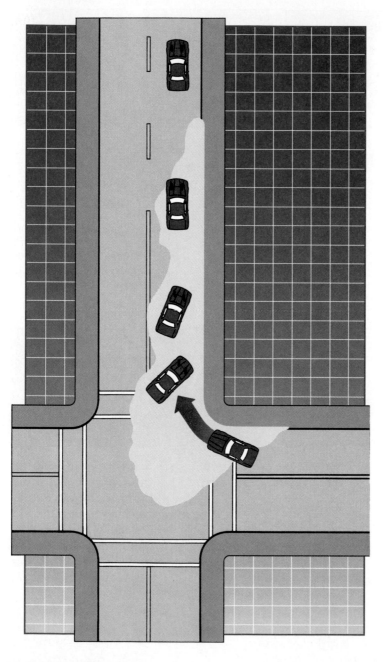

☐ **1.** Take your foot off the gas pedal immediately, but do not apply the brakes.

☐ **2.** With your hands in the 9 and 3 positions, turn the steering wheel in the direction you want the front of the car to go.

☐ **3.** Steer just enough to guide your car back onto a straight course.

☐ **4.** If you steer too sharply, the car may go into a counterskid. To correct a counterskid, steer in the direction you want the front of the car to go.

☐ **5.** Once you regain traction, continue to make small steering adjustments to center your car in the lane. When you regain control, apply the brakes if necessary to slow or stop.

☑ Check each item that you performed competently. Work to improve on the other items.

## Avoiding an Object in Your Lane

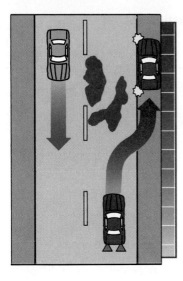

☐ **1.** If possible, straddle the object. If the object is too large, swerve to the right towards the side of the road. (Avoid swerving left into oncoming traffic.)

☐ **2.** Reduce your speed using controlled braking. (If traction is poor, do not use the brakes.)

☐ **3.** After you pass the object, check the mirrors and over your shoulder for traffic before moving onto the roadway.

☐ **4.** Then, signal your intent to move left, and move onto the roadway.

☑ Check each item that you performed competently. Work to improve on the other items.

## Avoiding an Oncoming Car in Your Lane

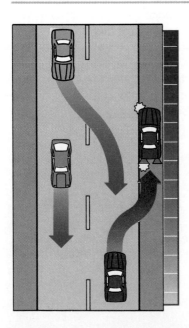

☐ **1.** Swerve quickly to the right towards the side of the road.

☐ **2.** Apply the brakes to reduce your speed. (Do not use the brakes if traction is poor.)

☐ **3.** When the car has passed, check the mirrors and over your shoulder for traffic.

☐ **4.** Then, signal your intent to move left and move onto the roadway.

☑ Check each item that you performed competently. Work to improve on the other items.

# Answer Key to In the Driver's Seat

**Chapter 1**

**Driving in the Highway Transportation System**
1. "David, the belt moves with you."
   "Jennifer, if you put the belt on carefully, you probably won't wrinkle your clothes. Besides, your safety is more important."
   "Marie, some other driver could create an emergency, and I'm not perfect either."
   A general response to all passengers: "Wearing safety belts is a rule to ride in this car."
2. a. Buckle up.
   b. Keep noise and distractions to a minimum.
   c. Keep hands and arms out of the driver's line of vision but always inside the vehicle.
   d. Never dare the driver to do anything illegal or dangerous.
   e. Help out by warning of hazards the driver might have missed.
   f. Give advance directions about any turns or stops.

**Chapter 2**

**Getting Under Way**
1. Before getting in the car, brush the snow off and clear all windows. Make sure headlights and taillights are clear. Check under and around the car—small animals often crawl under cars to sleep in cold weather. Once you are in the car, adjust the seat and mirrors and fasten your safety belt. Start the engine, turn on the defrost, and check the gauges. Once you are under way, you are likely to encounter slippery streets, reduced visibility, stalled or stuck vehicles, collisions, or road equipment. Turn on the headlights and windshield wipers, and drive slowly.
2. Because you are driving an unfamiliar car, take a few minutes to familiarize yourself with the location and operation of the controls, gauges, and lights. Also acquaint yourself with any adjustable equipment, including the seat and mirrors. Remember to fasten your safety belt. Once you have started the engine, listen to it carefully for a moment to determine whether it is running smoothly, and check the gauges to see that everything else is working properly.

**Chapter 3**

**Basic Driving Maneuvers**
1. a. No, the driver should keep the wheels straight while waiting to turn, so that the car would not be pushed into oncoming traffic if hit from behind.

b. Car A should turn into the nearest lane open to traffic going in that direction.

c. The driver of Car A must watch for oncoming traffic, traffic from the left or right going through the red light, and pedestrians crossing the street on the left.

d. Check over the left shoulder and in the mirrors. Signal left and move into the left lane when safe. Yield to oncoming traffic that could create a hazard and keep the wheels straight.

e. Possible hazards include traffic coming from behind, oncoming traffic, a traffic signal change, and drivers from the left or right ignoring the red light.

f. The car should be in the left lane with the turn signal on.

2. As you feel the engine slow, downshift to a lower gear for more power. Going downhill, you should also downshift to prevent the car from building up too much speed. Periodically—but not constantly—apply the service brake to keep your speed slow.

**Chapter 4**

**Traffic Laws for Safety**

1. Check your mirrors, slow down, and be prepared to stop. Watch for children who may try to cross the street from either side. Also be on the lookout for a crossing guard. A "school zone" pavement marking or warning sign would help to alert drivers to the possibility of children crossing. In this situation, the posted speed limit is not appropriate; you should slow well below the 25 mph speed limit.

2. a. You are in a lane that is designated for use by left-turning traffic. If you plan to turn left, continue in this lane; if you plan to continue through the intersection, make a lane change to the right after signaling and making sure the way is clear.

b. A red flashing light means you must come to a stop at this intersection regardless of whether any traffic is present.

c. The yellow crossbar indicates that the lane you are in is about to close. As soon as it is safe to do so, move to another lane that is open.

d. The center lane is reserved for left-turning traffic. Signal left, check for oncoming traffic, and when the way is clear, move into the center lane well ahead of where you want to turn left.

**Chapter 5**

**Natural Laws and Driving**

1. Driver A should release the gas pedal and steer to the right, but avoid oversteering. The service brake should be applied gradually, not suddenly. Driver B should brake and steer to the right, onto the shoulder if necessary, to avoid a collision.

**2.** A crowned road is an advantage to Driver A in this situation, since the road design would help keep the car on a turning path. Both drivers should reduce speed to a safe level and, if possible, downshift and brake before entering the curve.

**Chapter 6**

### A Strategy for Driving

**1.** Barbara should pump the brakes (the flashing brake lights will warn the driver behind that she is stopping) and steer slightly to go around the van. She got into this situation by following too closely considering the icy road conditions and the limited visibility created by the van. She also was not checking the mirrors often enough to see what was behind her. She might have avoided this hazard by maintaining a 4- or 5-second following distance and increasing that when the vehicle behind began to tailgate.

**2.** Student answers will vary but may include some of the following: pedestrians, vehicles turning left in front of oncoming traffic, vehicles not stopping for red light, cars parked on both sides of street, car in left-turn lane proceeding straight ahead.

**Chapter 7**

### Driving in City Traffic

**1.** Reduce your speed well before you reach the intersection. Identify the hazard—the truck partially blocks your view of traffic coming from the right. Predict the action of the truck—even though it is turning right, it may swing partly to the left to make the turn. Execute your move by proceeding slowly through the intersection only when you are sure there is no cross traffic. Avoid facing two hazards at once—the turning truck and possible cross traffic—by reducing speed.

**2.** Check over your left shoulder for traffic. Signal left and move out slowly around the truck when it appears to be safe. Be prepared to stop quickly—the truck driver may get out on your side. You could have been better prepared for this hazard by maintaining at least a 2-second following distance behind the truck so that you could stop far enough behind to see around it or by using a different lane if possible.

**Chapter 8**

### Driving on Highways

**1.** In this situation, the hazards are that Cars B and D may collide, or Car B may swerve into your lane. Car B may continue to pass or could brake hard and try to pull back into the lane behind you. You can flash your brake lights to warn Car B, slow to allow Car B to pass and pull in ahead of you, speed up so Car B can pull in behind you, or swerve to the right. Car D could fail to slow and increase the danger of a collision, slow to give Car B time to complete the passing maneuver, or slow and swerve onto the shoulder to avoid a collision.

2. You should slow, sound your horn to alert the driver of the backing car to your presence, move off the road to the right, and stop. Check for vehicles coming up behind you; these drivers may not identify the hazard at the same time you do. Continue on the exit ramp and get back on the highway at the next available entrance ramp.

**Chapter 9**

**Sharing the Road with Other Users**

1. a. The truck in the right lane makes it difficult for the motorcyclist to see or be seen. Traffic from the right could also create a hazard as the motorcyclist makes a left turn.

   b. The motorcyclist could pull out into the driver's path, since visibility is partially blocked by the truck. Also, the truck may have to make a wide turn partially into the car's lane and cause the driver of the car to slow and/or swerve.

2. You can predict that the bicyclist might swerve into your path to avoid a pothole. Stay in the left third of your lane and give the cyclist plenty of room. Pass the cyclist only when you are sure that oncoming traffic will not create a hazard.

**Chapter 10**

**Road Hazards and Vehicle Failures**

1. Release the gas pedal. Steer in the direction you want the front of the car to go. Once you have regained control, brake gradually to slow the vehicle. Avoid sudden steering or braking as you continue on the snowy surface.

2. You should not drive through the water at the present speed. Since the road is crowned, the water is probably deeper at the edge of the lane than near the middle. At 50 mph, the car is likely to hydroplane. You should slow to about 25 mph before reaching the water. You can use at least part of the left lane; if you slow enough, the truck will probably have gone far enough to leave the lane clear. After you have gone through the water, test the brakes. If they are not working, press the brake pedal while you drive so that friction will dry the brakes.

**Chapter 11**

**Driver Fitness and Highway Safety**

1. A few moments of light exercise before you get in the car can help prevent fatigue or drowsiness from becoming a problem. Once under way, drive at a reduced speed and keep a safe

following distance. Weather permitting, keep the window down to get fresh air. Play upbeat music on the radio. If fatigue becomes uncontrollable, don't drive—call someone for help, or pull well off the road and nap for a while.

2. You can predict that the driver ahead may turn, slow, or stop; be ready for any of these actions. Reduce your speed and drop far enough back so that you can stop safely if necessary. You can anticipate that vehicles following you may tailgate or try to pass.

**Chapter 12**

**Alcohol, Other Drugs, and Driving**

1. Based on BAC charts, Janet's BAC is .02 percent; Sergie's is .01 percent; George's is .10 percent. Janet and Sergie should convince George to let Sergie do the driving. They should plan to pick up Rosa in about 30 minutes.

2. It is not safe to ride with this person. The effects of the over-the-counter drug could wear off, and the driver could fall asleep at the wheel without warning. Tired drivers often make poor decisions, and reflexes may be slowed. Some of the alternatives include offering to drive yourself, getting another friend to drive, taking a cab, or using public transportation.

**Chapter 13**

**Owning a Motor Vehicle**

1. a. Sacramento is in grid M-9, and Stockton is in grid 0-10. The two major routes between them are Interstate 5 and Route 99 (a state highway).

   b. The national forest is Plumas. Camping is not permitted since the campsite symbol is not displayed. The color coding indicates other national forests which are not labeled. Students familiar with the area may recognize and be able to name these forests.

   c. Healdsburg is in grid M-6; Petaluma is in grid N-6. Accumulated mileage between them is 33 miles (52.8 km).

   d. Interstates 5 and 80 provide access to Sacramento.

2. Find a place to pull off the highway safely and check the map for an alternate route to your destination. Are there parallel highways or secondary roads that will get you where you are going? How far out of your way would an alternate route take you? Does the alternate route have service areas or towns along the way? If not, plan to make a fuel stop at the first opportunity.

**Chapter 14**

**Maintaining Your Vehicle**

1. Even though the belted tires are a bargain, Eduardo should buy radial tires. Mixing radial and bias tires on the same vehicle can result in serious handling problems.

**2.** Look over your right shoulder, signal, and move into the right lane. Pull into the breakdown lane or onto the road shoulder when it is safe to do so. Stop and allow the radiator to cool. Get out on the passenger side and check under the hood for a broken belt or hose. Check the coolant level. Do not drive the car if there is a broken hose or belt or if the coolant level is low. If possible, get to a phone and call for assistance.

# Index

An asterisk (*) indicates an illustration.

# Credits

**Photos**

Art production, cover and book design: Ligature, Inc.
Cover photos: H. deLespinasse/Image Bank, Russel Ingram. James L. Ballard: pp. 2, 4(t), 6, 7, 8, 9, 10, 11, 18, 19, 20, 25, 26, 28, 29, 32, 39, 40, 44, 46, 64, 65, 66, 76, 77, 85(r), 86, 100, 101, 104, 107, 111, 112, 113(b), 114, 127(l), 131(b), 132(r), 133, 135, 145, 147, 151, 158, 159, 161, 162, 165, 166, 167, 168, 169, 171, 178, 179, 180, 182, 186, 187, 189, 199, 201, 204, 205, 206, 214, 215, 222, 224, 225, 226, 235, 237, 238, 241, 247, 257, 258, 261, 263, 267; Frank Siteman: pp. 3, 4(b), 27, 45, 47, 66, 99, 109, 113(t), 123, 127(r), 132(l), 140, 141, 144(t), 148, 160, 184, 198, 203, 239, 243, 244, 256, 275; Gene Dekovic: pp. 5(b), 42, 50, 53, 62, 71, 85(l), 88, 124, 131(t), 143, 144(b), 183, 196; Beverly Dixon: pp. 5(t), 93, 181, 212, 242; Arthur Grace/Stock Boston: p. 59; Stacy Pick/Stock Boston: p. 78; Ellis Herwig/Stock Boston: p. 119; Bill Gallery/Stock Boston: p. 175; Arnold Crane: p. 190; Owen Franken/Stock Boston: p. 231; John Coletti/Stock Boston: p. 245; 4 x 5 Inc: pp. x, 60, 120, 176, 197, 217, 232.

**Art**

Amundson/Drabik & Associates, Inc: pp. 21, 22, 23, 24, 38, 63, 67, 68, 69, 70, 71, 72, 89, 91, 92, 149, 185, 200, 259, 260, 262, 264, 266, 268, 270, 286, 287, 288, 289, 290, 291, 292, 293, 294, 310, 311, 312, 315.

**Diagrams**

Ligature Inc: pp. 31, 48, 49, 52, 54, 56, 75, 88, 90, 103, 105, 106, 110, 126, 129, 130, 134, 142, 150, 152, 154, 163, 170, 192, 295, 296, 297, 298, 299, 300, 301, 302, 303, 304, 305, 306, 307, 308, 309, 313, 314, 316, 317.

**Map**

Rand McNally Road Atlas copyright 1985: pp. 248-249.